NOT ORDINARY MEN

By the same author:

Twice Around the World (Leo Cooper, 1991)

NOT ORDINARY MEN

The Story of the Battle of Kohima

by

JOHN COLVIN

LEO COOPER
LONDON

First Published in Great Britain in 1994, reprinted in 1995.
Published in 2003, reprinted 2005 and 2012 in this format by
PEN & SWORD MILITARY
an imprint of
Pen and Sword Books Limited,
47 Church Street, Barnsley,
South Yorkshire. S70 2AS

ISBN: 978 1 84884 871 9

A CIP catalogue record of this book is available from the
British Library

Printed and bound by
CPI Group (UK) Ltd, Croydon, CR0 4YY

Pen & Sword Books Ltd incorporates the Imprints of Pen & Sword
Aviation, Pen & Sword Maritime, Pen & Sword Military,
Wharncliffe Local History, Pen & Sword Select, Pen & Sword Military
Classics, Leo Cooper, Remember When, Seaforth Publishing and
Frontline Publishing

For a complete list of Pen & Sword titles please contact
PEN & SWORD BOOKS LIMITED
47 Church Street, Barnsley, South Yorkshire, S70 2AS, England
E-mail: enquiries@pen-and-sword.co.uk
Website: www.pen-and-sword.co.uk

To
MORANNA COLVIN

CONTENTS

ACKNOWLEDGEMENTS

My most particular thanks are due to John McCann, formerly 1st 18th Lancashire Fusiliers, for permission to quote extensively from his superb trilogy, *Kohima, Return to Kohima* and *Echoes of Kohima*.

I thank also Norman Havers (*March On*), David Rooney (*Burma Victory*), and the incomparable late Harry Seaman. Of those participating in the battle, I am especially grateful to Derek Horsford, David Wilson, Donald Easten, John Wright, Harry Smith, Peter Steyn, Gordon Graham, Jimmy Patrick, Stephen Laing, John Winstanley, Peter Franklin, Thomas Hogg and Masao Hirakubo. The Imperial War Museum (Rod Suddaby), the Public Records Office and the National Army Museum have given unstinting help and support.

MAPS

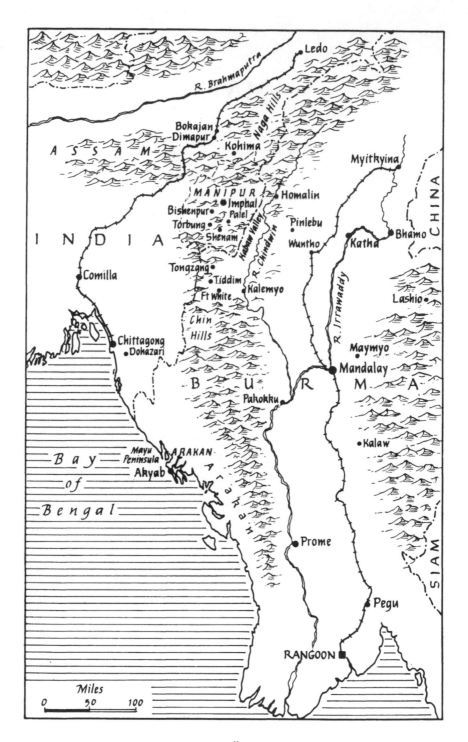

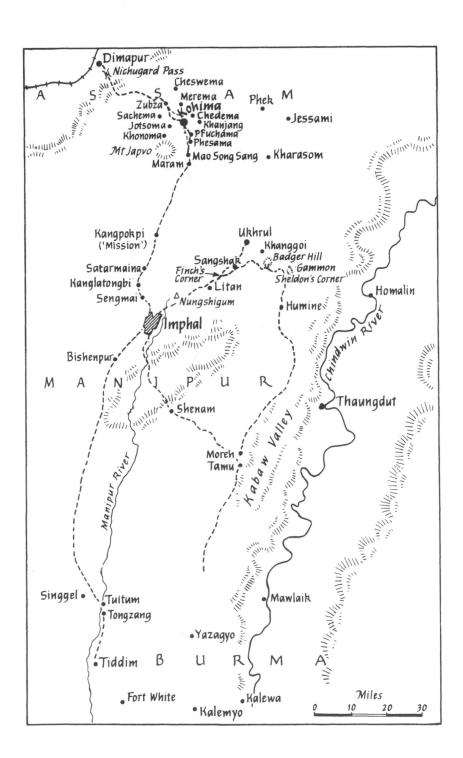

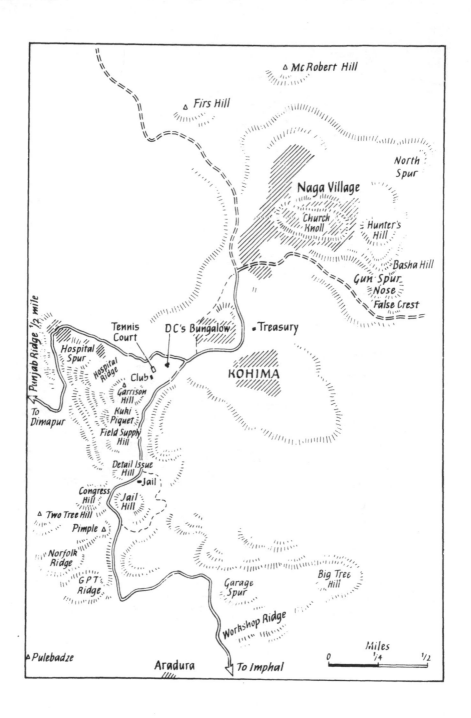

PREFACE

ON AN April evening in 1993 sixty elderly men met for dinner at Maidstone in the drill hall of a Territorial Army Regiment. They, and their comrades who were gone, had been meeting in this fashion for forty-six years to commemorate events that had occurred in 1944. There had never been many of them, and nine more had died since they had last met.

In this green, functional room they ate a proper Army curry-and-rice with grated coconut, peanuts, peach slices, banana, pickled eggs and plenty of currants. They sat on red plastic and metal chairs drinking beer at six-foot tables, surrounded by box-horses and wall-bars which they were certainly too old to exploit. But on the walls hung the gold cross on white ground of Montgomery's Eighth Army, the fern leaf of Freyberg's Second New Zealand Division to which they had been temporarily attached and which Rommel considered the best Allied formation in the Desert War. Here, closer to home, were the Red Ball of Fire and Gold Arrow of Briggs's and Messervy's Fifth and Seventh Indian Divisions, the shields of Stopford's XXXIII Corps, their own Slim's XIV Army, and the red-white-and-blue Phoenix of Mountbatten's South East Asia Command.

Although some wore suits and one a leather jacket, most of the men were in dark blue blazers with the White Horse on the pocket, and grey flannel trousers. They had been, those not disabled, artisans – carpenters, electricians, plumbers, builders, tradesmen, labourers, minor civil servants, simple but not 'humble' men. So were those younger veterans who, although not touched by their experience, were permitted to join them. They looked very ordinary, the old soldiers, neat, average, solid, mostly bespectacled, distinguished only by rather straight backs and an eerie, unspoken community. Later that night, on the railway station, they sang and shouted in the beery volume they would have used fifty years ago.

One of the men said to me, 'We couldn't have survived without the officers. Right from the start, we never had a bad officer.' One of the officers said, 'We could never have done it without the men. It was the men who did it, the NCOs and privates.' Both spoke flatly, as fact, without emotion.

1

They were *not* ordinary. They were the 4th Battalion of The Queen's Own Royal West Kent Regiment. Their motto was Invicta, the Unconquered. They held the line against the Japanese at Kohima, the most terrible battle of the Second World War. They were the inheritors of those Greeks killed to a man at Thermopylae with their commander, Leonidas, of whom Simonides wrote nearly two thousand five hundred years ago:

'Go tell the Spartans, thou who passest by,
That here obedient to their laws we lie.'

Peoples do not change. The Japanese today retain their virtues of tenacity, reach and forethought, although blind heroism is, fortunately, no longer suited to their strategies, and stupidity is anathema.

The British are not absorbent, not punchbags nor sandbags, not cannon-fodder, although they can sometimes hold a defensive line and sometimes not, retreating as in the Far East in gross non-combatant – if seldom combatant – disgrace. They are, on the contrary, when roused from lethargy, a barbaric people.

The common denominator of early defeats in the Second, if not the First, World War was lack of military preparation, the consequences of an overstretched Empire, a declined economy and the preferred intellectual posture of the ostrich. These attributes, whether material or psychological, formed the marshes in which the British soldier, ill-equipped and often inappropriately trained, first had to fight. It is surprising, in Burma as in North-West Europe, that he was as good as he was; at least, he was nearly always brave, and without any Shinto or Prussian ideological truss.

Nations are congeries of people, either of diverse races or of common descent, language, history and geographical limits. The former for a brief period was also a definition of the Empire, and the latter defined the United Kingdom itself until 1945, but no longer. The unity of the first was greatly aided by its armies, especially the Indian Army, in John Keegan's words 'the most durable and perhaps the most remarkable of Britain's imperial creations'.

The unity of the United Kingdom itself was provided by arrangements between its various races, English, Scottish, Welsh and Irish, the Kingdom's history thus leading to the Kingdom's constitution and customs, which in their turn subsumed the Empire and its armies. And the executors, leaders and inheritors of that bloody and ancient structure were the leaders of nation and empire, whether from Shrewsbury, Fort William, Carmarthen or Armagh. They were seldom soldiers, usually farmers, small merchants, lawyers, people like that, once called, with respect but not veneration, the middle class. They knew that the preservation, let alone expansion, of Empire was doomed and did not care much about it anyway. But, although without great windy causes, neither were they fighting – especially in Burma – *only* for Hearth and Home. They, and those whom they led, and who followed them, are among the subjects of this book.

We were then, in these islands, resilient, humorous, methodical but inventive and, in hard times, faithful. Peoples do not change.

Japanese determination and loyalty would be as marked. Since the twelfth century the prime component of that civilization has been a warrior class more or less subordinate to an Emperor, direct successor of the Sun Goddess; even after Perry or the Meiji restoration 'modernization' was made dependent on strong military forces. After the World Depression of the 1930s the economic progress of the Taisho era gave way to nationalism and foreign adventure, first into China and then inexorably toward South-East Asia and the Pacific.

Meteoric success ended in complete disaster. That also is the subject of this book. Since then demoralization and so forth have changed some of the institutions of Japan, but probably not the people.

Kohima was a point at which those two cultures met in battle and where, for the first time, the Western not the Eastern Islanders decisively prevailed.

On 19 April, 1944, a few hundred ragged, exhausted, wounded or dying British and Indian soldiers came down an Indian hill. For two weeks they had held, until they were relieved by their brothers of the 2nd Division, some thirteen *thousand* Japanese infantrymen with a background hitherto of unbroken victory. Now the County Regiments arrived, and Indians of the warrior races, to drive the Japanese out of their bunkers, across the Chindwin, and out of Burma at last.

I

THE JAPANESE SCREEN

ALTHOUGH THERE is no certainty about the origins of the Japanese people, apart from the Ainu aborigines, now a small minority on Hokkaido but once covering all the islands, their ancestors probably came from the Pacific via South-East Asia and from Central Asia. Insofar as the latter were of Mongol stock, and both philology and physiognomy have been interpreted to that effect, it would be tempting to ascribe to these roots the Furor Japonicus so frequent in the country's history, internal and external. But although Koreans find no difficulty in accepting a similar soft impeachment, few Japanese proudly admit Mongol ancestry and fewer still its consequences, even did their mythology not claim that the country was created by the gods, not by human genes, specifically by the Sun Goddess, ancestress of the first Emperor.

At all events, by the early years of this millennium the immigrants had established themselves in the Kyoto area of Honshu, under priest-kings, animist but owing allegiance to the Sun. Honshu is the main island of Japan which also houses Tokyo, Osaka and Yokohama. Their religion, Shinto, subsequently coexisted with Buddhism, as did their methods of government with systems imported from China and Korea. By the beginning of the brilliant Heian age (eighth to twelfth centuries), first Nara and, later, Kyoto became the Imperial home, both designed on the model of Peking.

From the twelfth century the strongest contemporary warrior family acted as the de facto rulers of Japan, albeit always appointed by the Emperor and governing in his name with the title of Shogun or 'barbarian-subduing generalissimo'. After the defeat of the Mongol invasions in the thirteenth century, largely accomplished by 'divine winds' or Kami-Kaze which wrecked their fleets, disorder, even civil war, led to a weakening of Central Government and the rise of provincial warlords, until the unification of the whole country under the Tokugawa Shogunate in the sixteenth century.

Tokugawa Ieyasu thereafter began to pursue from Yedo (Tokyo) a policy of national isolation, the 'Closed Country', with minimal foreign trade and hideous persecution of Jesuit and other Christian missionaries. In 1854 this concept, which did not, however, exclude a marvellous renaissance of art and craft, gave way to what might be called an Open Door, direct result of two visits to Yedo Bay by Commodore Perry's US squadron. Reluctantly, the Shogunate had decided to absorb such Western technology as would not affect the foundations of the Japanese spirit. Trading posts, consular and diplomatic Missions were established.

This conclusion was naturally perceived by some as an unacceptable loss of face. Fourteen years later the Tokugawa were overthown by a military coalition of regional leaders restoring in 1868 nominal powers to the (Meiji) Emperor. The latter removed to Yedo from Kyoto, but, in British constitutional terms, 'reigned rather than ruled'. Power lay with those warriors who had brought down the Tokugawa, but power executed in a modernizing, industrial mode. There was, of course, nothing modern about their attitudes to democracy. Shinto and Confucianism, projected through a system of state education, governed men's minds, enjoining loyalty and obedience to Emperor and hierarchies. Self-sacrifice and hard work were the rallying calls.

Even these changes, their rapidity and the dissolution of ancient customs, in particular the creation of a parliament (Diet), were too much for many in the Armed Forces. But victories over Korea, China and Czarist Russia (1904–05) restored domestic unity as well as considerably enhancing Japan's territories. Neither did the Japanese of that time forget that the Anglo-Japanese Alliance held the ring against intervention by Russia's allies in the Russo-Japanese War. But the defeat of the Russians caused the first doubts throughout Asia over white supremacy or invulnerability.

The Meiji and Taisho eras were periods of immense industrial advance based on both European and Asian markets. 'Democracy' too seemed to make headway against the old blind loyalties, although Emperor Hirohito's assumption of the throne was shortly to be accompanied by unharmonious events. The world depression had brought about a climate of violent nationalism, riots, attempted armed coups, the assassination of statesmen and political leaders including four Prime Ministers, and the seizure of Manchuria in 1931 by the Japanese Army, which had already occupied Shantung. Japan left the League of Nations in 1933 when Manchuria became Manchukuo, her virtual colony. The Armed Forces, the Army foremost, became again the dominant force in the political life of the country to the diminution, even elimination, of party government.

The Navy too became enraged, because of the replacement of the Anglo-Japanese Alliance in 1922 by the Washington Treaty which, at the instance of and with enormous financial disbursements by the United States, established a naval ratio of 5-5-3 for Great Britain, the US and Japan. From London's point of view, the Treaty gravely damaged this country's influence on Japanese policy and certainly diminished the close and admirable naval relations between Tokyo and ourselves. Few things were a better indication of our own consciousness of a reduced world position. The Navy's resentment was deepened by the London Disarmament Treaty of 1930 which extended the same ratio to auxiliary vessels; the Washington Treaty was formally denounced in 1936. Our lackeying to the US was of benefit neither to the Americans nor, more important, to the UK.

The Samurai, in collaboration with big business, had taken over the Government in an unbreakable centralized bureaucracy. Ruth Benedict, in *The Chrysanthemum and the Sword*, has said that that hierarchy, already the basis of society, created uncritical obedience to authority which, together with the Japanese fondness for regimentation and weakness for military display, easily enabled the Army to enforce military despotism. The revolutionary aspects of the Meiji Restoration had been affected too fast and from above. Political freedom was not one of its concepts since the Army exercised power in the Emperor's name, exploiting his mythology, 'the Supreme Command became almighty; God and Caesar in one'.

Japan, furthermore, lacked raw materials and had a population which more than doubled between 1890 and 1950. Emigration from the islands was almost excluded by legislation in most host countries, and the export solution to an inadequate standard of living was impeded by other countries' trade barriers and by insecure access to foreign natural resources. In the eyes of militant Japanese and of their subjects, expansion overseas, whether into China from 1931 or Mongolia/Russia (Japan's defeats of 1935 and 1939 at Halkhingol) were matters of self-preservation. It is, for example, extremely significant that a self-professed opponent of the military regime should describe the regime's policy as provoking 'the democratic powers to oppose our infringements on *their* vested rights in China'.

On 21 January, 1940, a British cruiser had stopped a Japanese steamer, the *Asama Maru*, bound for Yokohama, off Chiba Prefecture in Japan and removed twenty-one Germans of military age. (There was a corresponding action by a Japanese warship in Hong Kong waters against a British merchantman.) The Japanese Government (then neutral), claiming that such actions were permissible only towards armed belligerents, protested. Opposition to the 'Moderate' Yonai Government then led to its replacement on 27 July by an administration under Prince Konoye with strong military support. On 27 September, 1940, the Japanese signed the Triple Alliance with Germany and Italy, to be followed by a neutrality pact with the USSR in April, 1941, vitiated by the German invasion of Russia. In June Tojo succeeded Konoye and the stage was set for Pearl Harbour.

The Japanese Army visualized a Europe/Africa bloc ruled by Germany and Italy. This would be vigorously opposed by Great Britain which aimed, with India and Australia, to secure supply lines in the South Pacific. The US Navy, Japan thought, would expand, resulting in an Anglo/US Alliance in the Pacific, cutting off Japan from imported resources. Japan would therefore have to 'expand in the Southern Region'. For that purpose she needed security from the USSR, an early victory in China, a totalitarian homeland and speedy preparations for war.

The Navy supported the Southern Region policy, but opposed actual war except in the event of a total US embargo, US strategic use of British territories or heavy US and UK reinforcement of their colonies. Article 3, however, of the paper concluded at a conference between Imperial GHQ and the Government on 17 July, 1940, approved the employment of armed strength in the Southern Region under different conditions but, if possible, against Great Britain only. It was at the same time recognized that war with the US might become unavoidable and that thorough preparations must be made: the Navy registered lack of confidence in its own fleet's staying power should the US Navy resort to protracted war.

In the event, although the emperor had ordered that force should not be used, entry into French Indo-China (FIC) by Japanese forces, albeit agreed between the Tokyo and Vichy Governments, led to fighting at Langson on September 21, 1940. This agreement, initially in the north, was extended to the south in 1941. Thereafter FIC and, subsequently, Thailand collaborated more or less enthusiastically with the Japanese southward advance.

On 6 September, 1941, the Imperial Conference proposed continued negotiations with the US, Britain and the Netherlands, coupled with full readiness for war by October. The intransigent terms – according to the Japanese – of Cordell Hull's note of 26 November 'made peace impossible', but, in fact, on that day the Fleet had already left Hito Kappu Bay for Pearl Harbor.

In early December, 1941, Japan declared war on Great Britain and the United States. Pearl Harbor was bombed on 7 December, 1941, Singapore fell on 15 February and Batavia (Djakarta) on 6 March, 1942. On 18 January 55 Division, under Lieutenant-General Takauchi, crossed the Thai/Burmese border at Mae Sot.

II

THE ROAD TO KOHIMA

AS BRITISH Imperial strategy had been predicated on an 'invulnerable' Singapore, little had been done to prepare Burma against invasion. The forces available to Burcorps were 17th Indian Division, inexperienced and undertrained, Burma Division which had not before functioned as a whole and whose Burmese units progressively deserted, the magnificent 7th Armoured Brigade and, after Yenaungyang, the Chinese 38th Division.

In 1942 wireless sets, stores, the telephone network, Intelligence and above all Air power were wholly inadequate, and the roads often blocked by refugees and non-combatant soldiers. British troops were, too often, 'soft' and lacking motivation. In terms of leadership, General Wavell's belief that the Japanese were militarily incapable, that his 17th Division was already equal to the battle-stained Indian Divisions he had known in Africa, that Rangoon must be held at all costs, nearly caused the destruction of the Commander-in-Chief, General Alexander, and his troops escaping out of Rangoon from the advancing, 33rd and 55th Japanese Divisions. The absence of air cover, little artillery, dependence on the roads, contrary directives from India and complete inability to cope with Japanese tactics of encirclement and infiltration led to severe losses and incessant tactical defeats, not to say chaos. It is a pity, with hindsight, that Alexander did not accept Chang Kai Shek's offer of Chinese troops at the end of 1941.

BurCorps under its Commander, Major-General, later Field-Marshal, Slim – 'one of the great captains, in mountains, jungle and high plains, a man with the head of a General and the heart of a private soldier, the thought of whom was like home and safety' – was thus beaten over and over again on the long retreat to India. But despite hundreds of fresh cases each day of dysentery and malaria, precipitous tracks no more than eighteen inches wide, the monsoon, the frightful Kabaw Valley and 13,000 casualties, by late May, 1942, 'the battered scarecrow units of the Corps marched in the end with "proper pride" into India,' 7th Armoured, 48th Gurkha Brigade, 7th Hussars and 2 Royal Tanks. But the Japanese of the 33rd and 55th Divisions knew that 'the British were weaker than the Chinese. You surround them and they run away'. They developed a contempt for the Indian and British armies which fortunately became – after Wingate, Second Arakan, Kohima and Imphal – their own terrible nemesis.

In the meanwhile, Slim's tasks after taking command of the newly formed XIV Army were to save India, beat the Japanese and, in co-operation with Generals Stilwell and Chennault, build and maintain the rail, road and air links to China; all this at the end of supply lines from the UK greatly constrained by operational requirements in the Western Desert and elsewhere, not a Forgotten Army but an 'undernourished' one. The restoration of that Army's strength was the primary task, to rebuild 'the crumbling morale of our troops in the face of the Japanese'. A first step was to reorganize medical care, especially in malaria (84% of casualties), reducing the ratio of sick to wounded from 12:1,000 per day in 1943 to 1:1,000 in 1945. Rigorous twelve-hour a day training was the key, together with Slim's conscious effort to raise the fighting spirit of his men. Failure in the Arakan under Generals Irwin and Lloyd in 1943, on the pattern of earlier defeats, did not help in this regard. But, however slight the material results, General Wingate's first expedition into Central Burma in early 1943 certainly did, and the Press seized on the achievement. The Chindits were seen as proving that air supply could maintain an army in the disgusting conditions of North and Central Burma, and that British troops could match the Japanese at their own game. Jungle warfare had undergone a revolution, one which Winston Churchill did not comprehend, seeking an amphibious strategy to isolate the Japanese.

As it turned out, Wingate and the Chindits also convinced the Commander of Japanese 15th Army, General Mutaguchi, that if the British could handle the mountains and jungles of Northern Burma, so could he. Mutaguchi was the 'hero' of the Marco Polo Bridge at Peking in 1937, and a victor of Singapore. For him full-scale invasion of India via Imphal now became an obsession. That concept had hitherto rightly been opposed in Tokyo and by the Command in Singapore because of exiguous supply, the length of the lines of communication, as well as terrain considerations and, unless a leading role were given to the Indian National Army under the Bengali dissident, Subhas Chandra Bose, probable disapproval by Gandhi and Nehru.

Concurrently, Slim had by 1944 begun to believe that, despite the likely absence of a seaborne landing in Arakan, the reconquest of Burma might be achieved from the top down, from the north. The Japanese were visibly reinforcing on the Central Front, indicative of impending attack. Because of the appalling Burmese topography and the forthcoming onset of the monsoon, Slim intended to destroy the Japanese *before* he started his southern offensive. He chose the Imphal Plain as the killing ground, deciding not to go forward over one hundred miles of terrible country, but to pull back and concentrate 17th, 20th and 23rd Indian Divisions of IV Corps (Sir Geoffrey Scoones) in the Plain and win the decisive battle there.

The prelude was in the Arakan to the south-west. In February, 1944, XV Corps under General Christison defeated at the Battle of 'the Admin Box', with at least 5,000 Japanese dead, a diversionary attack planned by the Japanese 28th Army at 15th Army's request (Ha-Go) to distract British resources from the planned Imphal operation by 15th Army. (Here, too, a Japanese General, Sakurai Tokutaro ('Tokuta') dreamed of invading India, via Chittagong.) But after the brilliant destruction of the Japanese Air Force by Spitfires, a serious Japanese offensive – hindered by insufficient anti-aircraft guns, artillery and anti-tank weapons – was, for the first time, beaten by British and Indian troops, of the 5th and 7th Indian Divisions (9, 33, 114, 89, 123 and 161 Brigades), and the 81st West African Division. This was 'a victory about which there could be no argument, and its effect on the whole XIVth Army was immense.'

Then, in March, 1944, Wingate with 6,000 men and a considerably increased air component mounted his second expedition, to cut the supply lines of 18th and 56th Divisions facing the Chinese under the US General Stilwell, in order that the Ledo-Kunming Road could be built in security. Wingate himself crashed into a mountain and was killed. Casualties were severe. So were relations with Stilwell who, for an unfortunate period, actually commanded the Chindits as well as the wretched Merrill's Marauders, all forced by 'Vinegar Joe' Stilwell to fight on long after their health and strength were exhausted. Burma for the Americans was a base to service China: 'it was no part of their duty to help restore it to the Imperial power.'

Japanese air operations against Wingate did not really diminish the support which 5th Air Division had planned to provide for the Japanese ground forces at Imphal, but which they were soon to admit was impractical. Neither, on the other hand, was Mutaguchi's ground poten-tial against Imphal substantially diminished by the Chindit operation, with the exception of elements of 53rd Division whom he could not have supplied there anyway. Nor, on the other hand, was the Chindit role on Stilwell's behalf effectively diverted to the help of XIV Army. What Wingate did was drastically to change Mutaguchi's defensive strategy and induce him to an offensive against Imphal.

Both sides, then, were preparing for an offensive. XIV Army's withdrawal to Imphal from its forward bases west of the Chindwin was designed to destroy, with air supremacy and superior quality and numbers, Japanese infiltration and, eventually, the entire 15th Army, before the British/Indian advance across the Chindwin, the Irawaddy and on to Rangoon. This course, involving the cession of territory, was not initially popular with 17th and 20th Divisions or their Commanders.

The Japanese objectives were the destruction of British forces in Burma, the isolation of China and a separate peace; India was already ripe for revolution, open to invasion before the monsoon made supply impossible. (It will be recalled that the 'Quit India' movement had led by August, 1942, to widespread insurgency with serious loss of life, easily suppressed, but still grumbling in the background.) Supply, overwhelming British force, British flexibility, endurance and infinitely superior command would soon end that dream, which had been, only eighteen months before, a not impossible nightmare. It was, obviously, essential that the British withdrawals should coincide with, not follow, the first Japanese advances across the Chindwin. In fact, 17th Division, still under 'Punch' Cowan, its Commander during and since the retreat of 1942, moved late from the south, being nearly encircled and eliminated in incessant fighting with a reinforced Japanese 33rd Division before reaching the Plain, General Ouvry Roberts' 23rd Division in support. 33rd Division, under the sensitive Yanagida, never before in battle and hating the sight of injury and death, was then halted short of Imphal at Torbung, after being mauled at Tongzang, Tuitum and Singgel. Its eastern column, under Yamamoto, pursuing 20th Division, was held at the Shenam Saddle for two months of extraordinary mountain fighting. The British and Indians had stopped this famous Division, Yanagida being accused by Mutaguchi of cowardice and replaced by Tanaka.

The Japanese 15th Division from Thailand had been told to 'advance through the hills like a ball of fire'. It was under-equipped and in low strength, its commander, Major-General Yamauchi, westernized and gentle, mortally ill with tuberculosis. (He was also never unaccompanied by his European pedestal lavatory.) Nevertheless, after a 10-day march through the mountains over some 300 miles with little rest or sleep, one of his units took Mission (Kangpokpi) on 28 March, cutting the Kohima-Imphal road, and another, which supported 31 Division in the Sangshak battle, cut the road at Satarmaina on 3 April. But the Division, as well as failing to take Sengmai, was defeated with heavy losses at Kanglatongbi and at the hill battle of Nungshigum on 14 April against brigades of 5th Indian Division equipped with tanks and artillery. No Japanese forces of any consequence got nearer to Imphal than this. General Yamauchi was eventually dismissed by Mutaguchi on 10 June, his Division down to one battalion, for failing to 'take Imphal' by storm.

By this time 5th and 7th Indian Divisions, and 2nd (British) Infantry Division with its magnificent County Regiments, had arrived *by air* from the 'diversion' in Arakan, and by land from India respectively. (XXX

Corps under General Stopford had since been formed.) In this regard, the Supreme Allied Commander's 'diplomacy' and access to resources in acquiring adequate transport aircraft against the conflicting demands of both General Stilwell and the European Front deserve the most unstinting praise.

Units of 31st Japanese Division (General Sato) reached Kohima from the Chindwin on 3 April, with scarcely adequate supplies, and severe casualties from battle and disease, including beriberi. En route, Major-General Miyazaki, commanding the Division's Infantry Group based on 58 Regiment, took from 22-28 March to defeat 50th Indian Parachute Regiment at Sangshak, losing in the process almost one third of his troops, giving time for 5th Indian Division to reach Imphal and a garrison to be raised for Kohima.

Slim was not perfect, and he always admitted his mistakes. One was to assume that Sato's main target would be the large British rear base at Dimapur with its enormous reserve of stores, and that no more than a Japanese Regiment would be used against Kohima. Capture of Dimapur would cut off the US airfields in Assam which supplied China. This error was discovered through a captured Japanese despatch case at Sangshak, revealing plans for Kohima and the road to Imphal. It was immediately taken to Corps HQ. But it was too late. The Kohima garrison under Colonel Hugh Richards was very scratch indeed – Indian administrative units, 500 men from a convalescent unit, the only formed combatant troops the excellent Assam Regiment initially defending Jessami, Phek and Kharasom to the east of Kohima itself, and the raw Nepali Sher Regiment.

The seizure of Imphal, whose only pass with a good road was Kohima, was the main Japanese objective, although Sato's instructions were no more than to take and hold Kohima, not to go for Dimapur. It was not until 5 April, therefore, that less that 500 men of the 4th Battalion Royal West Kents, a Territorial battalion, debussed under heavy Japanese fire. The enemy then closed the ring round Kohima. For the next 16 days, in stench and filth, until the arrival of the 1st Battalion, Royal Berkshire Regiment, this British battalion, together with smaller contingents of the Punjabis, the Rajputs, the Assam Regiment and Rifles, defeated in hand-to-hand combat – with a little mortar capacity but with artillery only from two miles outside the perimeter – every effort by twelve to fifteen thousand soldiers of an illustrious Japanese division to secure their surrender and that of the garrison. It is hard not to agree with the Official Historian and with Japanese historians that 19 April – when the 'Dirty Half Hundred' (from 50th of Foot) were relieved – was the turning point of the battle of Imphal and, hence, of the whole Burma campaign.

'Probably one of the greatest battles in history, it was in effect the

Battle of Burma,' said Admiral Mountbatten, the Supreme Allied Commander, South-East Asia, although the Japanese did not abandon it for another two months. Anyway, it was a long way from the shambles of the sad retreat. In the latter context let us remember the words of James Lunt in *A Hell of a Licking*:

'Those of us who took part in the Retreat from Burma are unlikely to look back on that experience with anything but regret. It was a humiliating defeat. God knows, the British Army is familiar enough with retreats, thanks to its governments that so often sent it into battle unprepared and ill-equipped. But the Burma retreat was in a class of its own. It was horrible to witness a beautiful country being ravaged; to see innocent men, women and children dying by the roadside; to experience the total collapse of a civilised administration; and to have the feeling that so many of the Burmese were glad to see the backs of us after more than half a century of British rule ... But we learnt our lesson, found out what had caused it, went back and recaptured Burma.

> "Fight on my men!" says Sir Andrew Barton,
> "I am hurt but I am not slain;
> I'le lay me downe and bleed-a-while;
> And then I'le rise and fight again."

And in the end that is what we did!'

III

JAPANESE INTENTIONS
AND ORDER OF BATTLE

GENERAL SLIM believed that General Mutaguchi's aims were 'first, to capture Imphal, and second, to break through to the Brahmaputra Valley so as to cut off the Northern front and disrupt the air supply to China . . . A Japanese regiment would make for Kohima to cut the main Imphal-Dimapur road and threaten the Dimapur base . . . the offensive would begin about 15 March.'

In fact, HQ Southern Army in February, 1943, came to the conclusion that the Allies were preparing for an all-out offensive in the dry season after October, 1943, along the Hukawng Valley, Chindwin River, Mayu Peninsula and Yunnan fronts.

The reasons for expecting this event were, firstly, that British and Indian Forces in the Mayu Peninsula had made persistent and determined counter-attacks, albeit ultimately unsuccessful, between December, 1942, and February, 1943. 77th Brigade under Major-General Wingate had made a surprise penetration deep into Northern Burma, causing confusion in the Japanese defence system, considered to be a reconnaissance in force prior to a large-scale counter-offensive. A Chinese expeditionary force under the command of Chen Shin, furthermore, was assembled in Yunnan province, trained and supplied by officers and men of the US Army. The force was increasing daily and Chungking continually urged a counter-offensive in Burma in order to reopen the Burma road. The Chungking Army, which had retreated into Assam in May, 1942, had been reorganized into a more powerful operational unit with US equipment. The standard Japanese opinion of Chinese armies, however, was that they would not fight without a 5:1 majority; they would otherwise run.

The Japanese Army which had been so unexpectedly successful in operations in Burma in the spring of 1942 had relied for its defence on the difficulties of the Burma terrain, the effect of tropical disease and poor communications. But, owing to the changes described above, reorganization and reinforcement of Japanese forces in Burma began. It was never successfully completed owing to the increase in Allied air strength. The order of battle was: 15 Army HQ, Rangoon: Yunnan Front, 56 Division, HQ Manshih; Hukawng Valley Front and Jupi

Mountain Range Front, 18 Division, HQ Maymyo; from Kalewa-Gangaw Front to Central Burma generally, 33 Division, HQ Kalaw; Mayu Peninsula area, 55 Division, HQ Akyab. 55 Division had lost three-quarters of its strength in operations in January, 1943, and part of 33 Division sent as reinforcement lost half its fighting strength.

HQ 15th Army was reorganized as HQ Burma Area Army and a new HQ for 15th Army established. HQ Burma Area Army, GOC in C Lieutenant-General Kawabe, was the supreme command in Burma directly responsible for political affairs, the Indian National Army, railway units and the Kempei Tai, and for the defence of Southern Burma. HQ 15th Army, GOC in C Lieutenant-General Mutaguchi, was responsible for the defence of North Burma, Central Burma and Yunnan. HQ 55 Division, GOC Lieutenant-General Takeuchi, was responsible for the defence of the Arakan. No reinforcements were received, but the losses sustained by 55 Division and 33 Division were replaced.

The reorganization took place at the end of 1942 and 15th Army HQ was set up with an entirely new staff, completed by the end of March, 1943. The GOC in C 15th Army was made responsible for the defence of Yunnan, North Burma and Central Burma, and was to repulse any enemy counter-offensives along these fronts. For this purpose 15th Army was to occupy and hold the Salween River front in Yunnan, the Myitkyina-Mogaung-Pinlebu-Wuntho line in North Burma, and the Kalewa-Pakokku line in middle Burma.

Troops under the command of the GOC in C 15th Army, and their responsibilities, included 56 Division (HQ Manshih), defence of the Yunnan front: 18 Division (HQ Maymyo), general defence of North Burma. They were to occupy Myitkyina, Mogaung, Pinlebu and Wuntho and to send forward a detachment to Shadazup and the Chindwin River line to establish a patrol base. 33 Division (HQ Kalaw), responsible for the defence of Central Burma, was to fortify strongly the Mawlaik, Kalewa, Monywa, Pakokku and Gangaw areas, and to send forward a small detachment to establish a patrol base at the Stockade.

L of C troops: responsible for supplying 15th Army. Base at Mandalay.

Lieutenant-Colonel Hayashi, who had been Staff Officer Operations in Southern Army HQ, began, from about June, 1942, to advocate the advantages of an attack on Imphal as the putative main base for a British and Indian counter-offensive against Burma. He emphasized the need to exploit the successes of the Spring, 1942, Burma operations, before British and Indian preparations for defence could be completed. Southern Army and Imperial HQ concurred. 15th Army was ordered to make preparations for the proposed operation.

This plan was opposed by the Staff Officer Intelligence for the following reasons: scarcity of good roads in the India-Burma frontier area; ignorance of enemy strengths and of topographical conditions; incomplete preparations for supplying forward troops, and the danger that an advance by the Japanese Army into Indian territory would provoke political ill-feeling against Japan among the masses in India. Further, Lieutenant-General Mutaguchi, then commanding 18 Division, and Lieutenant-General Sakurai, commanding 33 Division on the front line in Burma, showed great reluctance because topography, communications and disease in the India-Burma frontier areas rendered operations in these areas almost impossible for either side. The plan for an attack on Imphal was therefore abandoned in approximately December, 1942. Instead it was decided to strengthen the defence of Burma by occupying strategic positions and constructing defence works.

The plan for Imphal was reconsidered in about April, 1943. Lieutenant-General Mutaguchi, commanding 18 Division, who had previously been opposed to the plan, now gave his support because of his deep impression of the exploits of Major-General Wingate's British and Indian 77 Brigade which had broken through the Jupi mountain range, previously considered impassable for operational troops. 77 Brigade had caused confusion in the 18 Division area and had also engaged powerful forces from 33 and 56 Divisions.

Mutaguchi now recognized that operations were possible anywhere in the North Burma frontier area in the dry season, if proper preparations were made. He preferred rather to attack and destroy the allied base for a counter-offensive than to stand on the defensive and attempt the impossible by defending a front several hundred kilometres long with one division. Appointed Commander of 15th Army in March, 1943, he thereupon began to advocate this plan strongly. The view was still opposed, nevertheless, by Major-General Obata, his staff, and the staff of Burma Area Army HQ, who, because of the scarcity of operational troops and the difficulty of supply, preferred a defensive strategy.

But Lieutenant-General Mutaguchi, who happened to be the only officer who really knew the topography of North Burma well, was adamant. As all the members of his staff had only been recently appointed and were ignorant of the area, they were unable to dissuade the GOC in C. The Chief of Staff accordingly decided to send staff officers to the front to reconnoitre the area, Major Fujiwara to the left bank of the Chindwin and Colonel Kinoshita and Major Takahashi to the Jupi mountain area. By this time some staff officers at HQ Southern Army and at Imperial HQ had begun to agree to the plan.

As a result of the reconnaissance of the Chindwin, it was found that the area was suitable for mule transport, that five or six battalions could obtain supplementary rations locally, and that the Chindwin River was easily passable by rafts in the dry season. It was therefore decided to advance the front line to the east bank of the Chindwin, though the main plan was still defensive in accordance with the orders of Burma Area Army HQ. When the Advance Line had been pushed forward to the Chindwin, the GOC in C became even more convinced that the offensive against Imphal should be undertaken immediately. The Chief of Staff, Major-General Obata, remained strongly opposed to the GOC in C on the Imphal offensive. When Lieutenant-General Mutaguchi pushed his line to the mountains on the western bank of the Chindwin in about May, 1943, disregarding the approach of the rainy season, Major-General Obata expressed strong opposition and was removed. He was replaced by Major-General Kunomura. However, Burma Area Army as such were still against the plan and it was dropped.

Meanwhile, Lieutenant-General Mutaguchi's plan was gaining support at Southern Army HQ and at Imperial HQ, partly because morale was low in Japan after the Solomons battles and because of the influence of Subhas Chandra Bose, who, in a recent visit to Tokyo, had strongly emphasized the need for action by Japan for the liberation of India. 15th Army began to make preparations for possible offensive operations in the following dry season.

Burma Area Army held an operational conference in Rangoon at the end of June, 1943, to discuss the Imphal operations, at which all staff officers of 15th Army and 28th Army, as well as the Chief of Staff and the Operations Staff Officer of each Division were present. Staff officers from Imperial HQ and HQ Southern Army also attended. The Japanese were aware of the airfields and the huge stocks of ammunition, fuel and supplies available to them in the Imphal plain after successful action, but after conferences on supplies and intelligence for this campaign in July and August, 1943, there was still cause for anxiety about supply. About three and a half divisions would be required, and the need to move 15 Division and the importance of the cooperation of 3rd Air Army were recognized. Burma Area Army ordered 15th Army to prepare for an offensive against Imphal and at the same time carry out defence duties. In September, 1943, GOC in C held a conference of Divisional Commanders to prepare operations.

The need to attack the Chungking Army which had advanced to the west bank of the Salween in Yunnan, and to seize the bridgeheads established by them, was also recognized in September, 1943. A sudden attack by the whole of 56 Division and the main force of 18 Division in the middle of October, 1943, was successful in this regard.

While the main force of the Army was engaged in the Manipur operations, the fronts to the east and north had to be defended by 56 and 18 Divisions, one division each against powerful Chungking and American-Chinese forces. Furthermore, as the Allied counter-offensive was to be expected after November, it was essential to lighten the pressure on, and ensure the safety of, these fronts for the forthcoming Imphal operations. The operations in the north and east were based upon this necessity and HQ 15th Army moved to Lashio.

15th Army recognized the necessity for the speedy accomplishment of the Imphal operations to push the line held by 33 Division to Mawlaik, Yazagyo and Fort White. Orders to this effect were given to 33 Division in October, 1943. These operations were carried out from the beginning of November to the beginning of December and 33 Division advanced its HQ to Shwegyin some 20 kilometres east of Kalewa.

18 Division handed over responsibility for the Homalin front to the newly advanced 31 Division in August, 1943, and its main force was assigned to the Hukawng front. Divisional HQ advanced to Myitkyina in September, but as the most powerful elements of the Division took part in the Yunnan operations decribed above, the concentration for the Hukawng front had not progressed much even by November. The roads in the area to the north of Mogaung were in a very poor condition owing to the rains. About 30 November, 1943, a small detachment of 18 Division which had advanced to the River Tanai was suddenly attacked by the American-Chinese Army. 18 Division collected all available forces in the area and attempted to counter-attack, but without success, surprised by the unexpectedly powerful and tenacious fighting put up by the Chinese Army. 18 Division intended to concentrate its main force in the northern part of the Hukawng Valley in order to launch a counter-attack. Requests were made to Army HQ for motor transport to supply and maintain this force. The demand could not be met as transport was required for munitions for the Imphal operations. As a result, 18 Division was ordered to carry out counter-offensive operations in the South Hukawng Valley. The Division was not in agreement with Army HQ on this point, and the operations in the Hukawng Valley led to indecisive and lengthy defensive battles, owing to an underestimate of the strength of the Americanized Chungking army, of Allied progress in the construction of the Ledo road and of Allied superiority in jungle warfare.

About 10 January, 1944, Imperial HQ's order to begin the Imphal operations was issued and Burma Area Army's order was promulgated in early February:

'15th Army will attack and occupy Imphal with its main force. In these operations, the Army will co-operate closely with the INA and support its operations. 56 Division in the Yunnan area will be put directly under the command of Burma Area Army.'

Lieutenant-General Mutaguchi was by now well satisfied that the view which he had advanced with such enthusiasm had been accepted and expressed his desire to extend operations to India, one of the reasons which caused him to assign so much strength to the Kohima area.

About 10 February 15th Army ordered strategic deployment of all the Divisions for the Imphal operations. The order read approximately:

'The offensive will start in Blitzkrieg style early in March; 33 Division will first carry out a surprise attack against the British-Indian 17 Division in the Tiddim-Tonzang area. A part of the Division, Yamamoto Force, will assume the offensive in the Moreh area, and by so attracting the attention of the British-Indian Army to this area, will also deceive them into the belief that this is merely a local offensive.

'Then, seizing a favourable opportunity, 31 and 15 Divisions will cross the Chindwin from the Homalin-Paungbyin Front. 31 Division will attack and occupy Kohima with its main force to hinder the reinforcement of the British-Indian Army. 15 Division will make an attack with its main force along the front north-west of Imphal; part of the division will attack the Imphal-Kohima road near 'Mission'. 33 Division will launch an offensive against Bishenpur in the Palel area.

'The Imphal operations will be completed in about one month and then the Kohima front will be reinforced with a part of the force employed in Imphal; 15 Army will then go over to the offensive.'

31 Division was to deploy in the Pinlebu, Tamanthe and Homalin areas, 15 Division in Wuntho and Paungbyin areas and 33 Division in Mawlaik, Kalewa and Fort White areas. To conceal their intention, only the minimum strength was to be kept in the front line. River-crossing preparations were to be kept strictly secret, and attempts made to persuade the Allies that the Japanese Army was constructing strong defence positions along the Chindwin.

15th Army decided to launch the Imphal operations on 8 March, 1944. Although Lieutenant-General Mutaguchi, GOC in C 15th Army, realized the need to take the initiative before the Allied counter-offensive believed to start about November, 1943, Imperial Headquarters could not reach a final decision to order the Imphal operations until February, 1944. Futhermore, since it was feared that there would also be an Allied counter-offensive from the sea on the coastal front of Akyab, Rangoon Bay and Tenasserim, and since there was political unrest in Siam, 15th Division, designated to come under the command of 15th Army, was held back in Siam and used to guard the Siam-Burma frontier road and the Bangkok area. (About this time, the numbers of Japanese forces in Siam and Malaya were almost negligible.) 15th Army, if it was to launch the Imphal operations, had to do so quickly. Even after 15 Division reached the front line, considerable time for reorganization, reconnaissance, training and acclimatization for operational purposes would be required. A request was accordingly made for 15 Division to be sent to Burma as quickly as possible and it was eventually despatched to the Burma front on foot; although the advance parties reached the field on 1 January, 1944, by the middle of March two infantry battalions and the Army Service Corps were still on the way. The Division, therefore, was scarcely ready for operations.

15th Army thus realized that it would need forty days to launch the Imphal operation, plus another forty days to take up new offensive positions, because of the inadequate preparations of 15 Division. Operations consequently had to be launched in March: if they had gone forward in December, 1943, or January, 1944, as originally planned, they would have developed differently or, at least, 15th Army would not have been in so desperate condition at the onset of the monsoon.

The attack was opened by 33 Division on 8 March, 1944. 31 and 15 Divisions began offensive operations by crossing the Chindwin river on 15 March. At the same time, 33 Army was formed by order of Burma Area Army with 56 and 18 Divisions under its command, well to the east of the main battle.

On 9 March, when the Army had launched the attack after all those months of waiting, Army HQ received information that British-Indian Army (Chindits) airborne troops of unknown strength were landing in the neighbourhood of Katha. The L of C troops in the Wuntho area were in a state of panic, and it was impossible to obtain any information about the location of the landing, its strength or the objective of its operations. The Army at first underestimated the strength of these units at two or three thousand, judging them to be nothing more than guerrilla troops. However, by the beginning of April it became clear from fragmentary information that they constituted a powerful operational unit, and the Army attempted to find counter-measures, firstly through L of C troops and units of the 15 Division, who were repulsed.

15th Army HQ, because of the Chindit operations, was unable to advance to Indainggy until the end of April. Owing to poor liaison between Division and Army HQ, ill-feeling and disagreements increased.

While preparing for operations, most of the MT was employed on the Wuntho-Homalin road, to be transferred immediately after operations began. The road was cut by the Chindits, and these vehicles could not be moved to other areas, causing supply for troops in the Imphal Area to become more and more difficult.

Part of 15 Division, 53 Division and another unit to be employed as reinforcements for the Imphal operations were absorbed by the operation against the airborne Division. 5 Air Division, which was to have been employed in full strength in the Imphal operations, was transferred to take part in operations against Wingate's airborne Division. The supply-line to 18 Division was cut, and, as a result, this Division, which had been fighting under difficult conditions, was faced by ever-increasing problems. All this had a very bad effect on the morale of Army HQ and on the Divisions concerned.

33 Division's operations about 14 March for the encirclement of 17 British-Indian Division in the neighbourhood of Tongzang failed, owing to an outflanking movement made by the Allied force, to tenacious resistance, and to the attacks of Allied reinforcements. The rest of the Division under Yamamoto was held by 20 Division under General Gracey in the Shenam Saddle.

17 British-Indian Division immediately withdrew to the Imphal Plain. 33 Division, not daring to pursue them at once, wasted several days, the first step to the fiasco of the Imphal operations; very serious ill-feeling grew between the Army HQ and this Divisional Commander.

31 Division was formed in Bangkok on 10 May, 1943, and consisted of the following units:

58, 124, 138 Infantry Regiments
31 Division Mountain Artillery Regiment
     „   Engineer Regiment
     „   Transport Regiment
     „   Signals Unit
     „   Water Purification Unit
     „   Veterinary Unit
     „   Medical Unit
Ordnance Unit
Total strength: approximately 16,000 men

58 Infantry Regiment and 138 Infantry Regiment were formerly known as 26 Infantry Brigade, formed in Shanghai in January, 1943, and sent to Singapore before being placed in 31 Division. 124 Infantry Regiment, which had taken part in the Guadalcanal operations in 1942, was in French Indo-China when the Division was organized. The first Divisional Commander was Lieutenant-General Sato Kotoku, a political enemy of Mutaguchi, replaced by Lieutenant-General Kawada Tsuchitare in August, 1944, after the Kohima operations.

Some HQ personnel flew direct from Bangkok to Rangoon, but most of the Division came by ship via Penang to Rangoon. Divisional HQ arrived in Pegu in May, 1943, moved up via Kinu and Wuntho in September, reaching Sakan at the end of December, 1943. During its three-month stay here, consolidation of its forces east of the Chindwin was completed, and preparations made for the attack on Kohima. The three infantry regiments moved up by rail as far as Wuntho and took up the following positions:

58 Regiment – Thaungdut – Tanga (HQ at Wayongon)
124   „   – In reserve at Banmauk
138   „   – Tamanthi – Thaungdut (HQ south of Sitsawk)

At the beginning of March, 1944, Divisional HQ advanced to Tomahe, (10 miles NE of Homalin), in readiness for the river crossing, all preparations having been completed. On 15 March 15 Army signalled final instructions. Two battalions of 138 Regiment were the first to land on the west bank; there they engaged with enemy forces who retreated after killing six men. 58 Regiment crossed south of Homalin; the other battalion of 138 Regiment crossed at 'Mampa' and Divisional HQ crossed at Maungkan followed by 124 Regiment which had been held in reserve. They encountered no resistance. Owing to the mountainous nature of the country ahead of them, the men carried only 120 rounds of ammunition each and sufficient rations for one month. Horses and bullocks were ferried across to transport supplies of food and ammunition, and some to be consumed.

As has been said, the 'conquest' of India via Imphal had become the obsession of General Mutaguchi, Commander of the Japanese 15th Army. Mutaguchi believed that if Imphal, capital of India's Manipur State, situated in a long high plain in the jungle-covered Naga and Chin Hills, could be captured, the opportunity would be provided for the Japanese-raised Indian National Army under their Bengali leader, Subhas Chandra Bose, to light a fire of revolution which would render India impotent as a base against Japan. Britain might be neutralized, the United States isolated and Japanese forces carried to a junction with Germany in the Middle East.

Although Tojo, who was both Prime Minister and Minister of War, believed that 'our main objective lies in India', others, including Mutaguchi's Divisional Commanders, and the Commander, Burma Area Army, Lieutenant-General Kawabe, said that there must be 'no mad rush into Assam'. Nevertheless, the original concept of a new defence line to defeat a British return to Burma had been superseded, at least in Mutaguchi's mind, in favour of his own ambitions. In particular, instead of authorizing only four battalions of 31 Division to attack Kohima, he had decided to employ the whole division to block British supply to Imphal and then move to India through Dimapur.

It should be noted, however, that under interrogation after the war, General Miyazaki, commanding 31 Division Infantry Group during the Kohima battle, said that the task assigned to 31 Division was only 'to occupy Kohima in order to cut off the retreat of the Allied troops in Imphal'. Whatever Mutaguchi intended, the Japanese Higher Command may not have seriously contemplated an invasion of India by land in 1944, only such a serious defeat of Anglo-Indian forces that Subhas Chandra Bose would be able to lead his Indian National Army into India and thus achieve a virtually bloodless conquest.

It might have happened had the Japanese not lost in the Arakan, had the Chindits failed, had 5th and 7th Indian and 2nd British Divisions been kept from the battle, had the British not held at Kohima, and had the Japanese not failed to provide for adequate air power, supply, transport and artillery, or to grasp the training, drive and morale of the new XIV Army. But, as we saw in Chapter II, the Second Arakan operation had been started too early by the Japanese and its value as a distraction from Imphal had been vitiated by Mountbatten's brilliant procurement of the enormous quantity of transport aircraft needed for the rediversion of 5th and 7th Divisions to Imphal. The Japanese were not only beaten in Arakan, but British IV and XXXIII Corps had time to prepare the ground in the Imphal area to the north-east, while the Japanese 15 Division ('Ball of Fire')* was still below strength.

Without Kohima, it would have been a damned close-run thing. For its part, the British command incorrectly supposed that, since the terrain towards the Chindwin across which the Japanese would advance was so impenetrable, the latter would attack Kohima in regimental strength only. This assumption was strengthened by the British belief that the main Japanese target was Dimapur, with its vast go-downs and railhead. In fact, although General Sato's orders were only to take and hold Kohima, his 31 Division *did* attack in *divisional* strength. His task was made easier by a secondary British road from Humine to Kohima recently 'opened' by General Ouvry Roberts, commanding 23rd Division. It was reasonable therefore for the British to suppose that 31st Division would reduce its efforts at Kohima in favour of Dimapur, if not that the 4th Battalion Queen's Own Royal West Kents would hold as long as they did.

In the end the Japanese did *not* reduce their efforts, but the Royal West Kents did hold out.

* Also the sign of the 5th Indian Division.

IV

THE CURTAIN-RAISER
AT SANGSHAK

THE 50TH Indian Parachute Regiment with three battalions was the country's first parachute formation, created against the advice of the old hands at GHQ, New Delhi. In 1944 it was commanded by Brigadier 'Tim' Hope Thomson, at 32 probably the youngest Brigadier in the Indian or British Armies. His long head, wide, smiling mouth and wary eyes under the glengarry of the Royal Scots Fusiliers topped the ribbon of an MC won in 1936 in Palestine. He was tall, reserved, imposing, rather silent, on the pattern of Wavell, and his airborne experience and skill were second to none.

His second-in-command was Colonel Bernard Abbott, with whom his relations were formal but correct. His Battalion Commanders were Lieutenant-Colonels Paul Hopkinson, formerly 2nd Punjab, and Dick Willis formerly of the Tochi Scouts, a celebrated Pathan formation from the North-West Frontier, and 1st Gurkhas, commanding 152 and 153 Battalions respectively. 154 Battalion had remained behind in India when the Brigade left for the Kohima/Imphal area.

Between 1 and 6 March the Brigade journeyed up the Brahmaputra in two river steamers. On arrival in Kohima, Tim Hope Thomson then visited the commander of 23 Division, General Ouvry Roberts, to receive orders which were in the circumstances not those for a conventional parachute unit. (It is, incidentally, about 50 Brigade that the legend runs of the Gurkha volunteers whose doubts about jumping from 800 feet were fully dispersed when they realized that *parachutes* would be supplied.) IV Corps' plan for the Brigade was to prevent Japanese infiltration by way of the Naga Hills and the Somra tracks. The Brigade, at that stage, thus also commanded 1 Assam Regiment, 3 Assam Rifles, units of the Burma Regiment and two companies of the Sher at Jessami, Kharasom and Phek, as well as 4/5 Mahrattas and others which fought at Sangshak.

The geographical command covered Ukhrul-Jessami, excluding the Kohima-Imphal Road and Kohima itself.

The Brigade then moved in stages from Kohima to mile 10 and mile 36 (from Imphal) where HQ was established on 17 March, Ukhrul to the north-east on the road to Jessami, Finch's Corner, Sheldon's Corner (10

March), 'New Guinea', 'Gammon', Point 7378 and, finally Sangshak. Sangshak was immediately SSW of Ukhrul, north-east of Litan (23 Division HQ), and of IV Corps at Imphal under Lieutenant-General Sir Geoffrey Scoones, most recently Director of Military Operations at Delhi.

At Sangshak, chosen as the point of last resistance, were ultimately collected part of 4th Battalion of the 5th Mahratta Light Infantry under Colonel J. H. Trim, 152 and 153 Battalions of 50 Brigade, two companies of the Kalibahadur Regiment, 80 Para Field Ambulance, 582 Jungle Mortar Battery and 15 Mountain Battery.

The Japanese 15th and 31st Divisions crossed the Chindwin River, east of which they had been hitherto deployed, on 16 March.

V Force, who were Naga, Lushai and Kuki tribesmen operating as scouts ('Watch and Ward') with their own W/T under British officers from the Assam Rifles and from other units, reported that the offensive had probably begun. The recipient of this message, 49 Brigade, was on the move south and no action was taken. British Intelligence, however, through an agent at Homalin of Z Force (British and Anglo-Burman stay-behind and infiltrated officers) had reported the crossing at 1300 on that day, when it was logged in by XIV Army and then in the IV Corps Intelligence Diary.

Intelligence distribution among British units was poor. Although IV Corps had seen from the Z Force report that a regiment of 31 Division was moving on 'an axis Homalin-Ukhrul to the Imphal-Kohima road to Kohima' on 16 March, the only message passed to the Brigade Major of 50 Indian Parachute Brigade by GSO1 23 Division, and that on 18 March, was that 'a column of Japanese advancing via Pushing, having attacked V Force HQ, was expected to bump 152 Battalion at Sheldon's Corner within the next two days'.

15 Division was commanded by Lieutenant-General Yamauchi, for nine years Military Attaché at Washington, a gentle, brilliant staff officer, dying of tuberculosis and, otherwise, dependent on western artefacts such as the notorious portable lavatory to which reference has been made. Owing to intelligence acquired by the British from a Burman agent of the Japanese, RAF Mitchells had already located and destroyed 4,000 men of this Division, while his 67 Regiment had been delayed, by the RAF in strikes against the railway. 15 Division's target was the Imphal plain, with one battalion sent as deception toward Tamu to join 33 Division against General Douglas Gracey and his 20th Indian Division, the main body to move against Imphal through Sangshak 'like a ball of fire'.

The 31st Division, as we have seen, was a recent formation, created from several Divisions of very experienced troops with service in China and Guadalcanal. The Division was formally organized in Thailand under the command of Lieutenant-General Sato Kutoku, with Major-General Miyazaki Shigesaburo commanding the Division's Infantry Group.

Their advance was to be in three columns, the southern under Miyazaki via Ukhrul, and the other two through the Somra Hills to Kohima and Dimapur. This odyssey, over the huge Alpine mountains, ridges and spurs, in thick jungle and forests on narrow precipitous paths, was accompanied by oxen, horses and elephants as carriers, as well as goats and 15,000 cattle, one for each man in the Division, food-on-the-hoof. Beasts slipped, fell and died on the ledges but, because of thorough prior reconnaisance, the artillery, or most of it, got through to Kohima. (After the march, the balance of provisions was intended to be provided by capture from the British.) Arrival itself was an amazing feat, executed by men with 50 kg loads of rice, beans, canned fish, biscuit and salt, as well as weapons and ammunition and with relatively little illness. It was not one envisaged by the British planners at Delhi and further east.

Miyazaki was a brave, passionate and able soldier who proved himself, after the battle, not to possess the more inexcusable attributes of his countrymen in relation to Indian and British prisoners and wounded. General Sato himself, although regarded by Slim as unenterprising, was a tough, aggressive officer. He had, however, distrusted and been distrusted by his Commander-in-Chief, Mutaguchi, since the warring political factors of the 1930s in Tokyo; and Sato had regard for his men.

On 19 March some 900 Japanese of III Battalion of 58 Regiment of 31 Division employing rifles, light machine guns and grenades, attacked 'C' Company of 152 Battalion, 50 Parachute Brigade, at Point 7358, a hill well to the east of Sangshak village. Sangshak had, as has been said, recently been vacated by 49 Brigade of 23 Division, sent to aid 17 Indian Division who were closing on Imphal from Tiddim according to Slim and Scoones' master plan. Their departure was, indeed, the reason for 50 Brigade's presence in the area. Major John Fuller, commanding 'C' Company, had 170 men, including seven officers, two medium machine guns and a section of mortars; he had received at least *some* Intelligence, for he believed the enemy to be forty miles away.

Three Japanese attacks were held. But by mid-morning, the Japanese War Diary reported that 'C' Company's 'fire had slackened considerably. Suddenly, from the top of the hill, a small group of about twenty men charged down towards us firing and shouting in a counter-attack, a charge which ended disastrously in a ravine across the line of advance. Seeing the débâcle, at the very top of the position, an officer appeared, put a pistol to his head and shot himself in full view of everyone below.

Our men felt deeply impressed by such a brave act . . . At Point 7378, III Battalion suffered 160 casualties, including three officers killed and four wounded. The British enemy had resisted with courage and skill.'

The attack was over by noon on 20 March with only twenty British Indian survivors. Attempts at ambush and outflanking by 4/5 Mahrattas and 'A' Company of 152 Battalion failed. Later that day most, if not all, companies of both 152 and 4/5 Mahrattas had become engaged in the area, at Khanoggoi at a road block and at Badger Hill and New Guinea. It was decided that a Box should be formed at Badger Hill. From Finch's Corner, the Brigadier warned Division that there would not be enough water.

In very heavy rain, it had been Hope Thomson's intention on 15 March to move the Brigade to Ukhrul itself, once the centre of Naga administration under the British. The village lay on a long ridge at about 6,000 feet, surrounded by pine woods. The settlement, other than the straggling Christian settlement, consisted of timber-fronted houses with huge overhanging porches, the roofs shingled, with roof horns, descending in stone platforms. In the event, he sent only a machine-gun platoon on 20 March, withdrawn on 21 March. (It must, unfortunately, be recorded here that Charles Pawsey, Deputy Commissioner for the Naga Hills, subsequently referred to the Brigade as undisciplined in its dealings with Nagas.)

On 21 March Captain Nagaya, in nominal command of II Battalion, 58 Regiment of 31 Division, having driven off the MMG Company of 50 Indian Parachute Brigade at Ukhrul, turned away from his line of advance to Kohima and on General Miyazaki's orders made for Sangshak. Miyazaki had learned that the British were about to be present here in brigade strength and was encouraged in this decision by a signal from General Mutaguchi plainly stating that 15 Division, *whose battle area it was*, was moving too slowly.

By 22 March the Japanese had cut the road to Sangshak from Litan, 23 Indian Division HQ. No supplies or military equipment could now reach Sangshak by road from Imphal at a time when the departing 49 Brigade had wholly failed to fortify the position or even to supply barbed wire. That evening the 152nd Battalion under Colonel Paul Hopkinson, the 4/5 Mahrattas – small, tough, funny, disciplined, calm but mischievous, Wellington's most determined opponents – under Colonel J. H. Trim, and the Gunner troop, marched in to Sangshak from Sheldon's Corner and other points whence they had been summoned by the Brigadier. Those of 153 Battalion who could get transport from Kohima, and were not stranded at Litan had also arrived, perhaps 390 men.

At Tim Hope Thomson's disposal were about 2,000 effectives from under-strength units, two-thirds of whom had been in action without rest for three days. The full-strength 3,500 referred to in the Official History is an illusion.

Sangshak village, unfortified and unimproved by its previous garrison, lay on a hill with a small plateau to the east slightly higher than the hill. Therein was a volcanic circular bank, unfortunately of obsidian, the crater of an ancient volcano, almost impervious to digging. Dense wild rhododendrons lay to the north and south, and thick woods to the east. A gully lay to the north-west. It was overlooked by the Naga's Baptist Church, initially in the Brigade's hands. There was little water within the perimeter and no wire had come, or ever would, from the division or IV Corps.

The perimeter was much too crowded for the numbers it held. Soon water was limited to a bottle a man a day; the main water point near the school was under continual enemy fire and rainwater had to be collected in tins and tarpaulins. Forty men were wounded this first day.

The topography of the Imphal plain varies from huge terraced mountains, green with rice shoots and blue-green with woods and forest once full of antelope and leopard, to the lakes, marshes and agricultural land of the plain itself. It is the envy, as a kind of paradise, of all visitors, but here, alas, all hell was about to break out.

The first Japanese attack on Sangshak was mounted in their usual way, grenade and 'charge', by 8, 5 and 6 Companies of II Battalion of 58 Regiment against John Sanders' (former 6th Gurkhas) 'C' Company of 153 Battalion. These were particularly accurate Gurkha marksmen who there and then killed ninety out of 120 Japanese. A young Englishman called Hobstock said that 'because of the mass downward movement of fifty or sixty tumbling Japanese bodies, the whole hill seemed to be moving upwards'. A second assault led to twenty more Japanese dead. Machine guns and mortars had added to the casualties. At the eastern end of the position, Havildar Sanbaji Bhningde, himself shot in the chest, and his Mahratta mortar crew drove off a contingent of 15 Division, now also arrived on the scene. From this point onward confusion is widespread about the respective accomplishments of the Mahrattas and of the Parachute Brigade.

Air supply to the garrison began on 23 March with depressingly consistent lack of success, most of the food, water and ammunition in blue, white and red parachutes falling to the Japanese, the aircraft with one exception flying too high and too fast. A break-out, because of lack of resources, had therefore to be excluded as did any form of attack on West Hill which the enemy now held. Encirclement at night, permitting regular Japanese bombardment and suicide raids of an officer and half-a-dozen men against tight defences, made sleep almost impossible. The predicament was exacerbated by the continued absence of wire. And, in that tiny basin, help could not be given to the wounded, since, even in the dark, movement over ground could not be allowed. Among the putrefying corpses, exhaustion spread.

That day Captain Nagaya's Battalion under Miyazaki, without waiting for the Japanese artillery, attacked, howling, in three-company strength, to be heavily cut about by British-Indian mountain guns and mortars. The (Gurkha) 153 Battalion supported by Hurricanes then attacked, inflicting severe casualties before being repulsed, but, on 24 March, 6 Company of II Battalion broke through in the south-west. Two Gurkha grenades landed near Nagaya and his Adjutant, Kameyama, who kicked one hard like a football, while Nagaya picked up the other and hurled it, shouting 'Charge!'

Shell bursts in this congested area caused hideous if inevitable casualties, devotedly treated by 80 Field Ambulance in a dressing station 80 × 20 yards, deep down in the old crater. The corpses of the Japanese rotted and stank all round the plateau. Water was reduced to half a bottle a day for each man.

After an abortive attack by III Battalion on 24 March, a joint II and III Battalion attack went in at 4 a.m. on 25 March against the Church and the north-west. According to 58th Regiment mémoires, 'some of the men broke into the position after savage hand-to-hand fighting, but then came under fire from the enemy on the left and right. Those who had entered were annihilated and the remainder withdrew with heavy losses in killed and wounded. So this attack ended in failure again.' The Church was sometimes in British and sometimes Japanese hands.

At least 300 men in each of the two Japanese battalions were casualties from this action, including most company and platoon commanders. Nearly *all* the British and Indian officers of 152 Battalion were either dead or dying by next day; only a handful of men were left.

The cautious Major Fukushima of 15 Division (III Battalion, 60 Regiment) had arrived nearby on 23 March; his attached artillery was reducing the British defences. On 25 March he contacted 31 Division, after being initially pinned down two hundred yards in front of 50 Parachute Brigade. General Miyazaki, in furious sadness at the losses of his *own* men, forbade Fukushima the right to enter Sangshak – 'soldier's compassion' or *'Bushi no nasake'*. He insisted that Colonel Fukunaga, Commander of 58 Regiment, march in, wrapped in the flag of the Rising Sun, for the glory of the final assault.

This was not to be. On 26 March, fighting in company strength between Captain Nishida's composite company from II and III Battalion and, after almost all other British officers were killed or out of action, Major Jimmy Roberts' Gurkha 'A' Company of 153 Battalion, continued for twelve hours. It was actually accompanied by the customary Japanese caterwauling, by two senior British officers with hunting horns, and by the guns on both sides. When it was over, Nishida had only eight men left out of one hundred and twenty, and Roberts had lost half his Company. British and Indian grenades were either useless or almost exhausted. Curried mule and apple was the hot dish of the day throughout this part of the battle. When the 60th Regiment attacked in the southwest, Fukushima lost thirty men and sensibly pulled back. But, in a rocky space of 400 × 800 yards, the Parachute Brigade's position had long been desperately vulnerable.

Then, *en clair*, came a IV Corps radio message, immediately challenged by the Brigade, ordering the Garrison 'to fight their way out, south and west'. This signal again apparently compounded the errors of IV Corps and 23 Division staff throughout the heroic battle: two battalions of Japanese 60 Regiment were outside Sangshak, one mile south. Nevertheless, after a final extended artillery shoot, the order was obeyed and, in various degrees of coherence, the Brigade moved out into the jungle, large areas of which had been set on fire by the enemy to 'drive the game'. The Japanese took over a position empty except for wounded, whom, however, unlike their colleagues elsewhere, they tended relatively well. Some they even released, in underpants and without shoes, at Kohima when they arrived there with their prisoners.

152 Battalion had lost 80% of establishment, including 26 out of 31 officers, 153 Battalion 35%, the Gunners 25%, the Machine-Gun Company and Brigade Defence Platoon 75%, Mahrattas some casualties and 100 men captured when they took 23 Division's order *au pied de la lettre*. At the time that troops left the position on 26 March 80th Para Field Ambulance had had in Sangshak 450 men in care, of whom 100 had to be left behind.

Scurrilous comment about the Brigade and its Commanding Officer began almost at once and circulated for many years throughout the Command and in India. Allegations of misjudgement and of a nervous breakdown, inaccurate Orders of Battle, denials that the Brigade had been deprived of timely information of the Japanese advance, were common if self-serving variations. These were on a theme that seemed to make the Brigadier scapegoat for mistakes that "nearly destroyed IV Corps and reversed the battle for Imphal itself". It is a happy thing that Hope Thomson, after reversion to the substantive rank of Major, subsequently held five active commands and won the DSO in Europe. He died in 1990.

A curious feature of this action was that the Order of Battle of both 15 and 31 Divisions was captured from the body of a slain Japanese Captain. This was instantly carried in two separate copies, at great risk, to IV Corps HQ by Captain Lester Allen and another. It is disappointing that the gallantry of these undertakings and their intelligence content – that Sato would concentrate the *complete* 31 Division against Kohima – mysteriously did not affect XIV Army's decisions about Kohima or about the tiny Assamese garrisons of Jessami, Kharasom and Phek, nonchalantly abandoned to their fate.

After Sangshak General Miyazaki gained considerable equipment and creature comforts from the battlefield. But the Japanese, because of the delay caused by Sangshak, lost the depot stores at Kanglatongbi. They also lost six out of eight company commanders and perhaps half the platoon commanders. 58 Regiment's total strength was reduced by half – 220 killed and 350 wounded – and one of its Companies had eight men left, all of whom were wounded.

The delay threw out 31 Division's Kohima timetable, enabled the town to be garrisoned from 5 Division flown in from the Arakan, and gave the British the Japanese Order of Battle for their Imphal campaign. Had Miyazaki not gone, as he should not have gone, to Sangshak, Dimapur and its enormous warehouses might have fallen. (It is, however, true that one Battalion of the 58 Regiment cut the Kohima-Imphal road on March 30.) The favourable consequences for General Yamauchi's 15 Division would then have been as great as the unfavourable consequences for IV Corps at Imphal.

Harry Seaman, in his magisterial and moving *Battle of Sangshak*, has told us that General Sato after the war dwelt bitterly on the loss he had suffered as a result of Miyazaki's unnecessary encounter with 50 Indian Parachute Brigade. The terms in which Ronald Lewin's *Slim* referred to this battle were: 'Another invaluable delaying action was fought, at Sangshak, by 50 Indian Parachute Brigade. Here, until 26 March, the Japanese were prevented from gaining further ground to the west'. The stand here was the first time – the second being the resistance of the Assam Regiment at Jessami and Kharasom – that Kohima was to be saved. In Field-Marshal Slim's words in August, 1944, '50 Indian Parachute Brigade bore the brunt of the enemy's powerful flanking attack, and by their staunchness gave the Garrison of Imphal the vital time required to adjust their defences.' This time was further extended by Japanese post-victory drunken pursuit of Naga women.

Perhaps therefore we may think with approbation about our country-men and about those Indians and Gurkhas who fought with them. The three Battalions of 50 Parachute Brigade later that year formed the nucleus for the new Indian Airborne Division of 50 and 77 Para Brigades and 14 Air Landing Brigade. Colonel (later Brigadier) 'Happy' Hopkin-son of 152 Battalion who was badly wounded at Sangshak but escaped to Kohima, commanded 77 until Partition, a slight, diffident, humorous, almost scholarly man, and a good soldier. He died in December, 1991.

V

THE NAGAS AND OTHERS

THE 1ST Assam Regiment, under mainly British officers, combined Gurkhas and hillmen (Nagas, Lushai and Kuki) with men from the plains: the terrain was familiar to them, as were the inhabitants. There was not necessarily much love lost between the different tribes, in particular between the Nagas and the Kuki who had raised rebellion in 1918 and more recently betrayed many V Force posts to the enemy. But within the Regiment, there was accord. By February, 1944, the only action this new formation had seen was in patrols along the Chindwin and in the terrible Kabaw Valley. Dysentery, scrub typhus and malaria had so depleted their strength that they had been pulled out to rest and recuperate.

Their commander was Lieutenant-Colonel W.F. ('Bruno') Brown, a tough little martinet of great physical fitness who, despite a genial and happy personality, demanded nothing but the best from his men. His tireless professionalism was rewarded by the Regiment's superb performance, now and in the main Battle for Kohima which followed, worthy partners with the Royal West Kents in the conduct of the siege.

From 1 to 16 February the Battalion had been training at Digboi in the Brahmaputra valley, where Captain Calistan, later to excel at the DC's Bungalow, took over command of 'B' Company. On 17 March instructions were received from IV Corps to prepare to move to Kohima and, after a conference of all officers, the regiment moved off with the M/T, sleeping the night by the road near Jorhat.

On 18 February they arrived at the gigantic stores depot of Dimapur, long thought by XIV Army to be the principal Japanese target on 15th Army's supposed march on Delhi. Brown went to Imphal for briefing at IV Corps, returning to Kohima on the 21st where 'A', 'B', 'C' and 'D' Companies, HQ Company and the Admin Company had meanwhile assembled under Major Thurgood. Here the Royal Corps of Signals handed over a Mark 22 W/T set. Lieutenants Peter Steyn, a powerful South African today living in Hong Kong, and the Welsh David ('Jonah') Lloyd Jones rejoined their companies. The mules and heavy (3 cwt) trucks were left in the Sher Regiment lines at Kohima.

The Battalion's orders, as carried from Imphal by Colonel Brown, were to take up the defensive at Jessami as a firm base with two companies outside as mobile striking forces, harassing Japanese lines of communication. One full company, 'A', now under Jock Young, a cheerful, hard-working, realistic young Glaswegian, whose captaincy had not been gazetted, was to man Kharasom, together with a 3" mortar section. Phakekedzumi (Phek or 'Fake') was garrisoned by a company of 1 Garrison Brigade Burma Regiment under Major Norman Giles of the Black Watch, later to be augmented by V force detachments under Lieutenant-Colonel R. A. Stanley.

The country in which these villages lay was considered to be that through which any Japanese invasion, however 'unlikely or small-scale', would have to pass en route to Kohima. Kharasom, Jessami and Phek were therefore the choke points in any attempt by IV Corps, at that time still in command of the area before the arrival of XXXIII Corps under Lieutenant-General Stopford, or of Colonel Hugh Richards, Commander Kohima Garrison, to stop a Japanese advance.

The landscape was of range upon range of hills, one behind another, grey and blue-green, 'as though the steep winter waves of the Channel had frozen suddenly on a vast scale. Featureless, cold and uncanny, they rolled on until they melted into the lowering sky' or into the haze of unmapped country to the east. The 2nd Field Company, King George V's Own Bengal Sappers and Miners, had recently improved the jeep track, but for the most part movement was by bridle paths on the bare spurs and round the folds of the hills.

On each ridge, or so it seemed, stood a thatched and tattered Naga village, grey and smoke-stained, and then more hills 'stretching away as far as the eye could see, in an ocean of peaks, a wilderness of steep fields, terraces, untouched forests, cliffs, gulfs and razor-backs which merged at last into infinity'.

Here dwelt the Nagas in bright plaids, red and yellow lunghis, scarlet blankets on brown shoulders, bead necklaces, elephant hair, ivory and polished brass bracelets on their arms, hornbill feathers in the hair, golden skin, page-boy haircuts, mongoloid, hard. Their women were magnetically attractive to some British soldiers.

Surrounded by these enormous hills, crags and gorges, the villages, with their huge projecting porches, faintly recalling Minankebau or Toba houses in North Sumatra, defended by stone walls, spiked palisades, dykes and thorn fences, offered shelter. Plum, pomegranate and pear blossom, pink sprays against the blue sky, white magnolia, rhododendrons, oak trees, alders. In the village the 'bachelor halls', three times the size of the ordinary houses, small granaries on stilts, patches of fenced garden, weathered grey thatch over the pitch dark interiors of all Naga houses, looked down upon wooden water troughs fed by bamboo pipes from hill springs, the sacred jumping stones, beside which the head-hunters used to bury their trophies, and the Genna posts commemorating ceremonial feasts.

Irrespective of the tribe or sub-tribe, the record of the Nagas during the Japanese occupation was one of extraordinary loyalty to the British, whether lightly, indeed inadequately, armed (mainly muzzle-loaders) in the 'Watch and Ward' Scouts of V Force, as runners, or in the construction of tunnels, caches and other 'holes' in the jungle warren.

At the worst point of wartime crisis, the anthropologist Ursula Graham Bower's personal Naga staff asked for leave. Well as she knew them, even she believed that they were unlikely to return. But they did so, twenty-four hours later, having gone home, made their wills, arranged for their families, given their heirloom necklaces to their sons, left beads for burial and come back to die, if necessary, with their English friend.

'After all, what was the better thing? To desert and live, and hear our children curse us for the shame we put on them, or to die with you, and leave them proud of us for ever.' Their plight today in an India where they are not at home is one of the saddest and most perplexing consequences of Empire.

Charles Pawsey, the Deputy Commissioner, said that when the Japanese first invaded the Naga Hills there had been universal conster-nation, and the whole population had been dumbfounded. In 1942 the threat had been real, but there had been ample time since then to prepare. The whole area was full of troops and for months streams of lorries had run day and night up the Imphal road. Then, almost overnight, the traffic had stopped and the troops cleared out. The Nagas as a whole probably did not realize that most of the troops evacuated before the forthcoming battle were non-combatants. What really distressed them was the evacu-ation on 31 March, after the first occasion that they had moved to Kohima, of 161 Brigade.

The shock was very great indeed. In some cases, the first thing the Nagas knew when they woke up in the morning was that their village was full of Japanese. The enemy did not at first treat the local population badly, seeking to win them over, to make them supply rations, carry loads and help the invasion. The Japanese thought that to show a Congress Party flag would bring immediate positive response, a curious idea in an Assam Hill district hostile to Indians. Moreover, the members of the Indian National Army, the Jiffs (Japanese Indian Fighting Forces) behaved disgracefully, far worse than the Japanese themselves. All cases of rape reported were found to have been committed by this rabble and not by the Japanese.

Both parties looted and stole, but, here too, Indians were the worst. The Japanese, however, plundered and stole pigs and chicken in Kohima Naga Village.

In areas far from British troops, Nagas had to supply rations and carry loads for the enemy. They could not be blamed for doing so when help was distant. Whenever there *were* British troops, the utmost help was given.

Their great value was in informing the British troops of Japanese dispositions, so that bombers and artillery could exploit the information. Again and again, although well camouflaged, Japanese camps were bombed or shelled with excellent results, extremely upsetting to Japanese morale.

The Intelligence supplied by the Nagas and other tribes was not the work of Government servants only. Ordinary villagers who noticed something unusual and reported it were as valuable as anyone. Before the fighting began, most Government servants had been sent to their villages with written orders to report to the nearest military formation. At Piphima, for example, Nikhalhu had been allocated to the area west of the road end, Zhuikhu to the area east of the road. A Dr Nandij also remained at Piphima. Later, when the British 2nd Division in armoured vehicles first came up the road, these three Government servants were on duty, although the rest of the security forces had been evacuated. Their information was invaluable. Similarly at Hanima, Lavi, a Head Clerk, was in charge. At Wokha, a Naga official called Ao with his gunner was in position and, together with Major Henchman, his work was of the utmost use. The gunmen and much of the Frontier Intelligence Staff were swamped, withdrawn or went underground, although at Chipkatami and Sakhazu they did well.

It was in this area that the Scouts and Levies were raised, of most use later to Perowne's Long Range Penetration Brigade in the north, covering the railway to Ledo after the first phase of the siege, with a free hand to deal with scattered Japanese. Again and again the enemy was ambushed, while British troops were never once ambushed by the Japanese. When the really heavy fighting in the Kohima siege was in progress it was, of course, impossible to acquire information from the Nagas. Just before the relief of the RWKs and Assam Regiment, Eric Lambert of the Indian Police arrived at the bypass road with 2nd Division and, with his Frontier Intelligence Staff and the local Nagas, organized and supervised an efficient intelligence system, in touch with the Southern Angamis in occupied territory by various routes over the Patkoi, and with Angamis in the villages around Kohima.

Help was rendered in other ways. Porters in hundreds helped 23rd Brigade. Round Kohima they carried for 2nd Division in the attack on

Aradura spur on the right flank and evacuated the wounded. As the 7th Division advanced along the Kezoma-Kidima range, Nagas engaged as porters and Scouts rendered invaluable assistance.

Pawsey always pointed out that, throughout the Japanese advance and subsequent defeat, the Civil Police also did extremely well. Ao was in charge of a section of the Frontier Intelligence work with headquarters at Wokha, and was awarded the Indian Police Medal. Two Constables did good Intelligence work in this area. On 2 April six constables were sent to Wokha: when our troops arrived, they acted as guides and escorted captured Japanese and Jiffs to Mokokehung. Also on 2 April, four constables were sent to Themokedima. The Japanese arrived on 9 April, and the constables then reported to the Honorary Magistrate at Wokha where they worked until the area was cleared of the enemy.

Constable No 47 Razuholie Angami was reported by the 2nd Division to have been very helpful during the operations which led to the recapture of Kezoma village and was thrice commended by the Army for good work. Constable No 30 Vihoi Angami was commended by the Army for his very great help in fighting in and around Kekrima village. He and a friend killed one Japanese and captured another.

Constable No 34 Khoylese Angami, with the assistance of villagers, captured three well-armed enemy agents. This constable had an exciting time. He and his friend, Merenungba Ao, an ex-sepoy, were caught by the Japanese, but escaped at the 15th mile of the Wokha Road, celebrating their escape by killing a Japanese at midnight at the 16th mile. Their wives had earlier been seized by the enemy as hostages. The men joined up with British troops in pursuit; the Japanese were hard pressed, and the wives got away. Constable No 29 Nigurohie and constable No 18 Dolhucha did very good intelligence work, keeping in touch with the South Angamis over the Patkoi Range while the Japanese were still in Kohima. They helped to kill three Japanese and caught one alive, collecting much valuable information about enemy dispositions and movements. Constable No 3 Khrulhel Angami and No 26 Menguzellie Angami did well with the Columns and were awarded the Indian Police Medal. Constable No 16 Khayakup Kuki did good work in the area between Dimapur and the Barak River; several enemy agents were captured in this area, and escaped prisoners of war were brought in. ASI Nivotso Angami (Frontier Intelligence) did very well before and after the battle, and was wounded. Constable No 33 Visopi Angami was wounded severely by the sword of a Japanese officer in a hand-to-hand struggle. He managed to get away in spite of great loss of blood. Constable No 4 Kelhikhrie Angami was sent to his village Tophema on 2 April. The Japanese arrived on 4 April. He remained in hiding until 18 April, when he reported to the Honorary Magistrate at Wokha with valuable information, returning to get details of enemy dispositions at Chieehama, which he reported to Lieut-Colonel Walker, the Column Commander, remaining as a guide to British troops until 27 May. Constable No 27 Jegesway Singh Manipuri was reported missing after the operations were concluded, and Constables No 55 Bishnudhoj Angami and No 1 Veeheyi Angami were captured and shot by the enemy while on intelligence duty.

Of the small Naga Hills Police Force, Pawsey was proud to record that nearly all were in the front line with our troops. Two were killed, two were wounded and one missing. Three Indian Police Medals were awarded. It is regrettable that these medals were not for gallantry, since the recipients showed great courage in the face of the enemy. The Police record during the fighting was excellent.

The Assam Rifles were founded in 1835 as a body of '750 ill-equipped, ill-armed, ill-paid, ill-trained men known as the Cachar Levy formed from Gurkhas, Nagas, Kuki, Lushai'. Their primary function was internal, but in pre-Independence wars they fought alongside the Army in defence of external borders. B. K. Nehru, however, Governor of Kashmir and Gujarat and an Indian High Commissioner to the United Kingdom after Independence, commented: 'Totally insufficient integration of tribes with the rest of the Indian community under the Raj gave rise to dissatisfaction of various kinds which have, in some parts, culminated in insurgency and insurrection . . . tribes were deliberately kept apart from the rest of the country for reasons both legitimate and illegitimate.'

The Rifles had five Battalions of fifteen platoons, each under the command of a Gurkha officer. This paramilitary force wore bush hats or black pill boxes with a badge and a red cockade, red and black lunghi/apron, green trousers and blue shirts. They marched with a quick, light infantry step. Four platoons from the Rifles were also seconded to V Force, that body of hillmen organized by Wavell in 1942 for operations against Japanese lines of communication. V Force had a central HQ and six groups, one for each Frontier operations area, each with its own small HQ. They included up to 1,000 tribesmen, living on the country.

The Naga Hills (Third) Battalion had its Commandant, Colonel G. A. E. Keene, in Kohima. Later, detachments of the Assam Rifles acted as scout and forerunners for the pursuit by XIV Army of the Japanese across the Chindwin. In peacetime they had, in exercising their internal security duties, conducted 'showing the flag' patrols from battlemented forts with quadrangles, like that at Ukhrul. In those days they communicated largely by carrier pigeon.

As Pawsey remarked, when war broke out with Germany the Third (Naga Hills) Battalion of the Assam Rifles had to provide drafts for regular Gurkha units and for the Assam Regiment. In these circumstances, the Battalion had to be virtually reconstructed.

On the outbreak of war with Japan their work was doubled and redoubled, the demands for their services never-ending. Four platoons were permanently out with 'V' Force in the Somra Tract, and had to be relieved, since work on the Chindwin in the presence of a population mainly sitting on the fence was arduous. To all intents and purposes, therefore, eight platoons were tied up with V Force. Reliefs could not be carried out regularly; some platoons spent over six months in the jungle, away from their own officers and battalion organization. It says much for their discipine and training that their duties were carried out as efficiently as they were.

In addition, there were four outposts and the guards for the American Observation posts, Nyassia, Shagot on the Patkoi, Wakehing, Donyo in Burma on the Patkoi, Lahe far inside Burma, and Mokokehung.

There were also escorts to be provided for the Senior District Officer Mokokehung on his numerous transfrontier tours. In 1943 detachments were sent to Nowgong for internal security when Congress was trying to sabotage British lines of communication. A detachment was in Manipur State in 1943 and there were numerous other guards and duties.

Very early on, the Assam Rifles had to vacate their own lines and make new ones in the jungle close to the water supply, without any assistance from the Army, so that their men were, even when in Headquarters, denied good housing. Nor were any of the other amenities available to the Army available to them.

Their final glory was the defence of Kohima. They had three British Officers, Lieut-Colonel G. M. K. Keene, MBE, Commandant; Major M. K. Smith and Captain D. Cleland, Assistant Commandants, plus their Subadar Major, Sardar Bahadur Bol Bahadur Gurung OBE. Night after night they were attacked by the Japanese and repulsed attacks without losing ground on Indian General Hospital Spur; according to their Commandant, their casualties were less than those of other units, because their defences were so excellent. For the last five days or so of the siege, a detachment under Captain Cleland with the Assam Regiment held the bump now levelled flat, overlooking the tennis court within a few yards of the Japanese. Here, too, they held on grimly till relieved, actually making ground. Pawsey and Buster Keene had adjoining dugouts. They met daily with Donald Cleland, white with fatigue from the night's fighting, and 'Smithy', and Pawsey's old friend Bol Bahadur, and talked of the night's events. They all carried on as if temporary removal from Permanent Officials' PWD residences only a few yards away were no more than rather a nuisance. So did the personal Staff, Buster's cook and Mhiasizolle (alias Sihu), and Kewhato, as well as the 3rd Assam Rifles

Office Staff. At one time, Pawsey had thought the Nagas would not stand heavy shellfire. He knew differently after the siege, even if the Nagas were indeed shaken when the kitchen got a direct hit in the early stages while they were making tea. Sihu did not approve of the disregard paid to the usual conventions of camp life. Even his little hedge and notice 'Deputy Commissioner's latrine – Private' was ignored!

Pawsey thought that he himself had a 'very soft time'. The honour and glory, he said, went to the Riflemen of the 3rd Assam Rifles, their brothers-in-arms in the Assam Regiment, the Royal West Kents and the so-called non-combatants, who held the front line night after night. A rustle in the jungle, a grenade rolled down the slope, a tin kicked, and a burst of Bren gun fire, hour after hour, the same thing; 'In the morning a line of dead Japanese a few yards from the front line'.

When the Assam Rifles were relieved after about seventeen nights of this kind of thing, Smith stayed behind with a platoon to look after the Assam Rifles' kit. The night after the relief was mysterious, deadly still, without a shot fired. Thereafter 'hell broke loose'. The Japanese had crept into the empty Assam and West Kent bunkers unnoticed and put all they had got into an all-out attack. Kohima was nearer then than ever before to defeat. Seven officers of the British relieving unit lost their lives. All honour to the Assam Rifles who had held so long without relief.

The memorial to men of the Battalion who died in the Battle of Kohima is north-west of Kuki Piquet on the small ridge forming the front line of the Assam Rifles Sector on Garrison Hill from which the enemy were kept at bay.

The following message dated 24 June, 1944, was sent by 'W. J. Slim, CB, CBE, DSO, MC, General Officer Commanding-in-Chief, Fourteenth Army', to His Excellency the Governor of Assam:

'Now that the whole of the Assam Province has been freed of the enemy, I think that it is an opportune moment to ask you to convey to the Nagas the appreciation which the Fourteenth Army and I personally so strongly feel for the loyalty, devotion and help that they have rendered to us. They have given this help without any thought of reward – on frequent occasions actually refusing reward. They have carried the wounded over long distances and difficult country, helped us in the porterage of supplies, furnished us with information and shown the utmost fortitude in enduring the cruel tortures of the enemy rather than betray us; in this their women have shown no less courage than their men.

'I would, therefore, ask you to convey to the Naga Chiefs and Headmen my very real gratitude and that of all ranks of the

Fourteenth Army for the magnificent services they have rendered, and our confidence that they will continue to show the same devotion to our common cause.

'When final victory is achieved, I hope that these loyal services will receive a tangible reward which they so richly deserve.

'I cannot conclude without reference to the whole-hearted and gallant cooperation which this Army has invariably received from the civil officials of the Naga Hills. Again, I would ask you to convey to them the gratitude and appreciation of all ranks of the Fourteenth Army and myself for their services.'

VI

THE ASSAM REGIMENT INTO BATTLE

BEFORE THE 1st Battalion of the Assam Regiment left Kohima for the outposts, Jessami, Kharasom and Phek, the Deputy Commissioner, Charles Pawsey (later Sir Charles), gave a party in the DC's Bungalow for their officers, also inviting nurses from the 49th and 53rd Indian General Hospitals. Bruno Brown insisted that his officers should attend in full battle order. In the then 'peaceful' conditions of the little hill station, the other guests regarded this with amused affection as an exaggerated, if not bizarre, gesture. It was a jolly occasion. Within six weeks, however, the Japanese would be on Hospital Ridge, both the hospitals closed and evacuated, the Spur strewn with dead and wounded.

Lieutenant Young and 'A' Company left for Kharasom on 23 February in four 15 cwt trucks, delayed by a broken bridge at Mile 10, repaired by local labour. The Battalion as a whole moved off next day, catching up with Jock Young later at MS 44, where they spent the night. On 25 February 'B' Company under Major Thurgood arrived at Jessami, while Young and 'A' Company continued to Kharasom. Battalion HQ, 'C' and 'D' Companies had reached Jessami by foot and jeep on 27 February, the advance party led by Major Sidiman Rai, a genial Gurkha also commanding 'C' Company, and the main party commanded by Major Askew, 'D' Company. The total strength of this Battalion was now 822 officers and men, of whom about twenty were British officers, including the M/T Platoon under Donald Elwell at Kohima.

On 8 March the regiment was visited by Major-General Ouvry Roberts, 23 Division, and Brigadier Tim Hope Thomson, 50th Indian Parachute Brigade, under whose command the Battalion operated, it will be recalled, before the arrival on 23 March of Colonel Hugh Richards as Commander Kohima Garrison, eventually under Lieutenant-General Stopford, XXXIII Corps. Hope Thomson ordered the garrisons to 'fight to the last round and the last man'. Roberts then 'opened' (by jeep) the newly made Kohima-Humine road, later to form a convenient additional route for Major-General Miyazaki and the 58th Regiment en route to Kohima. (Seaman doubts, indeed, whether had this road not been built, Mutaguchi would have decided to devote a whole division to Kohima.)

Immediately on arrival at Jessami, Brown set the Battalion to digging bunkers and fox-holes and the preparation of defensive positions *envers et contre tout*. The village itself was described in Ursula Graham Bower's *Naga Path* as 'a nest of wizards', the scene of a peculiar spell involving an egg in a bamboo to which adhered a piece of medical lint stolen from her dispensary. Jessami was also noted for the excellence of its rice beer (zu), perhaps of more interest to fighting men. It was approached from wooded ridges to fields and from the fields to a limewood reserve and then by a broad, worn path to the village gate.

The defences themselves were properly wired, with bunkers, outer and inner. They were not in the village itself but about half a mile south, with a bivouac outside the perimeter, although ammunition and food were within the defences. The position at the junction of two tracks was overlooked and did not have its own water, but it could at least monitor most of the approaches. Supplies arrived regularly by M/T from Kohima.

The Battalion had two platoon-strength patrols on permanent reconnaissance to the east, north-east and south-east, covering all tracks from the Assam-Burma border, at distances up to 20 miles from Base. (Soon after settling in at Jessami, Colonel Brown had sent a platoon from 'D' Company to reinforce Jock Young and 'A' Company at Kharasom.) On 18 March a patrol led by the Quartermaster, Jonah Lloyd Jones, met a party of Nagas near Molhe who claimed to be fleeing from a Japanese invasion of the Somra tracts. This news seemed improbable, but was later confirmed by the sight of 'torches moving toward a V Force stockade . . . panic was widespread, and villagers were leaving their homes.' Next day Charles Pawsey said that V Force HQ at Kuki had been taken.

Lloyd Jones reported accordingly to Jessami by runner, and to Imphal V Force HQ by W/T. He continued to patrol, exploiting ambush tactics. Major Rai and the remainder of 'C' Company were sent out to join him, while one platoon of 'D' Company under Peter Steyn moved off to Khanjang to watch the tracks and to cover Sidiman Rai. Major Thurgood followed later with half a platoon, while Calistan, who was married to an American and had been a guardsman in the Brigade of Guards, took two sections of 'B' Company with John Corlett to the north-east at Yisi. They found the enemy there and reported the fact to Jessami by W/T from a USAAF observer post. Major Calistan was then ordered back to Jessami. Corlett covered Phek and the Phek-Laruri track down which the Japanese were soon to come. Three Jiffs from the Indian National Army failed to take the pins out of three British grenades before throwing them at the British patrol. One Jiff was captured and shipped off to Kohima for interrogation.

As 'C' and 'D' Companies were patrolling, the defence of Jessami temporarily lay with only two platoons of 'B', plus Battalion HQ and HQ Admin Companies; a coolie train with reserve ammunition went from Kohima to Kharasom and Phek.

Lloyd Jones's tasks were to harry the enemy on the Molhe-Khanjang path and to protect a large party of Naga and other civilian refugees under the care of Deputy Commissioner Charles Pawsey. Jones's W/T team and all coolies withdrew. On 21 March he completed an ambush position up the track to Khanjang and removed all stores from a stockade which the enemy, in fact, attacked at 1130 that night. Reinforced by 'C' Company, over the next forty-eight hours the Assam Regiment patrols killed one Japanese officer and several other ranks in clashes with the enemy. Major Rai left for Khanjang on 24 March to cover the Wohong track.

Next day Peter Mountstephen, now an insurance executive in Melbourne but then Intelligence Officer of the Kohima Garrison, and one platoon of the West Yorkshire Regiment (Colonel Richards' old regiment, just arrived at Kohima) visited Jessami, believing it surrounded. It was not, but the Battalion was leaving the bivouac for the defensive position, storing water for five days in tins and tarpaulins, and stocking reserve ammunition. The visitors were also able to report, on return to Kohima, that all V Force units had fallen back on Phek. Major Rai and the remainder of 'C' Company returned to Jessami to stiffen 'B' Company defences.

The Japanese were at Layshi, 25 miles from Jessami, a column advancing under Colonel Toriaki later blamed by General Sato for attacking instead of by-passing Jessami, thus delaying the advance on Kohima of 138 Battalion as Nagaya at Sangshak had delayed that of 58. But 138 had got there in ten days from the Chindwin, an astonishing achievement, although they had lost *en marche* large numbers of transport animals and beef-on-the-hoof.

At Phek, where Steyn, Lloyd Jones, and Rutter and Best of V Force had arrived, the rumour that Jessami had fallen was denied by Michael Williamson, Assam Regiment Adjutant, on the telephone from Jessami. This was the last message to be received, the line to Phek then being cut. At Phek, apart from the Assam patrols and the 1st Garrison Brigade unit of the Burma Regiment, about 320 men of V Force were digging, patrolling and, so far as possible, harassing the Japanese advance.

In the meanwhile Colonel Richards had made a quick visit to his outposts, bringing a new W/T set, but, in response to Bruno Brown's estimate of an enemy attack in battalion strength the next day, no cancellation of the earlier order to 'fight to the last round and the last man'.

On 29 March Brigadier 'Daddy' Warren, commanding 161 Brigade just flown in with 5th Division from Arakan, agreed that it *should* be cancelled. He also ordered that, since the West Yorkshires, to Richards' great regret, were not allowed forward and had now been sent to Imphal, his own Brigade's 4/7 Rajputs should help withdrawals from Phek and Jessami at Kharasom. 1/1 Punjabis, another of his Battalions, should also help, together with the guns of the 24th Indian Mountain Regiment. None of the three garrisons had its own water supply. The Assam Regiment's rôle was delay, intelligence and harassment, which they had effectively conducted. No reinforcement was remotely in prospect; confrontation in main battle with the Japanese, now estimated by Pawsey's Nagas at a full division, was not contemplated. There was no military value in a fight *à outrance*.

That day Mountstephen was again sent out from Kohima, this time with signalmen to repair faulty telephone lines to the outposts but also to convey an order orally for all three garrisons to be withdrawn 'by the night of March 31/April 1'. On arrival at Phek, the nearest garrison to Kohima, he was told that the lines to Jessami and Kharasom were still down and that the radio had failed. Worse, he himself could not possibly make the journey to Jessami on the main track. He then discovered that his Sher driver had absconded with his jeep. On Mountstephen's trek back to Kohima, he found a basha with a cooking fire still burning, and the remains of a Japanese meal. A Naga, encountered en route, gave him some water, refusing payment. 'I am Naga, you need water'.*

Lloyd Jones and Corlett were, of course, extremely concerned that their Assam Regiment colleagues should be aware that the 'last man, last round' order had been rescinded. With a 24-man patrol they marched three miles through the hills until they reached a point from which Jessami was visible at a distance of two miles. The flash and roar of guns were clearly seen and heard. They also saw an aircraft, variously described as 'RAF' and 'wearing American colours', diving below the Jessami ridge in the bright sunlight before dropping a message which, in Corlett's opinion, would not have reached the perimeter. He was quite right. A second message also fell short, eventually being seized by the Japanese after brisk close-action skirmishing.

This garrison had no luck, a supply drop also falling to the enemy. As to the messages, it seems possible that the pilot or his guide, an officer

---

* When the war was over, Mountstephen was presented to Field-Marshal Slim, then Governor General of Australia, in Melbourne. In discussing the Siege, Slim asked him: 'Did you think I could ever get relief to you?' 'If you couldn't, I knew nobody else could. But I was bloody scared.' 'I gave you every reason to be.' 'I thought you were doing your best, sir.'

named Wemyss, did not know that the Battalion had left the bivouac for the final defences. The Phek garrison, however, and its V Force adherents under Lieutenant-Colonel R. A. Stanley left at 4.30 in the afternoon of 31 March under fire from the Japanese mountain guns, arriving at Kohima on 1 April.

In the meanwhile, 'B' Company of the 1/1 Punjabs, under Major Tom Ware with an RIASC jeep company and a mountain battery, who were intended to assist the withdrawal from the furthest garrison at Kharasom, bumped the 58th Regiment under Major-General Miyazaki, at last moving on Kohima after the Battle at Sangshak. In that ambush the Punjabis claimed one hundred dead Japanese to seventeen of their own men. Later at Mao Song Sang they lost twenty-five vehicles, mostly jeeps and a few trucks, against II Battalion of 58 Regiment, advance guard to 31 Division.

The Rajputs, under Jack Cargill, ordered to engage at Jessami and Phek, do not seem to have been engaged at all, for on 30 March XXXIII Corps ordered 161 Brigade back from the area to the defence of Dimapur at Nichugard Pass. Cargill had a magenta complexion and wore a woollen khaki camp comforter, a garment worn either as a hat or as a scarf, going into battle with a tin of fifty cigarettes in one hand and a dao* in the other. Once, about 120 feet up a foothill in the Arakan, when second-in-command, he insisted on smoking a cigarette but, unwilling to give away the battalion's position, ordered that his Rajputs remove their shirts and thus form a tent around him. The Rajputs' officers' mess carried their own silver and lace table-cloths on mules throughout the battles wherever they went. They were an original regiment; one company commander, loved by his men, red-haired, freckled, short and squat, marched backwards into battle in front of the sepoys, swearing at them. His name was Freddy Still, and he caused pleasure when complaining about an inflated testicle, due to a grenade splinter, but attributed to a 'Calcutta run ashore'.

The Punjabis reluctantly disengaged, and although the Rajputs stayed another twenty-four hours, unaware that Colonel Brown at Jessami had still not received the order to withdraw, 161 Brigade was away to the west of Kohima by dusk on 31 March.

We shall deal later with the reasons for this bewildering order which affected not only the outposts but, potentially, the fate of the Kohima Garrison itself.

From now on, in Slim's own words, 'The main weight of the enemy advance fell on this battalion (First Assam Regiment) in the first battle of its career. Fighting in its own country, it put up a magnificent resistance,

* Type of local knife or machete.

holding doggedly to one position after another against overwhelming odds and in spite of heavy casualties. Its Companies, although separated, never lost coherence. The delay the Assam Regiment imposed on the Japanese 21st Division at this stage was invaluable.'

VII

THE ASSAM REGIMENT: JESSAMI, KHARASOM, PHEK

IN JESSAMI, at five minutes to nine on the morning of 28 March, Major Askew, in charge of a platoon facing south, told Bruno Brown that twenty-five Japanese soldiers with an officer or warrant officer were approaching along the road from Kharasom. ('Hold your fire, old boy,' said the Colonel.) When these men reached the barbed wire at knee level across the road some forty yards from the Battalion's position, they all crowded round the officer, jabbering and pointing at the map held by one of them.

These were not the spavined, bandy-legged, bespectacled enemy of the cartoons, but all men of the Imperial Guard. Brown told James Askew to open fire. His Bren guns killed 23 Japanese, but the remaining two crawled wounded into the bush. (It was at this point that one of the party led by Lieutenants Steyn, Corlett and Lloyd Jones telephoned from Phek, and were told to stay there.) A Kuki Naik (Corporal) and a Naik from V Force volunteered to bring back papers for identification from the cadavers for despatch to Kohima. Both failed. One of the Naiks was killed. Major Sidiman Rai, with a whole platoon, had no more success, nor did the Naik survivor from the earlier attempt, who made a brave solo attack with grenades.

The Japanese then opened fire from all directions with small arms and artillery, obviously in order to pinpoint the garrison's LMGs, mortars and so forth. The Battalion, well-trained, its perimeter reinforced, booby-trapped and generally improved, with water, rations and ammunition, plus the last hot meal for many days, did not respond. But the garrison, with its superb vista of forested mountains to the Burma frontier, was completely surrounded.

When darkness fell, the enemy attacked at all points on the perimeter, seeking to find the weak spots with illuminating cartridges, machine guns and grenades, howling 'Banzai' as they charged. They were met with Bren and rifle fire, in assault after assault. No one from the Assams was killed, although the ground outside the defences was littered with Japanese; corpses were hanging over the wire. Enemy tactics against such stubborn resistance seemed inexplicable. The Japanese strained the defence to breaking point, but then suddenly broke contact. 'Rugged endurance baffled and upset them. The appearance of a new situation seemed to be beyond the ability of junior officers to overcome.

On 30 March the Japanese did not confine their attacks to the night. Heavy small arms, artillery and mortar fire continued throughout the day from what was plainly a reinforced column, which, it emerged, contained most of 138 Regiment, the whole 124 Regiment, Lieutenant-General Sato's 31 Division HQ, and 31st Mountain Artillery. The attacks, particularly grenade and artillery, were continuous, but although there were occasional infantry penetrations, those of the previous night had been sealed off. A Japanese flag, with other identifying documents, was taken by two jawans* to Kohima.

But the night attacks produced a degree of exhaustion in the defenders and, after the third night, the garrison was dangerously short of sleep. Machine-gun barrels became red hot, but still had to be changed with bare hands. Bunkers were exchanged with regularity, 'the grimy little sections strove to concentrate their sleep-starved eyes on the enemy'. The Battalion had also lost its only form of artillery, the 3″ mortars firing high-trajectory projectiles over 1,600 yards, and the 2″ infantry close support mortars, their gun-pits knocked out from overlooking ground. All communications, including those to Lieutenant Donald Elwell at Milestone 38, had now been cut.

An understrength battalion was facing, in its initial battle, two of the most experienced infantry brigades in the world.

Next day John Corlett, who had decided at Phek that only he could warn the Jessami garrison that the 'last man, last round' order had been rescinded, arrived at their perimeter after a hair-raising journey over some of the more testing hills on the Roof of the World. He was enraged to discover a Japanese officer sleeping in his bed but, on the other hand, was fired upon by his own Regiment at the perimeter check-point. He found his white dog, Kuku, but lost him subsequently in an ambush during the retreat to Kohima.

Colonel Brown, after severe interrogation of Corlett, eventually believed the order. Withdrawal that night was, however, impossible because of the difficulty of internal communication within the redoubt. Only after a series of ferocious hand-to-hand attacks next day in turmoil, blood and chaos, culminating in a large penetration of the defences, fortunately not properly exploited by the Japanese, did 280 men of the garrison, moving through ambushes in small groups, reach Kohima. (About 80 arrived under Bruno Brown and most of the remainder under Calistan.) Some remained and fought the enemy Brigades until they were killed or captured. Others escaped to Dimapur. Some were lost or

* Indian private soldiers.

killed on the way out by enemy and 'friendly' RAF fire. Although only twelve men of the Assam Regiment were killed at Jessami itself, the casualty list was lengthened by those who failed to win through during the disengagement, including those who fell to ambush during withdrawal.

Major Thurgood was captured in the retreat and was seen under escort by four brutal-looking Japanese soldiers. His boots had been removed and his feet were cut and bleeding. Across his shoulders was a blanket with a loosely knotted rope round his neck. He was later reported as having died of 'malaria' in Kohima itself.

A pre-war actor, Captain Nigel Stock, on the staff of 202 Area, who took a patrol round the Japanese right flank, was obliged to ditch his uniform on the Kohima-Imphal road when entering a village held by the enemy. He had a Naga pudding-basin haircut and smeared himself with soot and pig fat, spying for three days on the Japanese, thinking much of London green rooms.

One party, under the Kuki HQ Company Havildar Major Satkhusel, was reduced by ambush to six men. They were captured but escaped to Kohima and were there able to alert the RAF to a Japanese concentration at Sakhama which was rapidly bombed. One of this group, hands bound, taunted and jabbed by enemy bayonets, kicked out and knocked down a Japanese officer. The latter, eyes blazing, ordered him to his knees and executed him immediately with his sword.

The Adjutant, Michael Williamson, who escaped with Calistan's original party, lost his rifle and, in searching for it, lost his companions. He later found five sepoys and, after being told by the head man to leave the Japanese-occupied village, found himself in friendly territory. (In an Ao village, he was even offered a double bed with 'Home Sweet Home' embroidered on the pillows.) Many stragglers and escapees were saved by the Nagas. It was said of this Battalion that other units could perhaps have fought as well, but few, if any, could have fought their way *out* as did the 1st Assam Regiment.

At Kharasom, with 'A' Company, the 3″ mortar detachment and signallers, the little Garrison numbered no more than 120 men, including two British officers and three Viceroy's Commissioned Officers. Jock Young, the Glaswegian, decided to make his defence position among bamboo jungle and scrub on a small oval hill about 300 yards south of the village. As at Jessami and Sangshak, there was no water supply within the perimeter itself. There were, however, clear lines of fire except where an intervening hill cut off part of the village.

From 26 February Young had set the men to digging in and to stocking ammunition, rations and water. Double trip-wire was set up, as well as various other tactical obstacles. Patrols out to 7 to 20 miles reported nothing until, on March 20, Young was warned by Battalion HQ at Jessami that a Japanese advance had begun. On that day one platoon (30 men) of 'D' Company joined Kharasom and replaced 'A' on standing patrol.

Lieutenant D. B. Gurung has said that on 22 March an Assam sepoy reported 'a large enemy column moving north from the Burma/Assam Frontier'. On 24 March a party of Assam Rifles and V Force personnel with three officers arrived at the garrison; they were in bad shape and Jock Young sent them on their way to Kohima two days later.

In the early morning of 27 March the Japanese appeared from the Ukhrul road, turning west and then south towards Kharasom village. As they passed the Assam Regiment's position, 'A' Company caught them in the left flank with rifles and Brens from the east, leaving the road littered with enemy dead and wounded.

Young managed to report this to Bruno Brown's HQ before the line was cut. It remained cut throughout the action. The Japanese then attacked his position until ten o'clock and twice more that day, around noon and sunset. One VCO and a Havildar were killed, but there was no enemy penetration of the defence. At 1030 the Japanese gratuitously set fire to at least part of the Naga village at Kharasom, flames shooting into the sky.

Next day, between five and eleven in the morning, very determined enemy attacks were launched from the south-east and south-west, all repulsed with heavy casualties. Forty-five Japanese, including two officers, had been killed. At great risk, since the position was completely encircled, two jawans carried captured identification and other documents through the lines to Kohima.

The Japanese made further violent assaults from dawn onwards on 29 March, again beaten off with casualties, including three Japanese foraging in the village who were caught by riflemen covering linesmen working on the line to Mao. From 6.45 pm, through the night, the Japanese mounted heavy grenade attacks, followed by a penetration, enabling them to construct a small defensive position within the perimeter. Before ejection, the infantrymen in their peaked caps with the yellow six-point star, the light khaki field uniforms with the red rank badges on the collar, and their darker puttees, could be seen feeding on barley and other animal rations.

On the next day more determined attacks with LMG and MMG fire continued from dawn against the northern perimeter. Heavy automatic fire covered howling and yelling assaults from the south-east and south-west, again repulsed with Japanese losses. Two of the enemy penetrated the outer defences, where an Assam machine gun was out of action, but were cut down at the inner line. Sniping, as every day, continued all the time.

There was no dawn attack next day, and the garrison cleared away the stinking Japanese bodies, erected more obstacles and repaired the barbed wire.

Then, coming up on the garrison from the southern track, a large body of Japanese troops, probably in battalion strength, accompanied by elephants, mules, carts and coolies, 'a solid mass of soldiers', was observed on the march from 1130 to 1700, when they made camp on the river.

John Young, of course, did not know that the order to fight until 'the last man and the last round' had been cancelled. Despite his courage, good humour and Scottish pride, he was a young and inexperienced officer with no peers to consult. He knew, however, that the position no longer had any military rationale. Unable to defeat a battalion or more, by-passed by another, with diminishing supplies of water, food and ammunition, death and destruction could be to no conceivable purpose.

His decision was heroic. After summoning his platoon commanders during the latest major artillery and mortar bombardment, he thanked them and, through them, all the sepoys, but ordered them to break off the action and withdraw, after reforming at the river, on Kohima.

'I, however, shall stay. Since my orders were to fight to the last man, I will *be* the last man. And I could not leave the wounded.' In response to subedars who sought to stay with him, he refused: 'That is an order.'

Knowing that they were to evacuate Kharasom, some of the troops withdrew in less than good order, 'warming the bell' as the Navy says and not reforming on the west side of the Laniye River. But before they did so, they repelled yet another attack under mortar fire. Fifty-six men from 'A' Company and the 'C' Company platoon reached Kohima on the first of April.

A jemadar, in tears, later told an Assam Regiment officer that he had last seen his own officer 'standing on the firestep of his bunker, stacking tommy-gun magazines on the parapet, piling quantities of hand grenades around him and passing a Bren gun to a wounded sepoy who had dragged himself to Young's bunker'.

Nothing is known with certainty thereafter. Nagas reported an enemy dawn attack on the bunkers, the explosion of grenades, the crackle of British and Japanese machine-gun fire, then silence.

The Assam Regiment killed 250 Japanese at Jessami. There was no count of wounded, nor is there a casualty list for Kharasom, but the delay imposed caused one Japanese Regiment not to reach Kohima until 8 April.

VIII

ON THE EVE OF
THE STORM

WHILE XXXIII Corps was forming under Lieutenant-General Sir
Montagu Stopford, IV Corps under Lieutenant-General Sir Geoffrey
Scoones had the task of opposing Japanese 15th Army's aim, through 15
and 33 Divisions, to cover the Imphal Plain. The main road from
Dimapur was about to be cut at Kohima, that to Imphal had been cut at
Mission, the Japanese name for Kangpokpi, by 15 Division, while the
Bishenpur track to Silchar in the south-west was also severed.

IV Corps was now isolated by land. The enemy surrounded the Imphal
Plain. Scoones' objectives were to stabilize the position around Imphal
and, above all, to prevent the Japanese from securing a lodgement in the
plain, to mobilize the largest possible force from 17, 20 and 23 Indian
Divisions under 'Punch' Cowan, Douglas Gracey and Ouvry Roberts
against 15 and 33 Divisions. His effort to cut the lines of communication
to the east would be overthrown in the actions already described at
Ukhrul and Sangshak against 31 Division.

The XXXIII Corps area was about to be strengthened by the airlift, a
most unusual phenomenon in those far-off days, from the Arakan, of 5
and 7 Indian Divisions under Briggs and Messervy. It was also to be
reinforced by the imminent arrival of 2 Division, 'the Crossed Keys',
with its superb English, Welsh and Scottish regiments under Major-
General Grover. The defence of Kohima before battle began, or indeed
before there was clarity about the strengths of the opposing British and
Japanese forces, lay temporarily with Major-General R.P.L. Ranking.
But Ranking commanded an *administrative* unit – 202 Area – not an
operational command. General Sir George Giffard, Commander-in-
Chief, 11 Army Group, chose Colonel Hugh Richards, who arrived
there on 23 March, as Commander of the Kohima Garrison, reporting
directly to IV Corps which he visited on 22 March.

Richards was fifty years old and had commanded 3rd West African
Brigade under training for the Chindits. When Wingate discovered his
age, since the maximum for anyone on those operations was forty, he
deprived Richards of command. Richards had begun his career in the
Worcestershire Regiment, later becoming 2 i/c of the West Yorkshire
Regiment, before secondment to West African troops.

His orders from IV Corps read: 'You will be in operational control of all the troops in Kohima and of 1 Assam Regiment. You will be directly under IV Corps. Your job will be to hold Kohima and to deny area Jessami – Kharasom – Kohima to the enemy by the use of 1 Assam Regiment.' Brigadier Haynes' 253 Sub-Area under Ranking's 202 Area confused these responsibilities by retention of administrative command at Kohima, although, pending Stopford's arrival with XXXIII Corps, Ranking took operational control as well.

The Japanese advance on Kohima or Dimapur was initially thought by the staff of IV Corps to consist of two or three columns in battalion strength and, because of the demanding conditions in the Naga and Somra Hills, without artillery in any quantity. It was to contend with this relatively small force, and because he could not spare troops from the Imphal region, that Scoones had placed the 1st Assam Regiment at Jessami, Kharasom and Phek, with orders to 'fight to the last'. He also knew that, although he could not be certain whether Dimapur or Kohima was the ultimate Japanese goal, the two Indian Divisions and the British Division would soon be at Dimapur.

He was aware that the 161st Brigade, under Brigadier Freddy Warren, DSO, OBE, comprising 4th Royal West Kents (Lieutenant-Colonel John Laverty), 1/1 Punjab (Lieutenant-Colonel Neil Brodie) and 4/7th Rajput (Lieutenant-Colonel Jack Cargill), with 24th Mountain Regiment, 75 Indian Field Ambulance and 2nd Field Company Indian Sappers and Miners, would be the first major unit to arrive from Arakan. As we have seen, Slim sent it to Kohima and, on 29 March, Warren ordered that Punjabi and Rajput troops should help with the withdrawal of the outposts.

We have also seen that the next day General Ranking cancelled Slim's orders and sent, to the rage of the Brigade and its Commander, the entire formation back to the defence of Dimapur at the Nichugard Pass. This, of course, included the 4th Royal West Kents who were already digging in at Kohima itself by April Fool's Day. At this time, moreover, it was plain that the enemy was as large as a division.

The recall was based firstly on an appreciation by Stopford that the Japanese priorities in descending order were: (i) Dimapur, (ii) the Ledo Railway, and (iii) Kohima. The second reason was an RAF report, disputed by Pawsey and Warren, that a Japanese unit was outflanking Kohima on the north in the direction of the railway. In Pawsey's view, had this been the case, his Nagas would have reported it to him, and they had not. Pawsey was right: the 'unit' was a group of villagers returning home after work. The Brigade could therefore have been cut off by this non-existent 'column'. Warren pointed out that, once 161 Brigade was dug in at Kohima, they really could not be cut off since Sato would not risk leaving so powerful a formation behind him. But, in response to this argument, Stopford subsequently said that he had believed the Dimapur base to be too precious an objective to be hazarded for the defence of Kohima, which *could* have been bypassed.

But, according to General Miyazaki and, indeed, to the 15th Army tactical plan, the 31st Division was never intended, at least initially, to do more than 'occupy Kohima and check the British-Indian Army reinforcements expected from the Assam area', and/or 'to occupy Kohima in order to cut off the retreat of the Allied troops in Imphal'. There is no documentary evidence that, outside General Mutaguchi's dream of a March on Delhi, Dimapur was a designated objective for 15th Army, although it would certainly have become one had Kohima failed to hold.

On 3 April General Slim said that Kohima must be held 'since it would be hard to recapture, and its loss would undermine Naga loyalty'. On 4 April Stopford ordered 161 Brigade back to Kohima, but not before an RWK patrol in armoured carriers had reported that Japanese attacks were already developing from three sectors against the garrison. Had he not done so, the probable loss of the Ridge for a substantial period of time, the 31st Division occupying its entire length, would have led not only to enormous numbers of dead and wounded, but delay to, if not disintegration of, the Imphal battle itself. Richards and Pawsey were obviously pleased that neither the inadequate garrison nor the Nagas under British protection were to be abandoned to their fate.

On 1 April Ranking had told the Garrison Commander that if the Assam Regiment could get away from Jessami they would reinforce the Kohima Garrison. As we know, 260 of them from Jessami, Kharasom and Phek did so.

But after the original withdrawal that day of 161 Brigade and of the Royal West Kents, Richards had little left to fight with. On General Purposes Transport Ridge (GPT Ridge) was a platoon of the Assam Regiment under Lieutenant Peter Steyn, the tall South African now in Hong Kong and the Regiment's official historian; a composite company of Indian Infantry; some V Force troops and a company of Gurkhas under Captain Douglas Frew. A road block to the south of GPT was manned by a British officer and a few Gurkhas. There were, under the command of Major Reginald Lowe, 80 men of the Assam Regiment, including Lieutenants Brown and Corlett (A, D and HQ Companies), a rifle company of the 5th Burma Regiment and a Garrison company of the same, on Jail Hill. On DIS and FSD, Major Naveen Rawlley (now Major-General, MC, late Indian Army) had been sent by Richards to collect and command two platoons of 5/27 Mahrattas, 'the Kuriyan Platoon', more V Force men and another composite company of Indian infantry. Kuki Piquet, a hillock between DIS and FSD on the ridge, was held by Lieutenant James Barratt with one hundred Indian 'odds and ends' from the Reinforcement Camp. The DC's Bungalow sector was held by about 200 British convalescent and other troops, the Indian General Hospital Spur by the Assam Rifles under 'Buster' Keene, and by Major Calistan and Major Askew with 'B' and 'C' Companies of the Assam Regiment returned from the outposts. Colonel Brown was at Garrison HQ for the time being.

Troops of the 'State Battalion', the Sher Regiment, commanded by their own officers, but with three British liaison and training officers, Lieutenant-Colonel Gordon Borrowman, Captain Noel Lunn and Lieutenant James Hoyt were posted at Naga Village and Summer House (Garrison) Hill.

The Order of Battle included officers and men of the 24th Reinforcement Camp under Lieutenant-Colonel Malcolm Hepworth, 16th Punjab Regiment. The camp collected British and Indian replacements for casualties in the Imphal area, and also included convalescents from the 49th and 53rd IGHs, soon to be closed and dispersed. It also held non-combatant troops, many of whom were despatched to Dimapur before the battle. Although the combatants themselves were armed, they had neither their own officers nor their own formations before incorporation in the garrison's plan.

Richards had sent Rawlley to Detail and Supply Hill where he formed a 3″ mortar section from the Reinforcement Group, built and stocked weapon pits, while organizing his men into companies and platoons. He had only two infantry officers, an excellent Second Lieutenant Carrington of the Northamptonshire Regiment and Lieutenant 'Kuriyan', whose identity has never been positively established but who fought nobly. Also under Rawlley was an Indian Davis Cup player called Captain Savoor, who commanded a unit of 50 transport drivers and clerks. Regimental Aid Posts on several of the hillocks later to become battlefields were manned by medical officers and other ranks from the two IGHs, the 80th Parachute Field Ambulance, V Force, the Reinforcement Camp and the Hygiene Section.

Richards made Lieutenant-Colonel Borrowman his Second-in-Command. Borrowman was from the 4th Gurkhas, a friend of Slim's, a calm, experienced Scot of lean, distinguished appearance. Hepworth then took over from Borrowman as senior supervising officer of the Sher. Borrowman was recovering from a bad fall. Also on 1 April Major-General Ranking added to IV Corps' orders to Richards:

3. The garrison at Kohima will consist of: 1st Assam Regiment (if extracted from Jessami area).

The Native State battalion.
All other combatants at Kohima.

4. You will command the garrison of Kohima and will deny Kohima to the enemy as long as possible without being destroyed yourselves.
5. All unarmed personnel and all vehicles and stores not required for the defence and administration of Kohima will be dispatched to Dimapur immediately.
6. The decision as to the precise moment when it will be necessary to withdraw from Kohima must be made by you. You must, however, give me the longest possible warning of such an eventuality. It is emphasized that it is most important that Kohima should be held as long as possible subject to the proviso in para. 4 above.

Richards had no intention of withdrawing and never even mentioned that part of the directive to anyone except Gordon Borrowman.

For the defence, before Richards arrived, Borrowman from his sick-bed had devised four 'boxes' to protect the installations and stores. In the event, they were too far apart and imperfectly sited. The trenches and weapon pits, some of which were dug by Indian non-combatants and some by Nagas, were inadequate, as were the non-combatants supposed to man them. There was little or no wire, as barbed wire was forbidden by the Naga Hills civil bureaucracy. Most defence equipment had been directed to Imphal itself. There was only one gun, a 25-pounder which was subsequently found unusable because of the terrain.

As three of the 'boxes' were more or less irrelevant to command of Kohima Ridge itself, which Colonel Richards regarded as the primary Japanese objective, ('whoever controlled the Ridge controlled the road') he concentrated resources there and 'closed' the boxes, dismissing the non-combatant defendants to Dimapur. (It was, however, a pity that he closed the box at Workshop Ridge, as we shall see.) These, and as many others as could be identified, were issued with rifles before departure, not so much for self-defence as to deny them to the enemy. When the 'refugees' met 161 Brigade on the latter's return up the Dimapur-Kohima road, their protestations provoked the Brigade into regarding them as panic-stricken deserters from a garrison on the point of wholesale desertion. They were, in fact, for the most part, not even clerks, but 'coolies in uniform' without military training and precious little discipline either, but not representative of the fighting garrison, pathetically vulnerable though it was.

Because of the dual nature of command (operational under Colonel Richards, but initially administrative under Ranking and Haynes),

Richards had no control over the removal of units, stores, workshops and transport. One of the greatest difficulties experienced in preparing to meet the enemy was the constant fluctuation of the garrison. Many units were moved without reference to Garrison HQ. 'The size of the Box, the number of troops available to hold it and the facilities required were therefore almost impossible to compute.' With a small and unsatisfactory staff, Richards was besieged with insoluble problems, changing hourly, barely susceptible even to compromise.

There was neither the time nor the skilled labour, nor the knowledge of what units would finally be available, to plan properly sited dug-outs and trenches, water supplies or a centralized medical system. There were, however, correctly and well-distributed rations, ammunition (2″, 3″ mortars, grenades etc) and stores for between two and three weeks, either in the 'final' positions or to hand. Even the Royal West Kents when they came back were obliged to admit that some of these lacunae were due to uncertainty about the final battle dispositions. They were, however, not wrong, because they were a tough, experienced battalion with long service against the Japanese, about the poor quality of some in the existing garrison. But that was not the fault of Hugh Richards.

In the meanwhile, General Sato's Japanese 31 Division which had crossed the Chindwin on 16 March was approaching Kohima. On the right, the 138 Regiment, after advancing via Bombal, Kuki and Jessami, fighting V Force at Khanjang, and overthrowing Jessami and Kharasom between 26 March and 1 April, was on the outskirts of Kohima by 4 April, ready to 'fall on it and annihilate the enemy'.

On the left, after Ukhrul and Mao Song Sang where they cut the road, the 58th Regiment (Colonel Fukunaga) turned north to join 138. They captured Tuphema on 2 April, leaving 'C' Company with two machine guns and mortars to hold it and to guard the road to Imphal. I Battalion of 38 Regiment less one company went west of Kohima via Maram to cut the Imphal-Dimapur road in order to prevent British reinforcement. The II Battalion was to go to Kohima via Mao Song Sang and Kekrima, the left column to Kohima along the Imphal road. 11 Company of III Battalion entered Naga Village in the early morning of 5 April. It was expected that General Miyazaki would occupy Kohima without diffi-culty. He reached the hill station on 6 April.

The main body and HQ of 31 Division was at Khanjang 9 miles east of the town on 7 April, with 138 Regiment and 31 Mountain Artillery to the north-east. One company of 124 Infantry Regiment (Colonel Miya-moto) was sent to Rangazumi to guard the divisional flank against any attacks from the north, with the bulk of this regiment in reserve at the rear of the main column: it had been temporarily 'lost' by 33 Corps

Intelligence, who feared that it might be moving on Lyashi in the valley east of Jessami.

138 and 124 Regiments were not greatly regarded by the crack 38 Regiment with its long and victorious history, encompassing, inter alia, many years in China, tough, experienced peasants who had nevertheless just been through a stiff battle at Sangshak entailing the casualties already enumerated.

But Japanese spirit and morale were high and indeed it was the unanimous view of 31 Division's officers that Kohima could soon be taken and Dimapur reached, thus also severing the Bengal-Assam railway, vital to British survival and that of India.

Before leaving the Chindwin, Lieutenant Nishida, commanding 11 Company of III Battalion, had addressed his men: 'Let us now take farewell of our motherland'. General Sato, for his part, assembled his staff in the jungle and drank a glass of champagne with them: 'I'll take the opportunity, gentlemen, of making something quite clear to you. Miracles apart, everyone is likely to lose his life in this operation. It isn't simply a question of the enemy's bullets. You must be prepared for death by starvation in these mountain fastnesses.'*

* Louis Allen commented, 'Not the cheeriest of farewells, but Sato did not indulge in the Japanese habit of euphemism. The battle for Kohima might have gone differently if he had.'

IX

KOHIMA: THE NEGLECTED GARRISON

THE HILL-STATIONS of the Raj were enchanted oases for plainsmen from the humid valleys of the sub-continent far below. From the sticky, terrible heat of Punjab, Madras Presidency or Assam, cars and little railways carried sweating planters, officials and their families, visibly losing the red pimples of prickly heat, up terraced slopes, winding around the hills about Simla, Ootacamund and Kohima. Under oak and conifer, in cool, almost English landscape, the English rode and walked over the pine-needles in the woods and rides, played golf, billiards and tennis or danced in the Club. Agreeable dallying was enjoyed with the grass widows whom hill-stations not infrequently harboured, in villas named Wildflower Hall and such. It was innocent enough, the Englishman 'carrying his cool weather with him'.

No Simla, Ootacamund or Poona, more an administrative centre, Kohima village is on a saddle of the Naga Hills at about 5,000 feet between mountain ranges of twice that height. At its highest point rose the gabled houses and ragged attap roofs of the Naga village, approached by obscure, overgrown and tangled ways past stone walls and deep ditches to thick wooden gates, passage available for only one man at a time.

It was a town of little paths: poinsettias ten to fifteen feet high with up to thirty blossoms on the branch, fuchsias, hibiscus, geranium, mimosa, morning glory, canna, wild rose – blue, scarlet, yellow, pink, purple – and everywhere wild mauve orchids. Through this old straggling town of many villages, the largest in Assam, bamboo and jungle vine had worked their intrusive way, while eucalyptus, the Australian gum-tree with its blue-grey leaves, covered large parts of the Ridge itself.

To the south of and below Naga village was a wooden fort. In this ancient establishment, the garrison, including non-combatants, white women and children, a total of some three hundred souls, had in 1879 held out for two terrifying weeks against six thousand hostile Naga head-hunters armed with arrows and blazing flax, hurling human heads across the walls until driven off by a military contingent from Imphal. Major Johnstone had arrived not a minute too soon, the garrison's food and water almost gone. 'Coming events cast their shadows before.'

Within the old fort were the Government's offices, sometimes collectively known as the Treasury and sometimes as the Fort, not far from the quarters and barracks of the 3rd Assam Rifles, the paramilitary police body – not the Assam *Regiment* – under Buster Keene. Over the Treasury presided Charles Pawsey, Deputy Commissioner for the Naga Hills District of Assam, an Englishman of his time, apparently conventional, detached, cool, reserved, somewhat brusque, but with a comprehensive affection and respect for his charges. In the Kohima area itself were Angami Nagas, of undetermined origin, conceivably with racial links to the Celebes Sea or to the Dayaks of Borneo, but whose languages are yet thought to be of the Tibetan/Chinese group.

At the junction of the Treasury and the Dimapur/Imphal roads by the Military Traffic Control Post began the forested Kohima Ridge, the sides of which were terraced, all encompassed within the twisting, climbing road. On the highest hill of the Ridge, in trees and thickish undergrowth, was a gazebo or Summerhouse, authenticating the peacetime title of Summerhouse Hill. Before the War British children had played here, and British families gathered in 'the golden evenings' under the dark magnificence of the Japvo and Pulebadze Mountains to west and south. To the north, north-east and south-east ran wooded ranges of the Somra Hills, their rice terraces stretching away to the Chindwin River through Jessami, Kharasom and Ukhrul.

General Slim described the Naga Hills as 'those hellish jungle-mountains' by which he meant indifferent, destructive of body and mind, pitiless, containing the most virulent mosquitoes in the world, leeches of course, limitless variety of insects large and small, incubating vile dysenteries, malaria, typhus, cholera, every form of tropical horror, scabies and sprue, great suppurating sores. Even prickly heat festered, primitive scraping the only remedy, ineffective at that. Leopards, snakes and tigers lived in the undergrowth and the jungle slopes. Magnolia grew in the valley, oak and pine on the hill side.

On the next terrace to the north-east below Summerhouse Hill, or Garrison Hill as it became known during the Siege, was the Club House and behind it a flat-topped mound, both of which played significant roles in the battle. Below lay the famous tennis court, where the Japanese were finally held. The servants' quarters were on the next level, below which were Colonel Keene's bungalow, and that of the Deputy Commissioner, teak, stained dark brown, extremely comfortable, with deep verandah, steepish pitched roof, lawns, rhododendrons, cannas, groves of trees, beautifully maintained.

To the south-east lay the succession of hills where the battle was mostly fought, Kuki Piquet first, named after the Kuki tribe which had guarded the garrison against the Nagas in the rising of 1879. Next came

Field Supply Depot (FSD) Hill with sheds and bashas, and Detail Issue (DIS or Detail) Hill with its bakery and scenes of heroism by Lance Corporal Harman and others less famous. Opposite Detail Hill was Jail Hill, prison, ammunition and POL storage. To the south again was General Purposes Transport Hill (GPT or Transport Ridge), and the Aradura Spur leading to Mount Pulebadze, immortalized by the Royal Norfolks.

The 57th Reinforcement Camp under Colonel Hepworth was to the north at Merema, past Naga Village. The 53rd Indian General Hospital, until closed, lay on a steep bend in the road to Dimapur on Hospital Spur, to the west of and below Hospital Ridge. The position was not inaccessible to the enemy from the west, or via that Ridge and the Ladies Mile, a bridle path which ran from the Bungalow Sector along Hospital Ridge southwards. Ladies' Mile formed, in Cecil Lucas Phillips' words, 'more or less the perimeter line of the besieged British garrison'. In happier days, here the Europeans had taken their constitutionals.

We have seen that, because the Corps Commander and XIV Army could not initially believe that Kohima was seriously threatened, constant changes in the Garrison, frequently not even mentioned to Garrison Headquarters, led to inadequate defence works. Slim later admitted that he had made a mistake: 'I didn't believe that the Japanese could move on Kohima in divisional strength. Our soldiers saved our bacon.' Not many Generals are man enough to make such admission. To compensate, at least the Nagas under Charles Pawsey's Administration were of great assistance in emergency construction work. Pawsey himself became an object of veneration to all ranks, not only of the Assam Regiment and local units, but of the West Kents. He stayed in the Assam Hills until 1947, retiring to marry and to farm in Suffolk.

The Queen's Own (Royal West Kent) Regiment, the 50th Regiment of Foot, became the 50th (Queen's Own) Regiment in January, 1831, and assumed their full nomenclature with the amalgamation of the 50th and 97th Regiments of Foot on 1 July, 1881. One of their proudest battle honours, with 'Corunna' from the Peninsular War, is 'Defence of Kohima' reserved for them alone, whereas the Regiments of the Second British Division carry 'Kohima' only.

The Fourth Battalion (Territorials) fought with the British Expedition-ary Force in France and Belgium, being evacuated in the *Dorian Rose* from Dunkirk, then proceeding to Yorkshire, spending a total of 18 months in the UK. General Montgomery was at one point their Corps Commander. In April, 1942, they embarked in *SS Laconia*, a vessel designed for four hundred but now carrying some thousands of men, disembarking at Port Tewfiq in Egypt. In the desert they joined the 2nd New Zealand Division, regarded by Field-Marshal Rommel as the best formation he had ever opposed: Montgomery was this time their (Eighth) Army Commander. They sustained very severe casualties at Alam Halfa and First Alamein, before joining PAI (Persia and Iran) Force south of Baghdad, whereafter their motorized role became redundant.

They subsequently embarked for Bombay and a five-day journey to Ranchi where they were 'demotorized' or 'converted to animals', jeep drivers becoming muleteers and so forth, before taking part in XIV Army's first real victory in the Arakan. Here, as we have said, they again sustained heavy casualties, some from our own artillery. Before they had time to take the 'Tunnels', they had to proceed on foot, by paddle steamer and by air to India.

They were, as we have seen, then sent into Kohima, but withdrawn on April Fool's Day toward Dimapur. Their commander, Colonel John Laverty, sometimes referred to by his men as 'Texas Dan', then observed that it was as well that Jail Hill and GPT Ridge were held: 'If we lose those two hills to the Japs, the men on the Ridge behind us won't stand a chance.' It was noted at the time by the West Kents that the place was a muddle of combatants and non-combatants without central control. But this battalion, the magnificent 'Dirty Half Hundred', had been fighting for months in the Arakan, followed by their lightning journey to Assam. They were, although proud and confident in their own record against the Japanese, tired, frustrated – later to become more so – and without understanding the problems which had faced Hugh Richards. They and their colonel had a professional intolerance which may have overridden the need for professional co-operation with Richards: the will to survive was also a factor. But they met Auchinleck's alleged preference for Territorials rather than Regular troops: 'more enterprising, less hidebound', united by 'local' bonds.

It was on 3 April that the Garrison Commander had issued rifles to the labour force and other non-combatant Indian troops. As has been shown, to preserve small arms from the enemy, as well as to clear the garrison's terrain, he despatched as many non-combatants as possible to the rear. They unfortunately created en route the impression on 161 Brigade already referred to that these 'coolies' represented a garrison that was, in reality, remarkably staunch.

Although there was enough well-distributed food and ammunition for this minute, mostly gallant but ill-assorted garrison, there was no wire at all: 202 Area had been unable to cause the Naga Hills civilian veto on barbed wire to be rescinded. The provision of water, of adequate trenches and weapon pits, or of satisfactory medical arrangements had been precluded by the extreme fluidity of the garrison's establishment. Brigadier Warren (161 Brigade), by siting the 24th Mountain Artillery at Jotsoma, provided close support from the guns for Kohima. But Peter

Steyn, describing the atmosphere on 3 April, said, 'Tension mounted slowly and the question of whether Kohima could survive an attack was on everyone's lips. The answer lay in the realms of conjecture, but hopes and spirits were high. And so the last night of peace began.' It was extraordinary that, in the face of a Japanese infantry division, so gallant a statement could be made.

In fact, it was not the last night of peace. Fighting had already begun on Aradura Spur, to the south-south-west. And on 4 April Lieutenant-General Sato signalled to Major-General Miyazaki and his Regimental Commanders: 'Capture Kohima – at once.'

Far to the south, however, 17, 20 and 23 Indian Divisions were assembling back in the plain, ready for the battle with 15 and 33 Japanese Divisions which Slim and Scoones had planned on their own ground at Imphal. All would now depend on them, on the airlift to supply them and, above all, on whether Kohima could hold. But in Charles Pawsey's opinion, subsequently shared by the Japanese General Staff, the enemy had already thrown away three chances of victory, the first by diverting to Sangshak, the second by engaging, not bypassing, the Assam Regiment at Jessami, and the third by not attacking in full force at Kohima on 5 and 6 April.

Pawsey, although a civilian, had won a DSO with the Worcesters in the Great War. He believed that, had the Japanese pressed on at Pulomi, instead of waiting there from 4 to 9 April, they could have cut the main supply road between Imphal and Dimapur on 5 April, completely preventing the advance of 161 Brigade. They could also have cut the Rangapahar-Dhansiri railroad on 6 April. Had they done that, they could have held up reinforcements and supplies to Manipur Road, isolated the American air bases and the Chinese in North Assam, and created panic in India.

The Deputy Commissioner, after the event, indeed believed that the siege of Kohima itself, had been the decisive strategic mistake by Generals Sato and Mutaguchi, providing time for the safe arrival of 2nd British and 5th and 7th Indian Divisions and the eventual rout and destruction of 15th Army. Dimapur should have been the target.

In the meanwhile, Captain Jimmy Patrick of the 1/7 Gurkhas had been sent up from Dimapur with half-a-dozen other officers, including Barratt whom we shall see later, and Lieutenant Gould, subsequently killed. Patrick was told by Richards to command the 'Garrison Striking Force', a company from a State Regiment loaned to the government of India for L. of C. duties but not trained or adequately led for war. The troops were fine, but the officers were flabby, inadequate and of lower caste. He visited their positions and was almost at once under a hail of fire directed at 'nothing but a rumour'. A bullet passed through his hat, taking with it some hair, before he managed to persuade the men, in their own language, to cease fire.

Patrick was later sent to recapture the Treasury with this 'Striking Force'. The troops refused to pass the field of fire of a sniper and he had to double across before the others would follow. All crossed the main road safely in the glare of burning transport and advanced along the south side of the spur towards the Knoll, using the shadows cast by clouds crossing the moon. At 7.30 pm, having reached the line where the pine trees joined Treasury lawn, he gave the signal to advance. A Japanese then threw a firecracker and the whole company fled hurriedly, leaving Patrick alone on the lawn.

He went back to the foot of the slope and reformed the two platoons to try again. All ran away. After much effort he gathered together two platoons of the three that had started out and returned to Kohima Garrison to report failure. It is said that, after the war, their Maharajah executed one in ten of this unit.

For a short period he shared an inadequately covered trench with Peter Steyn of the 1st Assam Regiment, also sharing a tented latrine which, being well-disciplined officers, they used, although toward the end devoutly hoping that it would be blown up by enemy action. On one occasion, splinters from a Japanese mortar burst three jerry-cans of water above their heads in the trench, drenching them. They used to experiment with the angle of trajectory of a 2″ mortar until at the vertical the wind could have taken the bomb either way. Steyn, otherwise, retains from the Siege a passion for sardines and for thick Chakapurra biscuits, almost the consistency of dog biscuits.

Jimmy Patrick later served in 48 Brigade in 17 Division at Tiddim and southwards until the war ended. He returned to England, took his degree and joined the Malayan Civil Service, taking his Gurkha body-servant, Gunga Prasad, with him. (Gunga later served as chowkidar to the author of this book, and then emigrated to America.) Patrick helped to draft the constitution of independent Malaya and then worked in Whitehall until his 'retirement' to agreeable activities in Wadhurst, including editorship of the Regimental Journal of the 7th D.E.O. Gurkha Rifles.

X

THE ROYAL WEST KENT REGIMENT ARRIVES

CHARLES PAWSEY, on behalf of his Nagas, was not alone in his relief at the return on 5 April of the Fourth Battalion Royal West Kent Regiment under Lieutenant-Colonel John Laverty, the fiery, contentious Irishman.

On 4 April Pawsey's Naga scouts had already reported one advance on Kohima of a Japanese column in battalion strength from the south (Mao and Jakhama) along the road to Imphal. Hearing this news, Hugh Richards immediately moved out of Pawsey's bungalow with Lieutenant-Colonel Borrowman into the Garrison Headquarters and prepared bunkers with connecting trenches on Summerhouse/Garrison Hill.

First contact with the enemy had, in fact, been made on 3 April between a Japanese unit and an Assam Rifles patrol who claimed to have killed fifteen Japanese south of a road block near Transport Ridge. A State Regiment unit was also alleged to have produced evidence of success in the shape of three Japanese ears, but it is peculiar that these events, rather than the Nagas' report, did not act as the trigger for the Commander's move to his HQ.[1]

On 4 April a State Regiment patrol broke under attack from II Battalion, 58 Regiment, at Aradura Spur, south-west of Transport Ridge, and ran through a road block nearer to Kohima. Earlier that day two platoons of mixed British troops under Major Norman (Laurie) Giles of the Black Watch and Captain Maclachlan of the Burma Regiment were sent to observe and harass the enemy above Aradura. In the darkness, movement and digging caused them to realize that they were surrounded by units of II Battalion, 58 Regiment, in company strength but under the Battalion Commander. The patrol charged with fixed bayonets, killing a number of Japanese before reaching the garrison perimeter safely. Japanese 7 Company was nearly annihilated, but 6 Company, under Second Lieutenant Nakamura, held the position until his death.

By the evening 5 and 6 Companies had taken the whole area, chiefly thanks to the Yamamoto platoon. Sixty horses, released from their Assam Regiment stables, created incidents on the Kohima/Imphal road, racing in all directions.

In the early morning of 5 April, 11 Company, III Battalion, 58 Regiment, entered Naga village, killing the sentries at the store rooms and requisitioning transport. Captain Koboyashi of that Company had already remarked that, at first light, the resident troops did not seem to have even realized that the Japanese had arrived. When soldiers from the garrison came to draw the rations, they were all captured. The Japanese later 'rushed into action under cover of light machine-gun fire, throwing grenades as they went. 11 Company, even though the battle ended in defeat, was first into that place where the most fearful battles were fought'. Japanese military description has an invariable charge of frenetic energy.

Lieutenant Peter Steyn had been sent by Colonel Richards to reconnoitre Workshop Ridge as a platoon base in the southern part of the perimeter. This had been one of Richards' original boxes and, as the Nagas had built it to a battalion scale, Steyn had to report that it was useless for the present purpose.

Donald Elwell of the Assam Regiment Transport Platoon then found that the Indian composite company at the western end of GPT (Transport) Ridge had run away, abandoning its weapons, thus leaving the entire flank unguarded and exposed, isolating the Assam platoon in the centre. There had been, at some point, another major collapse by a State Company on GPT, leading to an attack on them with m.m.g.s by Gurkhas, perhaps those under Douglas Frew's Gurkhas and Steyn's Assam platoon.

Elwell, fired on by II Battalion's mortars as well as by friendly Brens from Jail Hill (known to the Japanese by code-word 'Goat') and from his flank, went back from GPT to Jail itself where Major Reggie Lowe gave him a platoon from the State Regiment under a reliable Subedar known to Elwell.

When he returned with this reinforcement to Transport Ridge, under mortar and Bren fire, the State troops 'had vanished as if by magic' into the nearest gulley, leaving the Subedar and a Naik. Climbing on through the scrub and undergrowth, after ordering the Subedar to rally the men, he found under persistent mortar fire that the bunkers and trenches he had so recently left were empty. Even his own Assam platoon, believing him dead, had withdrawn to Jail Hill under their Jemadar.

He therefore decided to follow them. Mortar bursts scattered the stones around him. Under steady Bren gun and other fire, from 'friendly' as well as enemy guns, with a grenade in either hand, he raced down the hill. He found no trace of the State platoon in the gulley on the way. His return was nearly fatal to John Collett who, sent by Reggie Lowe to find him, had made just enough noise and noticeable movement, however stealthy, to arouse Elwell's suspicion. It was only immediately before he pressed the trigger that the latter saw his friend's face through a parting in the lantana leaves.

Troops under Frew and Steyn at the east end of Transport Ridge had stood firm under increasing Japanese mortar fire from Aradura and artillery from a four-gun 37 mm battery firing over open sights from Workshop Ridge, commanding much of the main Kohima Ridge. The 3.7 inch mountain howitzers of 24 Regiment, Indian Artillery, were not yet in action from 161 Brigade's box at Jotsoma. There was, therefore, no defence, other than Collett's mortars, for the Assamese and Gurkhas on Jail Hill, unfortunately soon spotted and ranged. Their other flank being completely empty, Transport Ridge was evacuated on 5 April on the Garrison Commander's orders. It was a most serious loss, particularly after the failure, due to bad planning and shortage of resources, to defend Workshop Ridge, one and a half miles south.

Lieutenants Kuriyan and Barratt on Supply Hill and Kuki Piquet had seen the flood of deserters from the composite company, held them and turned away the mob before their panic could pollute their own stauncher Indian troops. None of the defecting officers was subjected to disciplinary action, nor is any inquiry known to have been conducted during or after the war.

Meanwhile on 4 April, a young subaltern of the Royal West Kents named Smith, had, with great courage, taken an armoured carrier patrol to Kohima in daylight. On his return to Dimapur,[2] he reported that the Japanese were moving on Kohima from the south with possible threats from north and north-east. Stopford then decided to send back 161 Brigade. The Royal West Kents would return from Dimapur with the 20th Mountain Battery, its screw guns, the 2nd Field Company KGV's Own Bengal Sappers and Miners, and the 75th Field Ambulance at first light next day.

The Corps Commander's order had been made easier by the knowledge that the county regiments of Major-General John Grover's Second British Division were assembling at Dimapur.

At this time the battle-hardened Japanese II Battalion was, of course, advancing on Kohima from the south, while III Battalion under Major Shimanoe was infiltrating into Naga village in the north. As III believed that Kohima had already fallen, they then pushed on northward to Cheswema – allegedly on Mutaguchi's orders countermanded by his superior at Burma Area Army, General Kawabe – before returning. 138 Regiment was moving in from the south-east with 124 Regiment in reserve: General Sato's headquarters was at Khanjang with 138. Although Slim and Stopford at XIV Army and XXXIII Corps still believed that the Japanese 15th Army's aim was the invasion of Bengal through Dimapur, we know that Sato himself had set as his objectives the capture of Kohima and seizure of the mountain pass there, the cutting of the road to Imphal and, *after* the capture of Kohima, reinforcement of 15 and 33 Divisions in the Plain.

The fight at Transport Ridge with its defenders from the Assam Regiment got under way. The Royal West Kents, with the 20th Mountain Battery, Lieutenant John Wright's Sappers and the Field Ambulance platoon began the long climb in three-ton lorries out of the steamy plain at Dimapur. Brigadier D.W. Warren DSO OBE, with the 24th Mountain Regiment Indian Artillery under Colonel Humphrey Hill, and its remaining batteries, the 4/7 Rajputs of large and noble stature under Lieutenant-Colonel Cargill, and the 1/1 Punjabis under Lieutenant-Colonel Neil Brodie, later under Lieutenant-Colonel Grimshaw followed them.

Warren later became an acting Major-General and, before his death in an air crash, commanded 5 Division. He led from the front. He was much trusted, even loved. The men knew that he would never ask them to do anything he would not do. When the Siege became really bad, they believed that since 'Daddy' Warren had put them in Kohima, he would get them out again.

The Arakan from which they had been so brusquely wrenched was a land of coastal mangrove swamps, 'the stinking, eerie jungle, the count-less little villages at the edge of the paddy fields . . . a constant series of nights and days in forest clearings by the side of wide rivers in queer, forgotten bungalows, in disused bashas and ruined village houses'.

In happier times, men remembered there the 'thump, thump of pounding rice, the boom of the monastery gongs, the shrill vespers of the village boys accompanied by the crooning of doves from the high *yar* at noon and the sleepy crow of jungle cocks answering the village roosters. Late afternoon brought the monotonous song of the harvesters and the sudden ring of laughter from the tea-drinkers across the way. There was the pulse and beat of the village orchestra, the charm of dark eyes and satin skin.'

It had not been much like that for the Royal West Kents, in that filthy jungle, stifling heat, among foul disease and a million insects, against an enemy whom British and Indian troops had for the first time, in Second Arakan, decisively beaten. Casualties, not least from our own artillery on one tragic occasion, had been severe.

During an engagement on the Maungdaw-Buthidaung railway, B Company of the West Kents had been devastated by ten or twelve rounds from supporting British 25-pounders, compounded by Japanese mortar fire of phosphorous smoke bombs setting the jungle alight. This, in turn, ignited ammunition and grenades in the webbing pouches worn by the dead and wounded lying where they had fallen.

After a long, thirsty night, the entire Brigade – Royal West Kents, 1/1 Punjabis and 4/7 Rajputs – moved on foot, by lorry and boat to Dohazari whence they were to be airlifted to the flooded runways at Dimapur. No one in the Brigade had any experience in loading fighting units with their equipment straight from battle into aircraft. The principle – one load to a Dakota and one to a Commando – was simple enough, but there were complications. The USAF refused to take the large Argentine mules. They were taken by the RAF, six to a Dakota tethered to a central rail running the length of the fuselage. Once on board, the mules urinated every time the aircraft engines fired, the liquid sloshing about among the electrical wiring with consequent danger to the aircraft. The stench was overwhelming. The gunners, for their part, had to dismantle guns which had not been broken down since Alamein.

Lieutenant-Colonel John Laverty was originally from an Irish Regiment, then with the Essex Regiment until his appointment as Battalion Commander of the Fourth Royal West Kents. He had won an MC in Iraq before the war. He led the Battalion solidly and well through hard victorious fighting in the jungles of the Arakan, in heat, disease and danger. He was a disciplinarian, sometimes distant, but quiet and human: he smiled with his eyes. He made plain on arrival that Kohima would be held until the last man and until the last round. There would be no surrender by 'The Unconquered'.

The 4th Battalion was a successful, confident formation which had mastered the Japanese in difficult successive actions. It had no doubt that it had the upper hand of this enemy. They travelled light and knew that the way to beat the Japanese was to get behind them. 'Once you did that, they left.' The Regiment itself, the 50th Regiment of Foot under the White Horse Rampant of Kent, was still largely Kentish, although diluted from other English counties and from a draft of South Wales Borderers.

Donald Elwell of 1 Assam Regiment, whom we have observed moving back on Jail Hill from Transport Ridge, defined them as what they were: 'proven warriors'. Because of casualties in the Arakan, the Battalion was seriously under strength, no more than 420 men and eighteen officers. They were, nevertheless, other than the gallant remnant of the 1st Assam Regiment, the only coherent and comprehensive body of men at Kohima with its own support and associated artillery. As Lucas Phillips said, 'Its structure was inviolate. Without its stubborn resistance, Kohima would not have survived. Had it not returned precisely on April 5, because of the capture of Transport and Workshop Ridges the garrison might not have held for more than another day. Indeed they held the pass at Thermopylae.'

But had 161 Brigade not been withdrawn by higher authority on April Fool's Day, a presence of three Battalions on the Ridge, not just the eventual one battalion (West Kents), might have altered the entire outcome of the battle, perhaps even 'la bataille de Kohima n'aura pas eu lieu'.

Laverty's second-in-command was Major Peter Franklin, also from the Essex Regiment, who became his close friend, occupying the command post with him. In Franklin's recollection, they were seldom, for obvious reasons, there together. Franklin described himself as 'rather good at sieges, Tobruk, Habbaniyah and Kohima'. He later went on to command the Battalion, before being blown up by a mine in March, 1945, receiving severe injuries to his back and to an arm. He subsequently served in the UK and the US, but because of a perforated eardrum he could not command again and worked for his family firm after service as a company commander in the Norfolks. He now lives in Colchester.

Douglas Short, red-haired with a red moustache, was an able, popular and conscientious Adjutant. An indefatigable smoker, he received large consignments of untipped Churchman No. 1 cigarettes, far more than the wretched seven a day allotted from Army rations. 'Dodo' Watts (Major P. E. Watts MC), in the Civil Service before and after the War, was a classicist who took his notes in Greek and did *The Times* crossword 'in his head' before entering the solutions into the boxes: he commanded 'C' Company after Shaw was wounded. In Alexandria, when most other officers were in night-clubs, he could be seen reading a volume of Greek verse while dining. Tom Coath, who led 'C' after Watts too was wounded, was a solid, genial countryman, much respected by all, a ranker who went on to command the Battalion after the War.

Major Tommy Kenyon commanded 'A' Company. He could not be said to have been happy about the appointments of two Essex Regiment officers as battalion commander and second-in-command, but he was a good officer, slight, outspoken, brave, particularly at the tennis court. Also at the tennis court, succeeding Kenyon, was John Winstanley, commanding 'B', tall, handsome, dark. He had been at St Thomas's as a student before the war, as well as being the longest serving Territorial officer, and is today a famous eye surgeon, living in a beautiful house on Richmond Green with his charming and capable wife, a former 'Nightingale' at St Thomas's. The first commander of 'C' Company was Major Bobby Shaw, formerly a stock jobber, analytic, exact, precise, wounded early and an inspiration to all the patients in the Advanced Dressing Station. He read his Bible and his Shakespeare and encouraged those who suffered with him.

Donald Easten, who worked in the City before the War and, after it transferred to the Regular Army, ran the Cadet Forces in Colchester on retirement as well as a pack of beagles, having hunted the fox before the War. He was wounded at Kohima when commanding 'D' Company and spent some days in the ADS, before joining the last battle there, that for Kuki Piquet, rallying 'D' Company in the face of overwhelming odds. His wounds were only repaired after medical treatment at Secunderabad lasting six months, of a blood-curdling unorthodoxy. He lives today at Wormingford in Essex, deep in the English countryside. Two of his daughters are married to naval officers, both of whom have been Attachés, at Rome and Oman. He himself remains active in a wide range of local and military associations: after 40 years, he received compensation for his wounds, with which he bought a field by a stream containing pike, chub, roach and perch.

The Admin Company was led by a Welsh Customs and Excise officer, Major Bryn Williams. He took the Battalion's transport out after they arrived at Kohima and brought it back again on relief by the Second Division.

Among the most memorable NCOs were Company Sergeant-Major Haines, blinded early on but fighting to his death, and Colour Sergeant Eves MM, still living, who fed the forward troops under fire. Sergeant King, in charge of the 3" mortars, had his jaw shattered by a shell splinter in the last Japanese attack on Kuki Piquet, but fought off their final rush. Sergeant Brooks had won the MM in France and held the Club and Mound under 'A' Company towards the end. Sergeant Williams, one of several 'absolutely first-class' Welshmen, commanded a 'C' Company platoon: also there was the splendid Sergeant Tacon of 'C' Company, wounded in an attempt to rescue one of his men.

There were many others. Lance-Corporal John Harman VC, the strange giant from Lundy Island whose tycoon father claimed Winston's ear; Privates Culmer, Mathews, Peacock, Heffernan (Laverty's batman, a stage Irishman), Boorman; Corporals Richards, Norman, Day and Gilbert; Sergeant Wells, Sergeant Parsons.

Padre Randolph, with his faith, austerity, hatred of war and blood, asceticism, his transcendant courage; Major R. de C. Yeo who commanded 20 Battery without which (and 2, 11 and 12 at Jotsoma) the Japanese would have conquered; John Wright of the Sappers, tough, civilized and as agreeable at 70 in Gloucestershire as he was at 22 in Assam. He had a long career ahead as consulting engineer in Malaya, Bhutan and America. When Sappers were on active service, it was assumed that one of their functions would be the construction of bridges and other tasks involving 'water'. In these circumstances, each man was entitled to a tot of rum. As all Wright's 65 Sepoys were Muslim, he became an even more popular figure in the garrison.

The Headquarters Company was commanded by Major Harry Smith. Smith was a history tutor, who later became Senior Master at Royal Russell School, Addington Palace, a Drapers foundation, and a master at Milton Abbey. He had fought at Alam Halfa and Alamein where Montgomery recognized him from the UK, and in Arakan where the West Kents lost seventy dead and two hundred wounded. He lives today with his wife at Winterbourne Strickland in Dorset, a kind, percipient, hospitable, gentle Englishman with garden, dog and well-loved children.

HQ Company consisted of specialist platoons: Mortars, Signals, Carriers mostly on their way up from Arakan, Pioneers, MT and the Battle Patrol, many on detachment to the rifle companies. The Battle Patrol guarded Battalion Headquarters, so that the troops on the ground numbered only about fifty, most of whom, 'splendid chaps, one and all,' had been with Smith since the beginning of the war. Smith used to refer to the mortar and other barrages as 'hum-guffery'.

His position was about two hundred yards behind whatever rifle company was holding, or not holding, the DC's Bungalow, about halfway up the slope of Garrison Hill, very exposed and continually swept by fire. Should the Company in front be overrun, Smith's was the only reserve before Colonel Richards' command post.

The Pioneers, under the redoubtable Sergeant Clinch, after the war to work as a carpenter in Chatham, Rochester and Maidstone, entrenched themselves in an elaborate bunker bristling with Bren guns, while the Company Sergeant-Major organized and commanded the remainder. The Company had no officers other than Smith, since they were out with the various rifle detachments. This Sergeant-Major received shrapnel in his head, penetrating his tin hat: 'Haven't the Signallers got any pliers?' he asked, before Smith escorted him up to Young's Dressing Station.

Unlike the rifle companies, constantly fighting off hand-to-hand assaults, HQ Company patiently endured the artillery and mortar barrages for the whole fortnight. On several occasions, firing over open sights from across the valley, a Japanese gun pounded their trenches with shell after shell; at such short ranges the missiles arrived before the report of the gun, a disconcerting experience. But Smith and his men frequently had the pleasure of watching the enemy artillery being blown to pieces by the Indian 3.7 inch guns at Jotsoma, brought down on their targets by Major Yeo from his O.P. within the garrison.

The Company had to provide the hazardous water-carrying parties from the little spring discovered within the perimeter. They had also to endure the constant sniping, the race down the hill through a storm of fire with boxes of grenades for the forward companies, the exhaustion – 'moving like zombies' – the dead bodies of friend and foe, the stench of mortality. The probability that the garrison would be overwhelmed was not, however, in men's minds: wherever the enemy gathered for another attack, the mountain guns could break them up.

Narrow escapes, nevertheless, were daily occurrences. Moving in daylight was very risky as the Japanese had ringed the positions with snipers. One morning, while inspecting his trenches, Major Smith stopped to relieve himself by a shell-torn tree under the impression that it was still too dark for him to be spotted. But a bullet cracked into the tree only inches from that vital section of his anatomy. The Japanese were poor shots. He was less fortunate on the last night of the siege when a mortar bomb exploded on the edge of his trench. A fragment struck below his eye, lodging in the front of his head, just missing the brain.

Inability to move around safely restricted acquaintance with other troops of the garrison. Men often only knew their neighbours. And, as Easten once said, it was unlikely, after spending one night in one place and the next in a different one, that men would know what day it was, let alone the names of all their companions.

Charles Pawsey accompanied Colonel Richards that evening down the Dimapur Road to welcome Lieutenant-Colonel Laverty and the Fourth Battalion and to guide the companies to their positions.

He was disturbed that Laverty's only remark to Hugh Richards should have been, 'Where is Kuki Piquet?', whereupon Laverty went forward without speaking further to the Garrison Commander. It is true that the garrison, through no fault of Richards', was in disarray. It is true that distinguished fighting units dislike dependence on any troops other than their own or brother formations. It is probably true that Laverty, despite Corps instructions to Richards, was establishing the paramount right to command. Warren himself would communicate only with Laverty as the 'tactical commander'.

Relations at lower levels improved as the battle became more and more a 'soldiers' battle', almost independent of the higher command. It was a pity that the contribution of existing units, particularly that of the Assam Regiment, but of many other individuals and groups, was later discounted, even traduced. Nor was it desirable that command should be divided, between Laverty over the Royal West Kents and odd attached groups and individuals, Hugh Richards over others, and Bruno Brown over the First Assam. Laverty's virtues, responsible for victory, did not include tolerance. He was a principled but single-minded man.

Notes

1. On 30 April, as the early morning mist lifted, the advance party of I Battalion of 58 Regiment en route for Pulomi encountered a 'British armoured vehicle unit' stopped for lunch on the road near Tuphema south of Kohima. Fighting took place, the Japanese capturing four tanks and sixty vehicles.

   There is no accessible record of this action outside the reliable Japanese history of 58 Regiment, *Burma Front*. An explanation offered by Harry Seaman, author of *The Battle at Sangshak*, is that the unit was transporting to Imphal some of the twenty-three Stewart tanks then held at Dimapur. If that were so, the unit would anyway have been stopped at Mission where the Japanese had already blocked the road to Imphal.

2. An *Army Quarterly* article by Stephen Laing described Dimapur and its Manipur Road railway station as they were in 1949: 'Manipur Road, little red brick station, the yards of which were deserted and littered with broken vehicles, ordnance crates, telegraph poles. There were no workshops, ordnance or supply depots, nor were there any military police. Wild elephants, monkeys in quantity, wild pigs and barking deer occupied the old ammunition depot. There was no Adjutant, no Quartermaster's store, no barber, no tailor, no shoemaker, no tanks or lorries, no mules, only two little Nagas driving cattle. The phallic monoliths still stood, and the brick tanks and buildings of the Cachari Kings of Assam.'

XI

COLONEL LAVERTY'S DISPOSITIONS AND THE TACTICAL DOCTOR

IT HAD been Brigadier Warren's intention that the entire 161 Brigade should occupy the Kohima position with firm bases at Treasury (Fort) and Naga Village which he had reconnoitred on the initial visit. Since April Fool's Day, however, things had moved on. The Japanese had occupied Naga Village, while a State Regiment NCO reported on 5 April that his men had engaged the enemy in the Fort itself. A Naga told Pawsey that the Japanese had indeed had a 'brisk fight' with the Sher company, after which 'they had then crowded in great numbers like rats in a field'. Although there were assertions that the Japanese killed most of the State Regiment in captivity, this particular unit was seen in Dimapur in late April.

Laverty's Battalion was not just the vanguard but for two weeks the main representative in Kohima of the Brigade, apart from the Gunners and Punjabi and Rajput detachments. Arriving on 5 April, after criticizing the administrative, medical and logistic arrangements undertaken by the garrison, they were guided by Richards' men to their positions. 'A' Company under Tom Kenyon debussed near the traffic control post and moved off to Garrison Hill. Here they found a State unit loosing off their rifles aimlessly into the air and other targetless directions. It was probably this detachment which had accidentally put a bullet through Captain Patrick's hat, removing a tuft of his hair: it is ironic that *sher* means 'tiger' in English. Kenyon then established his company cookhouse which, despite many casualties among the cooks, functioned until the Berkshires arrived at dawn two weeks later.

John Winstanley went with 'B' Company to the east side of Kuki Piquet to the south of Garrison (Summer House) Hill. Major Bobby Shaw took 'C' to Detail Hill (DIS), and 'D' Company under Donald Easten, regarded as 'too young' to be a Major, went into battalion reserve. ('D' Company was first up the road from Dimapur and had been under fire at Hospital Spur.) Harry Smith, the gentle schoolmaster, sited Headquarters Company between Laverty's and Richards' command posts. Bryn Williams took the transport out, or such of it as would run, and much later, brought it back.

Laverty's command post was dug by the Colonel and officers and men of his Headquarters, slightly above Colonel Richards' post, between the Deputy Commissioner's Bungalow and the top of Garrison Hill. It was deep, about nine feet long with overhead cover, accommodating four men, including Peter Franklin, and John Topham, the Signals Officer. It contained two W/T sets in two niches, for communication with Brigade HQ at Jotsoma, with Richards and with the West Kents' companies. Captain Topham was wounded and later killed: he and the Battalion signallers had been tireless in repairing line over the battered terrain.

In the increasing rain, wind and cold of that night, the sound of picks and shovels digging trenches and bunkers in the darkness could be heard from all the positions. Conditions that evening were not good. The original defence shelters were sometimes deep and large enough for twelve men, and with good cover. But many had only one small firing slit so that only one man could fire at a time.

Owing to heavy and accurate Japanese shelling of the West Kents' lorries when they arrived at Kohima, parked nose-to-tail on the road in view of the Japanese battery on Workshop Ridge, many men had lost their blankets and warm clothing. On leaving the trucks, they had taken only their weapons, ammunition and packs. Blankets were supposed to be collected later from the trucks, but many of those had been burned out under the bombardment, their drivers dead at the wheel or absconded to Dimapur.

On Detail Issue Hill (code-name 'Horse' to the Japanese) Bobby Shaw gave his men blankets taken from departing Indian Army Service Corps and other non-combatants. 'C' Company received 'no tiffin, dinner or tea' on that first evening. For breakfast next morning they only had biscuits and a tin of blackcurrant jam scrounged from a basha. Although the men never anticipated defeat, they were temporarily dispirited by the confusion and lack of rest after their mauling in the Arakan.

The garrison 25-pounder near Pawsey's bungalow had fired only one round, in an attempt to cover the disembarkation of the Royal West Kents, before being spotted by the Japanese gunners, ranged and destroyed.[1] Captain John Browning was wounded in the head and later killed. Major Yeo, commanding 20 Battery, then set up his observation post near Laverty's HQ with a telephone link to Richards. His four 3.7 inch guns, brought up, dismantled and later reassembled near Keene's and Pawsey's bungalows, were soon under fire from the Workshop Ridge battery and, since they were plainly visible from that position, never used.

It was not until 6 April that artillery could be brought down on Japanese positions. In an area of only 700 × 900 × 1100 yards, the Garrison's *maximum* perimeter, overlooked by enemy batteries of quick-firing anti-tank guns and 75mm howitzers, it was impossible to site guns safely in Kohima itself. Yeo dismantled two 3.7 inch howitzers, placing the parts in trenches, taking the other two to the peak of Garrison Hill. None were employed in the Siege and their gunners fought, and fought well, in an infantry role.

But 'Daddy' Warren, unable yet to enter Kohima where there was anyway no space for two more battalions or for any guns at all, had by 6 April formed a box at Jotsoma to contain his HQ, the bulk of the 1/1 Punjabi and 4/7 Rajput Battalions, and three batteries of three 3.7 inch guns each. The box was almost exactly two miles west of Kohima, the maximum range of the splendid Colonel Humphrey Hill's guns. Yeo, Captain Peter Kendall, Lieutenant Dickenson, and a gallant Sikh gunner, Lieutenant J.S. Punia, maintained a continuous 24-hour watch from OPs in the Kohima box.

Hill, at 24 Mountain Regiment, directed by these four, initially with ample ammunition, was soon able to answer from Jotsoma any request for defensive fire from the garrison, Richards or Laverty. At a later stage, Kenyon, Easten, Shaw, Winstanley and their successor company commanders could themselves call up DF via Laverty or Richards to Yeo in his adjacent OP, without the necessity for OPs in the infantry companies.

2 (Peter Hartley), 11 and 12 batteries, under Humphrey Hill, never failed the garrison. No shell ever landed on the British on Garrison Hill itself, despite a distance between friend and foe of as little, on the tennis court, as twenty yards, and despite constant changes of direction and range. Towards the end, the artillerymen in the box were so sensitive to Japanese sound and movement that they could anticipate the requests of company commanders. Japanese attacks were identified before they began and broken up over and over again. The Indian gunners, particularly after the RAF had dropped proper maps on the Jotsoma batteries, were uncannily accurate. There is no doubt that 24 Mountain Regiment thus contributed decisively to victory, both before and after relief of the garrison.

On the evening of the Royal West Kents' arrival it was evident to troops of that Battalion on Detail Issue Hill that the Jail Hill position was unlikely to be held. Assamese troops there were nevertheless firing two 3″ mortars over the hill on to the Japanese who, in return, were firing on Detail. About five mortar bombs landed ten yards from a West Kents' platoon HQ and one bomb only five yards away. Corporal Webber was standing on the edge of a weapon pit. Told to get into the pit, he jumped in as a mortar bomb exploded one yard from where he had just been standing. Native troops, possibly Burma or State Regiment, attempted to run away from Jail Hill, but were prevented by 'C' Company on Detail.

All in all, it had not been a happy day. There was, however, cause for gratitude that under the Japanese guns the Battalion had at least been able to get up the hill and into Kohima. Amongst the high trees, in the rhododendrons and the scrub, under the thick vegetation overhead and in the heat of the day and the cold of the night, the moon and the stars invisible in the forests, most would have no doubt preferred to be elsewhere. But this was a trained, steady, well-officered force, of great professional skill and experience.

The Regimental Commander of 58 had realized the tactical importance of Jail Hill. Fukunaga's assaults during the night of 5 April and the morning of 6 April meant that the position had to be abandoned. The Japanese of 5, 6 and 7 Companies, II Battalion, supported by mortars and infantry guns, yelling and blowing bugles, mounted an attack in greatly superior numbers, led by an officer brandishing a sword. A counter-attack by Lieutenant Peter Brown, nephew of the Bishop of Assam and a prewar tea planter, of the 1st Assam Regiment and Subadar Kapthuama Lushai failed. Brown was wounded, and although placed by Steyn in a lorry bound for Dimapur was found dead in the abandoned truck at Ms42 at the end of the Siege. The retreat of the Assam and Burma troops was followed an hour later by thirty British troops from the Convalescent Depot, where they had been found by the Japanese: nine out of ten Norfolks there had been killed by Jiffs.

The Assam Regiment lost two officers wounded and about twenty other ranks killed and wounded. Japanese casualties were, perhaps optimistically, estimated at 150 killed and wounded over the whole battle for Jail, but from start to finish it had lasted only one day.

Although 'C' Company believed that they were facing three Japanese battalions or 3,300 men, Laverty was under the misapprehension that only two *platoons* had been involved. He accordingly despatched 18 Platoon of Easten's 'D' Company in reserve, but, despite mortar support from Sergeant King, they and troops of the Assam Regiment were beaten back by Japanese already in the bunkers on Jail. 'C' Company managed to salvage two three-inch mortars and their bombs which the Assam mortar sections had left behind when withdrawing. Corporals Rees' and Webber's sections were now at the bottom of Detail, with Corporals Jimmy Beames' and Maxworthy's sections thirty yards higher on the hill. Communication trenches had been dug between them and Platoon HQ.

At 4.30 in the afternoon of 6 April, a Japanese reconnaissance aircraft circled overhead. Captain 'Dodo' Watts, MC, warned his men that dive-bombing might be imminent and that they should camouflage and dig in. Instead, thirty minutes later, the RAF bombed and strafed the Japanese mortar position on the heights of Transport Hill (no tiffin again and, once more, only hard biscuit and jam for dinner at 5.30 pm). At 6 o'clock the Company was mortared again with direct hits on its HQ. One broke Major Shaw's leg in several places, tearing the thigh, and the other caused shrapnel injuries to Privates Young and Sharpe. All three were evacuated to the Regimental Aid Post.

Mortaring and shelling began again at 9 pm and went on all night. 13 Platoon had no sleep, hearing also the clink of pick and shovel. Forty Japanese with entrenching tools and another fifty with weapons ready were engaged in digging within yards of the platoon. Dick Johnson, a bank messenger, Ernie Thrussel, book-binder, and Corporal Norman opened fire, while Sergeant Tacon grenaded the enemy. Corporal Webber's section alone killed ten, one poised to throw a grenade when the rifle bullet hit. In the area of Company HQ and 14 Platoon there was heavy firing; the Japanese killed Ginger Judges, the cook, injured Captain Watts and Sergeant Ward, slightly wounding Privates Woodward and Liddell of 14 Platoon. Jimmy Beanes (13 Platoon) took a bullet through his shoulder. He said that it was 'nothing serious' and refused evacuation. So did Captain Watts.

Perhaps it was from this moment that, in Captain Tom Coath's words, the Siege became primarily 'a private's battle, and our success was mainly due to the very high morale and steadiness of the NCOs and men'.

Many Indian stragglers had been caught, killed or wounded by mortar fire on Jail Hill and many among the Burmese units had deserted to Dimapur. (A Burma detachment did form itself on Garrison Hill under a new commander, A. J. Hoyt, replacing the dead Noel Lunn.) Richards disarmed all troops who had demonstrated lack of fire and other discipline. It was, however, very difficult to reform the composite companies from the Reinforcement Camp. Although some individuals and groups, such as that calling itself the 'Kohima Rifles', were not useless, Garrison Hill was becoming dangerously cluttered with ineffective and frightened men, hindering the fighting troops.

The Japanese were known and sensed to be moving in, all round the garrison, on the slopes, infiltrating through the trees, with little or no attempt at concealment. General Sato himself arrived in Naga Village, where III Battalion of 58 Regiment had returned from Cheswema. 31 Division's command post now directly overlooked the battlefield. To have lost Transport Hill had been bad enough, but the loss of Jail Hill put 'C' Company and Detail Hill in jeopardy, now not much more than fifty yards from the Japanese front line. Shelling of the Bungalow sector caused damage and casualties to the gunners of 20 Battery and to the composite British company there. It was fortunate that on that day (6 April), a company of the 4/7 Rajputs under John Wright's friend, Captain Mitchell, forced their way into Kohima to be added to the reserve and to make later a substantial contribution to the defence.

To the west, Warren had made his tactical mark on events by *not* moving into Kohima, where Humphrey Hill's howitzers would have been incapable of deployment. Nor was there room, as we have seen, for all the Punjabis and Rajputs, as well as the West Kents. The Jotsoma Box, in its present position and later on higher ground close to the village, may not have been a sound tactical site. It was overlooked, but the box was entirely justifiable in that it protected the best weapons at the Brigade's disposal, 24th Mountain Regiment's guns. It was also the ideal point from which to join the vital advance of Second Division from Dimapur.

On 6 April the extraordinary 'Tactical Doctor' arrived. Colonel John Young, tall, dark, hook-nosed, commanded the 75th Indian Field Ambulance. He had come personally because of warnings to Warren from Peter Franklin, Laverty's second-in-command, that the medical situation was deteriorating and would get worse without Brigade's facilities.

Young had studied art in Vienna before qualifying as a doctor: he played polo and was so keen an amateur soldier that he eventually gave up medicine and became a professional officer on the General Staff, hence 'Tactical Doctor'. He was, as a surgeon, 'neat, quick and daring' – although he had not practised for years – and, as a man and soldier, without fear. He knew India, spoke Urdu and was therefore extremely useful to the frightened Indians in the RAPs and ADS. He was an excellent administrator and able to combine the five aid posts into an Advanced Dressing Station on Summer House Hill, near Laverty's command post, although some RAPs remained with the companies.

The wounded men, for the most part, still remained in slit trenches, while the operating theatre was at first an open pit covered by a tarpaulin in the dusk, Captain Richard Glover, late of the garrison hygiene unit, Captain Abdul Majid, and Young himself began to operate on the initial seventy-eight cases brought in under fire by the stretcher-bearers. Shelling and mortaring, with the gruesome results that we shall see, continued unabated. Fifty-six patients were killed, rewounded as they lay outside, not to speak of those who died from their original wounds.

Young organized surgical and nursing teams, an entrenching group and stretcher bearers. In this he was greatly aided by James Barratt, an officer of the 1/17 Dogras, 123 Brigade, 5 Indian Division, that Division which also included the West Kents. Barratt commanded a composite company, one of those disarmed by Colonel Hugh Richards, not 'windy', but ill-disciplined. Richards had sent it to the west slope of Garrison Hill where Barratt had taught his men manners and instructed them in entrenching. He broke his hand on a mutinous Pathan's jaw and had no further difficulties. As his position was just below the ADS, he obtained permission for his men and those of another mixed company to dig trenches for the hospital, narrow and shallow in the rocky soil and spreading roots, or in wide bays for more than one patient.

His Company also made an operating theatre and a dressing station, one with a timber roof, the other with a tarpaulin, both 6 feet deep. In the faint light of hurricane lamps five hundred wounded were treated over a period of fourteen days. Surgery without proper instruments was the daily scene. Three doctors were killed and two wounded, but the 75th Field Ambulance War Diary records that 'the shelter of the trenches, slight though it was, at once raised the spirits of the wounded themselves'. And the wounded came in an unending stream. Glover's private diary speaks of the 'seeming futility of saving a life that was soon to be extinguished at the crash of the next shell', of 'awful nights, the stink of putrid flesh, terrible casualties'.

All of these had to be borne and succoured by the Regimental Chaplain, the Reverend Roy Randolph, a man who, because he had conquered very great fear, was not only of an ascetic sweetness, but of unbreakable courage, his tall, thin figure an example of goodness and belief to all his countrymen. He later became an Archdeacon of Johannesburg, but was last heard of in a monastic order.

The Adjutant to the garrison's 112 Works, Captain Stephen Laing, was responsible under Colonel Lander (CRE) for the large ration, ammunition, petrol, ordnance, engineer depots and for the bakeries, workshops, cattle drovers' unit, transport, pioneers and hygiene units. His NCOs were British, but his troops were 'virtually civilians in uniform', many without arms or training, supplemented by civilian labour provided by tea-planters engaged on road maintenance. Laing had been caught near Kalewa by the 1942 retreat and had made his way back via Tamu, Imphal and Dimapur.

After a longish period of training and a month as ADC to General Sir Alan Hartley, Acting C-in-C India, he was posted to Assam to supervise the construction of the Imphal-Kohima-Manipur road, a task of magnitude since, until the foundations were secured, it was continually swept away by landslides. Hitherto, the road had been confined to one-way traffic in opposite alternating directions, with 'gates' at Nichugard, Kangpokpi and Kohima.

On the arrival of the Royal West Kents, Laing realized that there was little for him to do at his assigned duties and, with his sergeants, went into the trenches with the RWKs until the end. His first position was on Jail Hill where, beside him, Sergeant Hewett fell dead with a bullet straight through the middle of his forehead. On Supply Hill, moving back, Sergeant Millichap described the situation as 'precarious': thirty minutes later he was killed. Laing moved further and further back towards the tennis court before being relieved with the rest by the Punjabis and Berkshires.

When he and George Lacky went down the hill, unshaven, no epaulettes or badges of rank, unwashed, their uniforms in tatters, a Military Policeman supervising the evacuation, crashed to attention in the salute.

On the Viceroy's orders, Laing was later appointed as Additional Deputy Commissioner to Charles Pawsey for nearly eighteen months, organizing commodities for Naga villages devastated by the Japanese. Wavell wrote: 'Captain Laing will stay in Kohima until I personally tell him otherwise,' a successful means of neutralizing other demands from Laing's Sapper superiors. When that was over, Stephen Laing qualified in London as a doctor in the hope of returning to the Nagas. But, by that time India was independent and in virtual civil war with Nagaland: New Delhi would only agree if he gave up his British passport for Indian papers. He did not wish to do so, and pursued a medical career with the Colonial Office, the London Mission Society, Taylor Woodrow, Bechtel, Unilever and Anglo-American, in Africa, the Middle East, South Asia, Latin America, South East Asia and as a ship's doctor. Now retired, but still doing voluntary work, he lives in an enchanted Sussex village with a stone bridge, a mill, a church and a little river.

NOTES

1. According to John Hill's *China Dragons: A Rifle Company at War, Burma 1944–1945* (Blandford, 1991), Appendix G, the principal Japanese infantry weapons were:

Mortar 91 mm (2.19 in.)	:	Range 2,000 yards max.
Mortar 90 mm (3.54 in.)	:	Range 4,150 yards max.
Battalion guns 70 mm.	:	Range 3,075 yards max.
Regimental guns 75 mm.	:	Range 7,500 yards max.

XII

THE ASSAULT ON
DETAIL HILL

BY 6 APRIL the Japanese had secured the road behind the garrison. Colonel Richards understood at the same time that the loss of Transport Ridge also involved the cutting by the Japanese of the garrison's water pipeline running from the Aradura Spur reservoir to Supply Hill. A very little water was then found at a point near the tennis court. Other sources included a small stream, a fair way to the west of the main position down a precipitous, forested slope, and a spring in a cliff near the DC's bungalow only accessible to men climbing up and down the cliff, encumbered with containers and personal weapons. Richards rationed water to one mug per man per day.

Barratt's Indian company had the responsibility for filling a large water drum in the Advanced Dressing Station from one or other of these points. Take-off could only be carried out at night and in hazardous conditions. Lives were lost. They themselves, and many others on the Ridge, had no hot tea throughout the Siege, subsisting on tinned grapefruit, oranges, pears, etc, collected at great risk from the depot on Supply Hill, and on the juice from tinned peas and beetroot. (John Wright always landed himself with pineapple juice, acid and without the gift of assuaging thirst.) Barratt's company was even more Spartan, enjoying no hot food either.

From Jail Hill, Captain Sato, after the death of Major Nagaya in an early attack on Detail,[1] led 2 and 5 Companies of II Battalion 58 Regiment against 'C' Company on Detail. They crossed the road in darkness between the two features twenty yards ahead of the West Kent lines, wearing gym shoes, their equipment muffled. There was no shouting, bugles or yelling. Assault was preceded by the common tactics of imitated British voices, 'Let me through, for God's sake let me through, the Japs are on me', and by single-shot sniping designed to draw an identifying response.

The first charge was severely cut about by the Indian Artillery from 24th Mountain Regiment at Jotsoma, by Sergeant King's 3″ mortars, and the Bren, rifle and tommy-gun fire of the defenders. But some of the enemy got through, and fierce hand-to-hand combat took place between sweating and desperate men firing and bayoneting on the edge of the rifle pits. The Japanese withdrew to Jail again, temporarily baulked.

Three more attacks followed in waves and in mounting numbers, this time with all the paraphernalia of yelling and bugles. Men rose up on the bank, at the end of 'C' Company's rifles, falling back, dead, wounded or to come on again. The moon had now risen as Captain Watts, wounded but in command after Shaw's departure, had hoped. The Japanese could now be picked out in the blackness against the silver roadway. The screams of an over-confident enemy could be plainly heard as the Jotsoma guns caught them and brought them down.

Some penetration occurred. 'C' Company's position was also out-flanked from the west by a Japanese approach up a steep, hidden, wooded slope. This attack seized the bashas at the northern end of Detail, earlier occupied by the Mahrattas and an Indian composite company. 15 Platoon was isolated from the action, and between Jail Hill and the 'ninety' Japanese in the bashas, Corporal Norman believed 13, 15 and HQ Platoons also to be cut off. At 11 am he and Sergeant Tacon, without any cover against the Japanese in front or the snipers behind, went out into the open ten yards from the West Kent's trenches and fired HE bombs into the bashas. Tacon left Norman there for an uncomfortable fifteen minutes while he consulted Captain Watts. Norman was fired on by both sides. Behind him, Private Stirling received a bullet in the side of his neck.

As the gap between Supply and Detail Hills was under fire from Japanese 75 mm, Donald Easten, commanding 'D' on Supply, ordered Lieutenant Doresa, aged only 20, full of dash and spirit, to move with his platoon through dead ground to the east and take the bashas from the north-east corner of Detail. Another 'D' Company platoon gave sup-porting fire against the bashas from the base of Supply, until Peter Doresa, CSM Haines and Company HQ troops, together with five unknown Gurkha volunteers, mounted an assault 'with bayonet and grenade against the unsuspecting bashas'.

Between them, 'C' and 'D' Companies fired the huts, forcing out terrified Jiffs and Japanese amidst the crash of grenades, rattle of Brens and explosions from an ammunition dump on Detail blown up by British grenades or Japanese 75 mm from Transport Ridge. The enemy, bursting out of burning huts, started to fall everywhere or run helter-skelter under rifle and tommy-gun fire, their bodies piling up all over the hill. 13 Platoon claimed that seventy Japanese were killed and twelve wounded, the Gurkhas cleaving three men's heads from crown to chin with kukris.

Easten moved his second platoon from the foot of Supply to Detail, relieving it with the third and remaining 'D' Company platoon. He then took over both 'C' and 'D' Companies. Captain Watts had been wounded again, this time in the arm and now was evacuated to John Young's Dressing Station. It was another cold and windy night. 'C' Company had eaten nothing but biscuit and jam. Captain Tom Coath, the ranker who commanded the Battalion after the war, was now sent from 'B' Company to command 'C', which, as well as Shaw and Watts, had incurred at least forty casualties during these actions and was to suffer many more. But it had been a classic operation.

As a Good Friday, 7 April had left much to be desired. When Coath arrived on the Hill, 'C' Company was again under mortar bombardment. His men were firing at Japanese visible in the moonlight. An attack began from the same quarter, Jail Hill, but the Jotsoma 3.7s caught it before it developed. Another began against the DC's bungalow, driven off by the British composite company there. Unfortunately, 24 Mountain Regiment two miles away did not have the range to hit reinforcements in Naga Village, including guns drawn by elephants.

Although the Japanese had added quick-firing 37 mm anti-tank guns to their artillery on Transport Ridge, the problem on Detail was a machine gun close to the burning ammunition basha in the northern sector. (The anti-tank guns were invulnerable to the Jotsoma guns. Their shells, incidentally, arrived before their noise, allowing no time for evasion. They also caused airbursts among the trees necessitating head-cover which, in turn, limited 'C' and 'D' Companies' fields of fire. Covered trenches were the answer, but, before they could be completed, many lives were lost.) The Japanese were still in the bunker on the morning of 8 April and, if another attack were to be mounted, the machine gun would cause havoc among the West Kents.

Donald Easten, commanding 'D' Company, and his CSM were approached by Lance-Corporal John Harman. Harman had left the Life Guards after mechanization because, he said, he preferred horses, but nevertheless ended up as a sniper with 'D'. He had advised Easten in the Arakan to stick with him. 'A man in Spain told me I should live to be at least seventy. Stay with me and you'll be all right.' Easten replied that the man in Spain had said nothing to *him*.

On another occasion he had asked Easten for his permission, bully beef stew, biscuits and jam becoming monotonous in the Arakan, to kill a steer from among cattle who used to graze in no-man's-land, returning to their owners at night. Easten told him that Battalion HQ had refused, adding, 'except if one of the animals breaks a leg or something like that'. Only minutes later, there was a burst of machine-gun fire. When Peter Franklin from HQ came down to investigate, the peace-time meat inspectors and butchers in the Company had so disposed of the steer that no trace was visible. Steaks were distributed that night to neighbouring West Kent company commanders, as well as within 'D'.

Harman told Easten and Haines that he knew how to get at the bunker. He ordered his section to cover him with the Bren, crawled out of his position, ran first slowly, then with gathering speed for thirty-five yards until he flung himself down at the very mouth of the bunker under the fury of machine-gun bullets over his body. Easten saw him take out a four-second grenade and throw away the clip. He then heard 'one-two-three' before Harman threw it into the slit. The two Japanese gunners were killed instantly and the Lance-Corporal returned to his rifle pit with their machine gun. When asked why he did not take a commission, he would reply only that he was an individualist.

A similar act of courage had been accomplished during Easten's brilliant infantry attack with Doresa on Good Friday. A large building on the east of Detail Hill had been identified as a bakery, with one brick and three bamboo walls plus a tin roof. It was occupied by Japanese, including another machine-gunner who had deadly coverage of 'C' Company from the south. The bakery contained six ovens. Grenades failed to dislodge these soldiers, but the 'C'/'D' Company operation to clear Detail could not be said to have been accomplished until they were disposed of. The building had no windows, only slits between roof and walls behind which the enemy was sheltering securely in the ovens or in the lee of crates and boxes, relatively safe from grenade or automatic fire.

The only way to get at the target was by destroying the walls. Easten consulted John Wright of the Bengal Sappers and Miners. Wright had already designed Laverty's command post, including the timbering, shown Barratt how to build slit trenches to take stretchers, advised how to protect dug-out walls with crates, improved the range of Sergeant King's mortars and built several other devices.

The lids of ammunition boxes on poles being too flimsy for the purpose, Wright tied twenty-two slabs of stiff, hard gun-cotton on to an old discarded door which one of his men had obtained from the Hospital and added a detonator and fuse. He and Easten charged the bakery uphill at the double, slammed the door against the brick wall which was also the back of the six ovens, pulled the ignition and ran back. A tremendous explosion resulted, smoke and dust with bricks and other debris flying through the air, including a tin of grease which landed on Wright's tin hat; the Japanese bolted into the waiting guns of 'C' Company. Two Japanese were left alive in the bakery, a gravely wounded officer who died shortly after, and a corporal who was persuaded to give away the Order of Battle of the 58th Regiment but later committed *sepuku* (suicide).

The Japanese Battalion Commander described these actions as 'a crushing defeat for the 58th Regiment . . . even worse than Sangshak'. Wright deserved a VC: his Naik was awarded the Indian DSM.

58 Regiment had numbered five thousand men. The total of effective British fighting men in Kohima, including formed units as well as British and Indian soldiers without officers, was now down to about six hundred and fifty. Against this paltry figure, the Japanese could muster no less than three Regiments, 58, 124 and 138, which although somewhat reduced, numbered perhaps twelve and a half thousand. This was heavy odds and it is perhaps fortunate that even the garrison command posts were unaware of the true situation and even luckier that Sato did not exploit the preponderance. A battalion attack on a broad front, although the terrain was against it, would have been much more difficult to resist than night attacks by 31 Division in platoon or company strength, even with mortars, grenades and artillery on the widely spread trenches, this from all directions except the west, against a voice-warfare background.

Sato, of course, did not believe that the tiny Allied garrison could hold for long against the ever-victorious Imperial forces. He saw no reason to change inflexible Japanese tactics. Most of the Kohima battle was at the end of a rifle or hand-to-hand, the enemy materializing suddenly out of the blackness straight in the sights of British and Indian infantrymen. The lack of Dannert wire was a great help to Japanese methods of infiltration and, once within close range, snipers roped themselves into trees at least until tree bursts, in themselves producing heavy casualties, removed leaf cover. Above all, the Japanese aimed to create exhaustion in their enemy, themselves sleeping by day while their artillery kept the garrison alert and awake, mounting their infantry assaults by night.

At night the tired Allied troops stood to in the dark before the moon rose, prey to every false perception of movement, each rustling of a leaf the indicator of Japanese infiltration behind or at the flank, waiting for dawn and its relief from real or imagined fears. Japanese 75s, 37s, anti-tank, mortar or grenade fire had been particularly bad on Good Friday, killing or wounding patients in the ADS, and inflicting casualties in those trenches from which cover had been removed in order to provide maximum fire. (Stephen Laing calculated that from the plop of a grenade being fired to arrival on its target, the interval was fourteen seconds.) Enemy artillery was most active at first light and at sunset, hammering regularly at the nerves as well as at the objective. This produced in troops permanent apprehension that, when they awoke, 'the occupants of the next weapon pit might be Japanese', or that the Japanese might swarm over the field hospital, with unthinkable consequences.

Charles Pawsey had chosen to remain with the garrison. He did not want it to be thought that he had abandoned the Nagas. In his white shirt and grey flannel trousers, his bungalow a ruin, he moved about Kohima, always guarded by two Naga followers in red blankets with spears and daos. Although, despite his Great War experience, he had no military function and little contact with Naga friends and informants outside the Ridge, he kept as close contact as he could with the troops, in particular with Buster Keene and the Assam Rifles.

He thought highly of Colonel Hugh Richards ('first-rate'), as did Major Harry Smith and the Royal West Kents HQ Company. So did Richards' second-in-command, Slim's friend, Gordon Borrowman. When the Garrison Commander made his daily visits to the units, often under sniper fire, the West Kents cheered him on, calling out, 'Come on, Sir, you're winning'. Major Easten remarked that Richards encouraged the troops, 'a good British officer walking about, looking unafraid'. Captain Elwell and Major Rawlley described him as 'under strain, but understanding, considerate, never rattled, often laughing and joking under fire'. There may have been a moment, after his W/T sets had been knocked out, when Richards' resolve was challenged.

Pawsey and Keene kept their dogs throughout the Siege, as proper Englishmen should, Pawsey's a mongrel and Keene's a shitzu. Laing had to shoot his, with sadness and regret; it was white and conspicuous.

In the Royal West Kent's command post Laverty and Franklin knew that they were under attack all round the perimeter without any early chance of reinforcement and certainly not, so far, of relief. The water supply was negligible, the men still restricted to a pint or less a day. The casualties in Colonel Young's Dressing Station and field hospital were mounting, their survival uncertain under constant bombardment. Their suffering, mostly borne in silence, was a continual concern to Laverty. He was tired and would become much more so, but he led his men firmly, cheerfully and responsibly to the very end.

Although he could not get to the lines as much as he wished, he made the men feel that what lay ahead was not just a battle but a great adventure. The 'bloody-minded Irishman' who came through a test of leadership that few anywhere have passed grew in authority from a good but unexceptional leader to a great battalion commander.

NOTES

1. Major Nagaya was killed by a grenade after taking a British bunker, armed only with his sword. His body was taken to the rear, covered in white flowers by his soldiers.

XIII

THE LAST EASTER OF LANCE-CORPORAL HARMAN

VARIOUS WAR Diaries give dates ranging from 7 to 10 April for what follows. Colonel Laverty was under Japanese artillery fire in his blacked-out command post on Garrison Hill during the lengthening shadows of the evening. He asked John Young whether he could handle the current numbers of wounded in his Dressing Station. Young said that he could not, nor even shelter the wounded in slit-trenches as opposed to stretchers in the open; since his position was under continual fire from 75 mm howitzers and quick-firing 37 mm guns, trenches could only be dug at night. There were already thirty men on stretchers in the open. One hundred walking wounded should therefore be evacuated without delay.

Although Young had come into Kohima along the peaks of the ridges, he doubted whether the same route could be followed by weak and slow-moving wounded men. He suggested nullahs, but these were almost indistinguishable from one another, steep and rocky. He and Major Peter Franklin, Laverty's Second-in-Command, accompanied and guided by Peter Corlett of Jessami and by one of Pawsey's Nagas, decided to lead their stumbling party on a compass bearing in pitch darkness through valley, forest and jungle.

A platoon of Rajputs under a Jemadar formed the escort fore and aft. The wounded kept slipping in the wet earth of the jungle, some falling, opening wounds which ached, burned and freely bled. The officers, fearing that the Indian wounded, once down, would never move again, refused them rest. Through the dense undergrowth, up and down uncountable slopes, they covered seven miles in seven hours.

The Assam Rifles, who formed the flank guard at Ms42, the dangerous crossing of the Dimapur-Kohima road, came under heavy fire, but Young and Franklin handed over their party intact to Major Richard Pilcher, Young's second-in-command, who sent them all on in lorries to Dimapur and Zubza. The Japanese cut the road next morning.

The Doctor and his companion tried on their return journey to turn back a hundred non-combatants who had followed the route used by the wounded leaving Kohima on Hospital Spur. Young did not know that they were not fleeing, but that Hugh Richards had sent them out deliberately in order to clear the ground of ineffectives.

There were still over a hundred 'lying-in' patients in the ADS, thirty gravely wounded. The day saw forty more admissions from Detail Hill.

On 8 April Colonels Laverty and Richards were faced with separate but concentric threats. The first consisted of night attacks by Japanese infantry, 138 Regiment under Toriaki against Colonel Keene's Assam Rifles at Hospital Ridge. This part of the Ridge was just to the east of Hospital Spur, west of Kohima town. (It was down that spur that the wounded had limped to safety.) On this occasion, although the enemy were beaten off with rifle and kukri, several with split skulls, some were able to entrench on the lower spur, a sensitive and dangerous side door for a major assault on the Ridge. On 9 April, however, a two-platoon Assam attack, preceded by mortar fire but without artillery, recovered ground taken earlier.

A second attack developed against the DC's bungalow. It was preceded by the severest artillery bombardment yet sustained, and by more mortaring. The original defenders were British and Gurkha troops from the Reinforcement Depot. Even without their own officers, they fought well. Major Yeo's Gunners held firm. Two of them, Punjabi Mussulmen, died defending their dismounted guns to the last Bren round.

The Japanese charged in company strength from dead ground, storming both Pawsey and Keene's bungalows, driving the garrison troops back to the twenty-yard-wide terrace. Here lay the asphalt tennis court, running north-south above the two bungalows and surrounded by the high wire netting enclosing tennis courts anywhere. At the east slope it was commanded on the next higher level by the Club and adjacent mound. From none of these terraces, except at their extremities, was any lower terrace visible, although the command posts on Garrison Hill virtually surveyed almost the entire area.

To the north-west of the tennis court was a large tarpaulin water tank. One of the take-off points for Barratt's gallant band of water collectors was one level down to the south. Japanese 9 and 10 Companies, with 11 to follow, dug in near the water tank twenty yards from the Royal West Kents.

The Japanese destroyed a British machine-gun post opposite the tarpaulin, killing the crew except for one man who shammed dead so effectively that he was trampled on by the enemy in establishing their positions. Two British sections dug in along the wire netting opposite, with the rest of the unit on the terrace above by the Mound and at the Club. Richards, at this critical moment, sent in one platoon of the Assam Regiment under Subedar Kapthuanas Lushai and a Burma platoon of 1/7 Gurkha Rifles. The whole party was commanded by Jimmy Patrick. The

Burma platoon reached Pawsey's bungalow in a well-planned and covered attack, but then could make little or no progress; isolated, Kapthuanas' platoon had to withdraw. Patrick's total command numbered only twenty men with two Brens and, although they actually captured the position, heavy Japanese grenading and the failure to arrive of a platoon promised by the West Kents enabled the enemy to recapture it.

Laverty now told Sergeant King, to whom he had given five replacements for his mortar unit from the Replacement Depot and the Quartermaster's store, and five more who were carrier drivers, to switch his mortar fire from Jail Hill to the DC's bungalow. The fighting here, across the rhododendrons and cannas, was hand-to-hand, the enemy advancing in screaming waves until halted at the tennis court where the mob was held.

'A' Company, under Major Tom Kenyon, hitherto in reserve on Garrison Hill whence he had heard and seen the early Japanese attack on Hospital Spur, was moved to the DC's bungalow. The first platoon into battle was led by Sergeant Brooks who held the Club and Mound, the Japanese on the other side of the court temporarily stopped by 'A' Company's fire. Lieutenant Hinton's platoon went to the left of the tennis court and Kenyon put the third platoon in front of the Mound. Only from that place could one see down the hill.

A novel about Kohima claims that for the rest of the Siege 'they played with each other on the tennis court, but the balls they were using were grenades, and these were followed by bullets and shells whenever anyone on either side moved'. It was only by night, free of infantry but not artillery assault, that soldiers could eat, improve head cover or work on their trenches. Japanese attacks were often preceded by accurate mortar fire causing casualties to the Royal West Kents and to the composite companies now functioning efficiently under Tom Kenyon. On the Japanese side of the court there was excellent dead ground, but the hideous noise made by the enemy in attack enabled precise fire from the Indian Mountain Batteries to be called down from Jotsoma and from King's mortars, all landing just the other side of the court and never with injury to Allied troops.

But Japanese did get through, singly and in small groups, on to the tennis court. Against these, the only defence was Bren-gun fire, grenades and, sometimes useless against sudden apparitions, the rifle.

'A' Company was in position by dawn on 9 April. At first light, the British soldier who had pretended to be dead at the machine-gun post destroyed the day before, leaped out of his hole across the court and raced into the West Kent's trenches. He provided useful information about the enemy's weapons and defences. Major Kenyon's batman at this time shot a Japanese who had thought he was in dead ground and was walking about to demonstrate his good fortune.

Part of the Japanese 138 Regiment under Colonel Torikai was now moving from the Merema Ridge in the north-west to block the movement of British reinforcements for Kohima. Torikai put troops athwart the Dimapur-Kohima road at Ms36 north of Zubza. 161 Brigade was now cut off by 138, while Major-General Miyazaki of 58 Regiment began to move in from the south on the right flank.

In Kohima, the water ration had just been cut to three-quarters of a pint per man per day.

The third threat was on Detail Hill where 'C' Company had four hard biscuits and some cold mutton for breakfast. In the early hours of that morning there was little activity out of Jail Hill and only two snipers, one of whom nevertheless hit Sergeant Cathorn in the forward trench at the bottom of the slope. Corporal Norman fired six smoke bombs to cover Cathorn's stretcher-bearers, but the Sergeant was dead on arrival at the aid post.

The men had had no tiffin and the same monotonous diet for dinner at 6 as for breakfast. There was no char all day. The Company stood to from 6.30 to 7.15 when it got dark, at which time the Japanese mortar barrage began, followed by a bellowing infantry attack in company strength. This assault was halted by rifle and machine-gun fire from four weapon pits on Detail, ten yards back from the Jail-Detail Hill road. 58 Regiment tried to raise ladders on to the side of the hill under the fire of British grenades; three separate assaults of two hundred men each were mounted. The Japanese failed to capture any part of the hill.

The firing was ferocious, the Bren-gun barrels red-hot and frequently changed. Ammunition supply to the forward pits was under great difficulties. There were four pits for 13 Platoon in this sector, one pit to 15 Platoon under Corporal Maxworthy on the left. Corporal Rees, Privates Wells and Skingsley in one pit were 'knocking the Japanese down in batches'. Next was Lance-Corporal Hankinson's pit with a Bren gun and a Bren group of three privates, Lawrence, Goodall and Naylor, above another position containing Corporal Webber and four privates.

The attack ended at 10 pm. At 11 pm Naylor heard a jeep on the road and left his pit to report it to Sergeant Tacon. One of his companions saw him coming up the hill, assumed he was Japanese and shot him in the leg without challenge. Sergeant Tacon took Naylor to the ADS. Corporal George Martin was killed by mortar bomb. 'C' Company had suffered heavy casualties, but had inflicted even more on the 58th Regiment.

It was on this day that Captain Coath observed that his men 'were beginning to get a bit determined'. In the twenty yards 'frontage' of his front trenches, manoeuvre, movement, and repair were very difficult, even impossible. Coath had been able to do little more than mount eight Brens in interlocking fields of fire in the Bren group and in Hankinson's pit, ensure ammunition supply, and 'place faith in his men'. On Easter Sunday the men continued to justify that confidence.

At midnight on 9 April 'C' Company heard digging. At 2 am a mortar[1] began to fire on them from the point where the Japanese had entrenched. This mortaring, and a bombardment from a 75 mm above them over open sights, together with a quick-firing gun, continued for forty-five minutes, the worst pasting so far. Private Walker, Lieutenant Phythian's batman, was killed when the pit was struck, but, falling on Phythian, saved his life, the officer receiving only slight leg wounds.

When the barrage lifted the Japanese attacked. The Indian 3.7s from Jotsoma caught them once more. One of those shells landed on Corporal Rees' pit killing Wells, burying Rees and Skingsley, who, however, dug themselves out, moving to Corporal Beames' pit, which included a man from 14 Platoon and a convalescent in the 1/1 Devons. Shells, grenades and mortars exploded all round the forward trenches. Two grenades landed in Allchin's Bren-gun pit which collapsed, killing him. Another wave of two hundred Japanese came in and again they were mown down. But when Corporal Rees evacuated his pit, and Allchin was killed for lack of British fire-power on the ground, other positions had also to be given up. When the assault ended at 4 am, the Japanese had a foothold at the bottom of Detail Hill and were digging in twenty-five yards forward of 'C' Company's second line.

Although 15 Platoon's Bren group, half-way up Detail at the level of a 13 Platoon pit, had its weapons covering the entrance to that pit, 13 could not move in daylight, or even put their heads out. Jail Hill was covered by 'thousands of Japanese' whose snipers could see every movement on Detail. A sniper from Jail hit Nobby Hall in the head; no one from the Aid Post could reach the position. Hall died, after a few hours, in Norman's pit; the crew then moved into Beames' position which was more or less attached.

Sergeant Tacon was behind and had some freedom of manoeuvre, although his platoon now numbered only six out of thirty-six. Easten had brought up a platoon of 'C' Company; his company's Lieutenant Phythian was in the front trenches. The Rajput platoon under Captain Mitchell then took over 'D' Company trenches at the bottom of Supply Hill men commanded by Major Naveen Rawlley. Mitchell's body was later found by John Wright when digging near his own position. One of the disconcerting things about the Siege was the endless confrontation between contiguous living and dead.

Lance-Corporal Harman who had earlier destroyed the machine-gun post on Detail came up with 'D' Company reserve platoon. Five Japanese with machine guns and two automatics overlooked the whole British position.

Captain Easten saw Harman, covered by a private in his section, 'hurtle down through the trees, rifle in hand and bayonet fixed'. Despite fire from Jail Hill, he jumped the ridge in front of the Japanese machine-gun post, shot four of the Japanese in their pit, then disappeared, when only a glimpse of his rifle rising and falling could be seen. He re-emerged from the pit, some describing his return as already a stagger, others as a dash for home, or a run broken by a hit, or as a ruminant stroll.

At all events, this huge and complex man was finally brought down by a Japanese bullet which landed in the base of his spine. Donald Easten raced across to him and brought him in, trying to remove his equipment as the blood spurted from him.

'Don't worry about that, Sir. It was worthwhile. I got the lot.' He died within a minute and for this action and that the previous day he was awarded the Victoria Cross.

While this was in progress, Corporal Rees stood up to watch it from the edge of the pit. The Japanese had fixed lines on the position. Rees was hit twice in the side. Sergeant Tacon shouted, 'Hang on, Taffy, I'm coming.' When he crawled towards Rees, he in turn was hit in both arm and leg, fracturing the latter, but just managed to roll out of the line of fire.

The men started to talk to Rees but, although he was in a dip only two yards away, could do nothing for him. When he told them that he was paralysed, they knew that there was no hope. He was soon delirious, and for eight hours screamed, shouted, prayed and called for his mother and father. Tom Coath tried unsuccessfully to lay down a smoke-screen, so that the stretcher-bearers could get him away.

The fourteen men left were helpless beneath the continuous mortaring, shelling and sniping, 'like rats in a trap'. At 5 pm they were told that 'B' Company was about to take over their positions and those held by the Japanese at the bottom of Detail. At 7 pm a platoon of John Winstanley's 'B' Company arrived. They failed to take the objective and withdrew. Lance-Corporal Hankinson then, without orders, evacuated the remainder of 'C' Company's existing pits. Those who left were instructed to reinforce 16 Platoon (Sergeant Stammers). One section accompanied Corporal Guest to recapture their old pit. The attack failed, Private Shipp wounded in the leg. Japanese mortaring continued, killing Sergeant Boxwell and seriously wounding Captain Easten, who was succeeded in 'D' Company by Fred Collett. Tom Coath now took over the whole depleted 'C' and 'D' Companies' area. Easten went back to ADS but, in great pain, came out to reinforce his old 'D' Company at the very end.

Easter Day had been rainy, wet and cold. One of the men taking part in these remarkable actions added only that he had a 'hell of a headache, as well as a nasty head cold'. It was on this day or the next that the troops heard that Odessa had fallen; one of the sector commanders had a radio with which he used to broadcast the news twice daily by putting the handset next to the loudspeaker. It was also the day that Ukhrul was incorrectly rumoured to have been retaken, and that on which the first rumours began, so damaging to morale when proved false, that relief by the Second Division was imminent.

On 10 April the Japanese English-speaking radio announced that the Kohima Garrison had 'fled in disorder on 6 April'. Two Jiff propagandists, one speaking Punjabi, the other Gurkhali, harangued the Indian troops, imploring them to surrender and, to the latters' delight, complaining about Jiff and Japanese casualties. Patrick's Lushais thought them very droll, despite the truth of their claims that the water supply was now almost nil, that there wasn't all that much food, that the garrison hadn't washed for days, and that the wounded lacked medical care. Nobody seemed to want to accept the Jiffs' invitation, although it promised 'abounding comfort and sustenance'. British and Indians dismissed the broadcasts with abuse and derision. Fear, at first continual, had been 'replaced by a detached air of faith in a continued existence'.

In fact, 6 Company of the Japanese II Battalion had been wiped out on Detail between 7 and 8 April, forcing the Regimental Commander (Fukunada) to reinforce with 5 Company and his Signals, Ordnance and Regimental HQ Companies. When the peak was eventually taken at noon on 8 April, the unit's strength was almost exhausted.

On that day I Battalion of 58 Regiment under Major Morimoto which had started from Mao Song Sang on 3 April without 2 and 4 Companies, arrived at Jotsoma (161 Brigade HQ) via Maram and Pulomi. In the afternoon of 9 April 3 Company advanced on Jotsoma Hill and, after confused fighting, occupied part of it and tried to disrupt traffic on the Dimapur road. A platoon commander, Lieutenant Miki, was later found dead in British trenches.

XIV

NOT GOOD, ANYWHERE . . .

NOW THAT the northern exit to Kohima at IGH Spur had been closed there could be no further evacuation of the wounded. There was, furthermore, nowhere in the ADS that was not under enemy observation or shell and mortar bombardment. Forty more wounded men were killed as they lay on stretchers in the open or in slit trenches. The doctors operated crouching, the hospital theatre only five or six feet deep and ten feet in diameter. Medical equipment was stored in subsidiary trenches off the theatre, the operating table itself a stretcher or trestles still lit, as in pictures of HMS *Victory*, by shaded, flickering hurricane lamps.

Blankets for shock cases were badly needed, but could not be taken from the fighting men. Doctor Young was also short of blood plasma and other supplies. Escorted by four Indian Sappers, he moved down the steep hill close to enemy troops of 58 Regiment climbing up. He reached five abandoned trucks by the DC's bungalow and also the old Indian General Hospital, returning with medical stores including plasma and about one hundred blankets. Young was now also able to add a Resuscitation Group to his hospital team under a Captain J.A. Hunter, with one and a half sections from the IGH. But the number of patients, after the fierce fighting of the past two days, had risen to two hundred.

The water ration, at half a pint, was a restriction bearing heavily enough on the combatants in the line, but worse on the wounded and dying in the Dressing Stations. Barratt and his Indians did their best, the water platoon working through the night.

All over the area, in the rocky ground, under attack most of the day, burial was difficult, the consequences bizarre. If burial could not take place until dark, rigor mortis caused arms, legs and parts of the torso to stick stiffly out of the shallow ground. The Japanese often could not bury their dead at all. The stench of rotting corpses poisoned the air, the smell of Japanese cadavers and the absence of sanitation adding to the horror.

On Detail Hill Tom Coath put 14 Platoon forward, again covered by interlocking Bren-gun fire, with 13 in the rear. Japanese attacks in full strength, supported by grenades from discharger caps, more effective and of greater range than hand-thrown, were continuous in the darkness and pouring rain. Allied artillery could not be brought down. Those men left in 'C' Company had only their rifles, Brens and grenades to repel yet one more mass assault. Hand-to-hand fighting took place right up to, and even into, the forward trenches until everyone there was dead. When the Japanese moved in at dawn on Easter Monday they poured paraffin on the bodies of the dead West Kents and burned them.

At 1230 Corporal Norman, Lance-Corporal Hankinson, Privates Lovell, Johnson, Thrussell and Gordon were informed that 'C' Company really would evacuate Detail Hill that evening. They were sent forward 150 yards to within ten yards of the Japanese with orders to stay there until 'D' Company and the remainder of 'C' Company, 'red-eyed, exhausted and soaking men', could be withdrawn to Supply Hill. These few men were surrounded on three sides by hundreds of Japanese who, had they looked over the side of Jail, would have annihilated them. The purpose of this suicide squad, as the men called themselves, was to provide time for the Sappers under John Wright to lay mines and booby traps, to destroy food and other stores, and to burn the remaining bashas. In the interval, snipers on Jail Hill mortally wounded Lieutenant Gordon Inglis and less seriously wounded another officer. 13 Platoon heard the Japanese laughing.

At 6.20 pm the 'suicide squad' started to crawl back to those few companions still on the feature. Wright lit the fuses to the bashas. One of the explosions was of sacks of flour which formed a 'ball of fire' in the sky of startling proportions, 'like Hiroshima' in retrospect for Wright. About fifteen minutes after the huts had all blown up, the Japanese started mortaring, followed by an infantry assault. But by that time 'C' and 'D' Companies were clear of Detail and had gone back to Supply Hill (FSD), where they reinforced 'B' Company, short of men since the Arakan.

For six hours they had endured the last trial of those four days on Detail. The platoon had, however, managed to get tinned peas for their breakfast at eight that morning, after standing to from 5.40 to 6.15 am. For dinner they ate bully beef stew, tomatoes, pears, tinned milk and half a cup of tea, the first hot meal since arrival. Perhaps it was brought in dixies by massive Colour Sergeant Eves and his dwindling brigade of cooks.

The men now had, that cold, windy night, three hours' sleep. Although these soldiers, NCOs and junior officers were no mercenaries, still

'Their shoulders held the sky suspended
They stood and earth's foundations stay.
What God abandoned, these defended
And saved the sum of things for pay.'

Not all of them believe that what they saved endures in the shape for which they fought.

Neither did the rain and the overcast that night neglect the tennis court, where the Japanese 37 mm Q.F. and 75 mm guns concentrated their fire with a thunder to match that of the elements. On Garrison Hill the water poured down on the wounded in their open stretchers and shallow trenches, filling them with liquid mud beyond the capacity of the bearers to contain. It was very cold on the hill. To the north, at Hospital Ridge, 138 Regiment back from Pulomi flung in another attack against the Assam Rifles and Assam Regiment. It was driven off with rifle fire at point-blank range. Identification on the bodies now confirmed the presence also on the Spur of 124 Regiment. Three regiments, in British terms three brigades, eight or nine thousand Japanese, were therefore confronting a British perimeter which may not have contained more than five or six *hundred* unwounded fighting men. A further three thousand Japanese soldiers of General Sato's 31 Division were closing in on 161 Brigade and on the first units of 2nd Division near Jotsoma, Zubza, Merema, Phesama, the Dimapur and Imphal roads, not many minutes march away.

The odds had thus shortened further, a calculation which the West Kents and garrison staffs made, but which most seemed, even then, to discount. That peculiar refusal to admit the possibility of defeat which, on land, sea or air does not appear to operate among the British until all is nearly gone or, rather, until the first awful stages of unsuccessful battle have passed, had now begun to emerge.

In the DC's bungalow area the men collected the rain in tin hats, waterproof sheets, dixies and so forth. Artillery bombardment began as light failed. When the barrage lifted 58 Regiment, in wave after screaming wave, came at their objective with the storm in full spate, halted or checked by the extraordinary accuracy of 24 Mountain Regiment's 3.7 inch from Jotsoma, directed by Yeo and his other three OPs. As the Japanese rose up over the bank from the dead ground below the tennis court, 'A' Company under Major Tom Kenyon with rifle and grenade held off attack after attack coming in that day almost every thirty minutes. Sergeant Brooks at the Club, although his platoon was dangerously short of ammunition and losing men to Japanese fire, was ferocious in defence. By dawn on 10 April a soaked and battered 'A' Company still held the line.

This was the sixth day of the Siege. The soldiers were terribly tired, faces drawn, haggard, unshaven because of the lack of water, dirty, unwashed, huge eyes with great bags underneath from exhaustion and vigilance. Their lives were centred on survival and, apart from that, on water, food, clean weapons and ammunition. They thought of

'England, Home and Beauty' and wondered why they were where they were.

To the west that morning, the 1/1 Punjabs were at least fully integrated into the 161 Brigade box. But the Brigade was held – as firmly as the Kohima Garrison – by 58 and 138 Regiment on the Dimapur road. Second British Division had, as we have seen, arrived at Dimapur, but not all its formations were yet fully ready to move: the Ledo railway and its link to General Stilwell, the Americans and the Chinese were thought threatened by 24 Regiment. But to the tiny Kohima Garrison it seemed as though an entire Japanese Division was about to divert its attention from the obvious strategic objectives of India via Dimapur and the north-east via Ledo to the insignificant alternative of Kohima. The whole weight of 12,500 men in all their Shinto rigidity was coming at them. The men no longer believed in promises; there was no prospect of early relief.

That evening another bombardment began all along the Ridge. Even the West Kents, let alone the less tested 1st Assam Regiment, the Assam Rifles or the composite British and Indian companies, had not hitherto endured its like in their varying experiences of this awesome campaign. None of the Companies was well placed to receive it. 'C' and 'D' Companies, which had not been at full strength on departure from Arakan, had since lost over 50% of their men on Jail, Detail and Supply Hills. Our own artillery in the Arakan, as we know, had accidentally killed thirty men in 'B' Company, not to speak of other casualties incurred by that unit. Sergeant Brooks' platoon of 'A' had lost many at the tennis court. Perhaps the Royal West Kent Regiment numbered three hundred effective fighting men. The Assam Regiment and the Assam Rifles may have mustered 150 fit men: the British and Indian composite companies from the Reinforcement and Convalescent depots counted perhaps one hundred unwounded. Two depleted platoons of 4/7 Rajputs remained with the Garrison.

'A' Company was in well-dug weapon pits, trenches and dug-outs on the western edge of the tennis court, most with head-cover. As the guns began, so did the thunder, preceded by huge flashes of lightning in the impenetrable sky. The rain crashed down in a solid wall, drumming on the earth, drenching the men to the skin while shells and bombs from captured three-inch British mortars burst around Kenyon's Company. Jotsoma's 3.7 inch shells fell among the Japanese forming up thirty yards away on the other side of the court. Then came the hail of enemy fire and the waves of infantry, driving with yells across the court, hurling grenades, drifting back, coming on again right up to the British trenches, until the red-hot brens drove them back for that night.

The bombardment had killed some in Tommy Kenyon's Company

and wounded many others, some of whom went back to the beleaguered Dressing Station. Several were shell-shocked and there was little that Major Kenyon or his subordinate commanders could do about that, apart from encouragement and assurance. In the little sector forty yards by forty where 'A' Company had to stand, many collapsed in exhaustion, others trembled and shook, weapons neglected. Two bombs exploded in the operating theatre nearby, killing the young surgeon, the orderly and the patient. The bursts among patients in open stretchers and shallow trenches outside the dressing station could hardly be endured in the driving icy rain. Wounded men were repeatedly hit again. Without bedpans, the stench was appalling. In the daytime flies, attracted by the excreta, settled on men's wounds. Sepsis and gas-gangrene spread.

Young and his surgeons worked tirelessly. So far, there had been adequate dressings and anaesthetic, but conditions were barbaric and the operations, including amputations, would have been serious enough in Base hospitals. The patients' morale was remarkable. Everyone helped his neighbour. Major Bobby Shaw ceaselessly set an example of cheerful calm and courage. And among the fighting men, the fate of their colleagues in the Dressing Station was an additional motive, rooting their determination never to allow the enemy to get their hands on the wounded. Humour and confidence, despite everything, were still there.

Supply Hill now housed the 46 remaining men of 'C' Company – 12 men in 13 Platoon, 20 in 15 Platoon and 14 in 14 Platoon under Captain Coath who divided the survivors into two platoons. It also housed Major Naveen Rawlley's composite Indian Company, two platoons of Rajputs and Lieutenant Kuriyan's Indian platoon. The Rajputs were badly shaken by Captain Mitchell's death by shell fragment on the evening of 10 April, but rallied under Subedar Sultan Singh, fighting vigorous close combat battles until almost wiped out. The hill was heavily mortared and shelled, one bomb falling on 'C' Company's position, gravely injuring Ginger Hankinson in the back and wounding Private Murray in the arm. Japanese snipers were also active, but no assault developed. 'C' had been told that the Second Division was at Ms43. They waited anxiously for their arrival but, like all previous hopes, it was not to be. Coath told his men, from prisoner interrogation, that there was one Jap brigade in the immediate vicinity, of which two battalions were on Jail Hill and another occupying the DC's bungalow area with Battalion HQ and mortar depot.

Coath said that there was 'a Division of three Japanese brigades in the column', one brigade about 8 miles away, one in Kohima itself, and the third in reserve, with its supply base at Mao Song Sang. This information, since it also included the incorrect statement that a 'British Independent Brigade' had wiped out the Mao base and occupied it before recapture by a Japanese Battalion withdrawn from Kohima, seems typical of wartime 'buzzes'. It probably referred to the Chindit Brigade operating locally.

On 11 April 13 Platoon on Supply Hill had hard biscuits, fried tomatoes, baked beans and half a cup of tea for breakfast; salmon, jam and tea for tiffin, and, for dinner at 1800 bully beef, fried tomatoes, pears and milk, but no tea. They learned, for the first time, of Captain Easten's injury on 9 April and of the death and wounding by mortar bomb of Corporals Willy Want and Gilbert of 'D'. They also heard that Sergeant Stammers' 16 Platoon of 'D' on Supply Hill only had three men left.

Brigadier Warren told Laverty on 10 April that Victor Hawkins' 5 Brigade of 2 Division was ready to advance. When it could link with 161 Brigade, Warren would be able to move on Kohima. But, unfortunately, although his Cameron Highlanders battalion had overthrown a Japanese road-block at Ms32, Hawkins was faced with several more on the way to join 161. Warren himself was to meet yet more en route to Kohima. (It will be remembered that 138 Regiment had cut the Kohima road at Zubza on 8 April). There were too many messages, however well-intentioned, promising early relief. At least the officers of the garrison understood that the Jotsoma box holding the vital Indian 24th Mountain Regiment with its 3.7s should be held until the link with 2nd Division had been made.

On 10 April Warren was so pessimistic about the situation within Kohima that he suggested withdrawal of the garrison to Ms43. Major-General Grover rejected the proposal. As Warren could not clear the road-block at Ms32, 5th Brigade sent two companies of the Worcesters forward and, on the 11th, followed them to the perimeter which they had formed in Zubza village. Here a Japanese 75 mm caused damage and casualties. The Divisional Commander and Brigadier Hawkins on reconnaissance here found the country so formidable that, although the 5/161 Brigade link-up remained the aim, an operation by *both* brigades would be planned. The Cameron Highlanders now moved up to a village called Khabvuma, while the Worcesters spent the night in Zubza. On 12 April the Camerons moved on to Sachema toward a Japanese position known as Bunker Hill which they, with the Manchesters' machine-gunners, the Worcesters and artillery support from 10 Field Regiment, did not take until 14 April.

It is instructive that throughout these and forthcoming actions, all Commanders were criticized by their immediate superiors for too slow a conduct of their operations, Major-General John Grover, commanding 2 British Division by Lieutenant-General Sir Montagu Stopford, XXXIII Corps, and Brigadiers Warren, Hawkins and Shapland (161, 5 and 6 Brigades) by Grover. In reverse, all of them were considered overcautious by the Kohima Garrison.

XV

SUPPLY HILL HOLDS,
JUST . . .

A VERY severe bombardment, in part again afforded by the British 3" mortars which the Japanese had captured at the Treasury, was mounted at dusk on 10 April. The fire was again all along the Ridge, in particular against Dr John Young's Advanced Dressing Station with its hundreds of helpless casualties, John Laverty's Headquarters and 'A' Company at the tennis court. Here terrible wounds were inflicted, damage to bunkers and trenches caused and weapons destroyed.

The infantry attack which, as usual, followed the artillery with lavish use of grenades, was close contact, even hand-to-hand, beaten back by the grim and determined West Kents, desperately cut about in earlier fighting on this bloody, rain-sodden earth. Tommy Kenyon, despite his Company's magnificent performance against incessant Japanese assaults over the past two dreadful nights, now asked for a relief. 'I don't know how the men stuck it, nor how any of us were left alive,' he said later. After the numbing, pulverizing hours of bombing on a tiny confused space in pouring rain followed by the violent onslaught of yelling Japanese in greatly superior numbers, it was almost an understatement.

His men remained spirited. They were well led. They had dealt with the hordes by experience and training, by Sergeant King's mortars, by the expert use of cross-fire from Brens and rifles, and by grenades. Each time the little groups of attacking enemy had dwindled to single infiltrations, to none at all, to a silence, although a temporary silence.

John Laverty, although Franklin and the Adjutant, Douglas Short, took as much off his shoulders as they could, was very tired. He listened, thanks to the skill and stamina of Captain Topham, his Signals Officer, to the reports of his Company Commanders, but spoke little except to transmit his decisions.

In the ADS shells had burst everywhere. The cries of the wounded in agony for want of pain killers, the pleas for help, the noise of the working parties clearing and 'separating the shattered bodies of those not yet dead from those which had been blasted to bits' were difficult to endure for others wounded but not yet rewounded by the incoming mortars. Seventy men had been rewounded that night. Because of the increase in wounded and the impossibility of evacuation, the ADS trenches were now only 200 yards from the tennis court. The feeding of the wounded presented grave problems, although Barratt's Indians gave up a large proportion of their rations. Blankets, plasma, drugs, morphine and serum against gangrene and, above all, water, were dangerously short. On 12 April Colonel Richards asked 161 Brigade to arrange an RAF airdrop to supply these commodities, together with ammunition for the garrison's weapons which was, similarly, running short.

Also on 12 April Laverty decided to relieve Kenyon's Company by 'B' Company, hitherto posted on Kuki Piquet where the action had not yet been as savage as elsewhere on the Ridge. (Captain Tom Coath, now commanding 'C' Company since the wounding of Shaw and Watts, had come from 'B' Company.) Their Commander was John Winstanley, the former St Thomas's Hospital medical student. He was, like many of the others, a Territorial, one who had served with the West Kents since 1938. He had two subalterns, Victor King and Tom Hogg. Sergeant Glyn Williams from Pontypridd was the senior NCO of the draft from the South Wales Borderers which 'B' Company had received to fill earlier gaps. The Company was still gravely below strength. On Kuki water was short and, although there had been no hand-to-hand combat, shelling and sniper fire had been incessant.

At 1000 on 11 April firing had been heard from Punjab Ridge. Fighting was seen to be in progress. The garrison assumed that 161 Brigade had been able to open the 'door' in the Jotsoma Box and, unwisely, that message seems to have been passed by Laverty to the West Kents. Some minutes later Brigade could only tell him that although 1/1 Punjab *was* attacking, pressure on 161's flank and other attacks on the Box made further progress impossible. Victor Hawkins with 5 Brigade was temporarily stopped at Ms38, and no further action took place at Punjab Ridge that day.

This was another disappointment. Morale remained unbroken, but it had not been improved by these continual rumours of early relief. Another factor adversely affecting security of mind was that no wound, however grave, earned a safe or comfortable bed with consistent surgical and nursing care. To be wounded meant continued, even more fearful exposure to danger. All the leaf cover on Garrison Hill, and most of the ground cover too, soon disappeared under artillery and mortar fire and the ceaseless coming-and-going of hundreds of men. Snipers, as well as the guns, had a clear view of the wounded. Trenches were not deep enough; stretchers were even more vulnerable. The poor non-combatants were, of course, defenceless, as subject to Japanese fire as the fighting men, soon forming a sizeable and expensive proportion of the wounded.

Nor were the Jotsoma guns always able, despite first-class spotting and direction from the Kohima OPs, to counter enemy mortar fire from

Jail and elsewhere. The Japanese moved their weapons with impunity from site to site after a few rounds. The 3.7s were thus too often striking at targets which no longer existed. The garrison's mortars were no substitute, since their use in daylight would bring down annihilating enemy fire on stocks which were too low anyway and were primarily needed at night.

In 'B' Company, the platoon under Victor King was placed on the right near the Club and the Mound. The Mound, under Kenyon, had been equipped with a Bren gun manned by two unidentified 'old soldiers', probably from the British composite company based on the Reinforcement Camp. Both were excellent and both were killed during 'A' Company's tour at the tennis court. Lieutenant Thomas Hogg took the centre and Sergeant Glyn Williams the left of the position.

The Company moved silently into their dug-outs and trenches, Kenyon's 'A' Company succeeding them on Kuki Piquet. The evening bombardment had just concluded. The platoons, having crawled and sidled into the positions, evading Japanese snipers, soon heard the voices of the enemy and the sounds of their weapons as the first assault formed up in the dead ground on the east side of the court. 24th Mountain Regiment's 3.7 shells were immediately among the Japanese infantrymen, but the attack came in with unquenchable fury against rifle and Bren guns on fixed lines, grenades flying through the air like cricket balls into the now wavering mass of the enemy. It was at this point, when the Japanese broke off their first attack that evening and returned back across the tennis court to their trenches in the Deputy Commissioner's garden, that 'B' Company realized that British guns had been switched to the defence of Jotsoma and the mortars to Supply Hill. To break up the Japanese before they began or as they returned had to be done without outside aid. The defence for a little while became concentrated on grenades, which were themselves in short supply, having to be supplemented from other Companies. Accounts, nevertheless, that suggest that 'B' Company was outflanked or bypassed, or that a 'hut' dominating the left flank was seized by Japanese, lack documentation or other evidence.

More attacks followed throughout the night under grenade-dischargers and mortars, all of them head-on and all defeated, but inflicting severe casualties on the defenders. Nor was the enemy, infiltrating through such bushes as still stood, always visible or at least not until they chose to be, when they charged with high-pitched, cursing voices. Japanese were all around Winstanley's men, stamping through the shrubbery, groaning, sweating, grunting until going down under the Brens and, time and again, withdrawing back across the tennis court.

By the time 'B' had arrived, all the ground east of the tennis court, including the DC's bungalow, had fallen into Japanese hands. 'A' Company was still holding the Club House itself and the top edge of the tennis court, but well-concealed Japanese snipers were established in some large cherry trees just beyond the court and to the left, where they had a good view across the back of the Club House. This made movement particularly dangerous. 10 Platoon under Thomas Hogg lost several men before establishing exactly whence the fire was coming. Between the Club House and the foot of Summer House Hill a level parade ground had been constructed. The excess soil had been heaped up to form a hummock about 20 ft high above and on the south side of the parade ground. On 'B' Company's arrival, 10 Platoon was sent to occupy this hummock where they found more badly constructed defences in the form of so-called 'bunkers' with roofs of corrugated iron covered with a thin layer of turf. This proved no protection against 75 mm shell bursts and more men were lost that first night. After darkness, when the Platoon had first moved into this position, but before the shelling had started, it was joined by a BBC reporter equipped with a microphone connected by wires to recording equipment in a vehicle on the road below. He did a wonderful interview and commentary, but subsequently discovered that the recording equipment had not been switched on.

On this occasion a local Naga, probably an Assam rifleman who was in the bunker, delighted in going out by himself for several hours each night, returning at first light with a wide grin to show his trophy of Japanese ears threaded onto his bayonet. This seemed an enjoyable substitute for head-hunting, discouraged for years by the interfering British.

Next day John Winstanley moved 10 Platoon down into a central position to hold the Club House itself. By now the Platoon was reduced to eight men, three Bren guns with a crew of two men each, Hogg's batman and a runner. Hogg sited the Brens around the building, one each at the NE corner, where some steps ran down to the tennis court, one at the NW corner, near his own position, and the third at the SW corner, where there was a kind of gateway between the building and the hummock. In this way Hogg thought he could defend both sides of the building and provide supporting fire from his central position to each of the other two. However, he quickly lost both of the gun crew at the NE corner, where the main Japanese attacks seemed to concentrate. During darkness, therefore, he took over this position himself and returned for the daylight hours to the central position near the NW corner, so that he could still move about.

The Japanese started to attack on both sides of the Club House at the same time, so that both forward guns became committed together. The right gun, in the gateway, had a good field of fire along the south side of the Club House past the tennis court below and across an open grassy slope. It also had a reliable crew and attacks along this side soon faltered. The Platoon was not so fortunate with the left gun whilst Hogg was in charge.

As the full moon came up at about 2 am, Hogg heard the drumming of unshod feet on the tennis court. A dozen Japanese rushed forward with fixed bayonets. He aimed and pulled the trigger, but the gun action slid forward too sluggishly to fire the first round and one of the attackers lunged at him with his bayonet, luckily catching the double thickness of his webbing belt, causing no more than bruising and a nick in the right side of his waist. He re-cocked and put the whole of the 25-round magazine into his assailant, who did not fight again.

The main attack developed. Forty or fifty men were involved in two parties, one charging up each side of the Club House. There were too many to stop and it began to look ugly. Hogg had the uncomfortable feeling that he was being overrun. However, John Winstanley to the rear dealt effectively with this penetration. For some time there was fierce fighting behind, and the platoon was mightily relieved when Winstanley appeared.

Usually attacks of this size were preceded by much shouting, but this attack was surprising in its silence. There were, however, frequent 'pleas' in English: 'Johnny, you must surrender now, you are surrounded and have no escape – for your own sake lay down your weapons and move forward with your arms raised.' But the men knew what happened to those unwise enough to surrender.

The following day when Hogg had returned to his daytime position near the NW corner of the Club House, his remaining NCO, Lance Corporal Hill, wanted to know, if, when it came to 'every man for himself', he could accompany his commander. They were under heavy grenade attack at the time and, unseen by Hogg, one grenade had fallen into Hill's end of the slit trench. Hill turned his back on it and sheltered Hogg completely: it took three weeks for him to die from his wounds.

During these actions, Major Peter Franklin took the night party of sepoys from the 75th Indian Field Ambulance to the water point forty yards away from 'B' Company. There were twenty men in all, each with two chagals or canvas bags holding a gallon, each of which took eight minutes to fill from the tiny spring. Five hours were needed to collect twenty-six gallons in this way, eleven distributed to the ADS and fifteen to the Companies.

During this night also, Colour-Sergeant Eves kept the men in the trenches fed with warm food, moving staunchly from trench to dug-out to trench with his dixies, defying gun, mortar, grenade and sniper.

During daylight on 12 April 'C' Company, the Rajputs, the Kuryan platoon and Major Rawlley's men on Supply Hill were severely shelled and mortared. One direct hit landed on 'C' Company's position, wounding Lance-Corporal Ben Russell and an attached signaller named Norton. A daytime infantry attack followed in Company strength. After it had been repulsed, 26 Japanese dead were counted in front of the Rajputs' position. A rumour reported later by Corporal Norman alleged that the Assam Rifles during the night of 12/13 April had killed 130 Japanese, bringing back their ears on their bayonets. There is no record of this in Pawsey's papers or in Steyn's work, the latter admittedly on the Assam Regiment, but with references to the Rifles. An action on 13 April may have prompted it.

Corporal Norman as usual, was forthcoming on the rations: hard biscuits, one sausage, baked beans and half a cup of cold tea for breakfast; for tiffin at 1230, biscuits, salmon, jam, no tea; bully beef, fried tomatoes and half a cup of cold tea in the evening. 13 Platoon managed to get hold of a packet of Australian coffee biscuits and a few tins of pears and milk. During the night Norman slept for only three hours because of the noise of small-arms fire from the bungalow area. Later that night, according to him, the Assam Rifles were supposed to recapture the DC's bungalow, 'but they did not'.

The defence held that night on Supply Hill. The opposing lines were so close together that Lieutenant Punia, the Sikh Mountain Battery observer on Hospital Ridge, 'brought down the Jotsoma 3.7s on targets scarcely fifteen yards from the troops he was supporting'. Sergeant-Major Haines of 'D' Company was blinded by enemy fire. He refused to go to the ADS and, until he was killed, moved about the Company with the help of a private soldier, encouraging his men. Meanwhile, the guns on Jail Hill were firing directly into the Allied trenches opposite.

There was a serious problem of command. Colonel Richards' choice as Sector Commander for Supply Hill was Naveen Rawlley. There was, however, mutual ignorance between Rawlley and the West Kents of, on the one hand, his presence and that of his units, and of the Royal West Kent companies on the other. 'No effective attempt at co-ordination seems to have been attempted, the West Kents operating autonomously with little regard,' according to Major Kenyon of 'A' Company, 'for others who might be able to help or were helping.' It is possible that, had the British battalion been less autocratic, Supply Hill might not have fallen.

But one of the more notable features of this action was, indeed, the 'autonomous' nature of almost all its scattered components. The intensity of Japanese fire in that tiny space made movement between units impractical, if not impossible, except at night and in silence. Very few of the men, who had not, unlike the Royal West Kents, worked together before, knew anyone other than their next door neighbour in their own slit trench. Very few had any grasp at all of events on other sectors. Most remained strangers to each other. One officer of the West Kents, in the thick of the action, was, until April 1993, unaware of the existence of the Assam Regiment which relieved him at the tennis court. Kenyon, for instance, was 'only vaguely aware that there were some troops on his right, and had no positive knowledge of the existence of Rawlley's troops'.

Next morning the bombardment got worse and the stand-to became less an 'Action Stations' than a permanent state. Relief was not in sight. The airdrop later that day was far from a success. The Japanese from Detail Hill penetrated at the second attempt the weakened Rajput lines on Supply, occupying a basha. At Colonel Laverty's request, Hugh Richards sent in aid 9 Platoon of the Assam Rifles under Subedar Uttam Singh, which wiped out the Japanese before withdrawing with casualties under heavy machine-gun fire . Perhaps this was the action which so impressed Corporal Norman.

The dressing station was bombed again in the early morning with two direct hits. There were, for the time being, only ten stretcher-bearers for over 200 casualties. Captains Moti and Sadiq had been killed as they worked. John Young had been wounded. Twenty-one patients were killed and thirty-one rewounded. By noon, with the help of the Royal West Kents Pioneers, the ADS had been, astonishingly, reorganized and reconstructed. Damaged instruments and equipment had been repaired and cleaned. Captains Thomson and Glover had re-established dressing parties. With Colonel Richards' agreement, a well-entrenched part of the State Regiment's area was taken over by the ADS for the accommodation of patients.

The ADS was hit again, this time by 30 3" mortars, at 6.30 pm. Captain Lahir was killed, as were ten wounded men. Captain Majid and many patients were rewounded. The dressing station reopened at 3 am, but, as the medical staff were becoming exhausted, on a shift system. The ADS was hit again at 5 am, killing twelve men in the theatre and outside, and wounding twenty in a dug-out. Young immediately chose a new site for construction by Barratt's Indians and the Royal West Kents; the new dugout was ten feet long, six feet deep, with a splinter-proof roof and four feet deep communication trenches to the casualty area. It received a 3" mortar bomb which caused little damage, though slightly wounding Captain Glover.

Now, due to earlier damage to the containers, the water situation had become very serious. Much depended on the airdrop later that day.

In the dark that night on Supply Hill one of Fred Collett's platoons had lost two men in hand-to-hand bayonet fighting with Japanese infiltrating between Coath and the Rajputs. He lost a further two under parachute flares in an attack on a basha which he was unable to repel. Assam Regiment reinforcements the following morning cleared the Japanese from the basha with grenades, but were badly hit by two machine guns from Transport Hill. The enemy were still on Supply Hill, too close to the Allied positions on the forward slopes under direct fire from Jail. Laverty knew then that Supply would, sooner or later, have to be abandoned.

XVI

'THE BLACK 13TH'

ON 13 APRIL the pre-selected dropping zone was encumbered by Indian non-combatants who had to be cleared off. The strips were laid out under sniper fire in the shape of a yellow 'T'. The reception party heard the aircraft engines ten minutes before their ETA, but the pilots did not reply on the frequency. Peter Franklin fired the green Verey cartridges which were to give the order for the drop. Three Dakotas circled after coming in straight and low but, presumably because their pilots did not see the green flares, passed on to unload their coloured parachutes carrying the garrison's ammunition into the Fort, despite the red Verey lights now fired by the West Kents to dissuade them. The garrison would feel the effect of this error by the time the first Japanese bombardment came in that night. But now it was 2.30 in the afternoon.

The second flight was extremely accurate, despite the encroaching hills. The parachutes landed on the ground or in the trees. Unfortunately, the loads were exclusively of the 3.7 inch ammunition that should have been dropped to the 24th Indian Mountain Regiment at Jotsoma, useless at Kohima. This, of course, meant that there would be no grenades, so desperately needed to repel enemy assaults at the tennis court and on Supply Hill, nor mortars for Sergeant King. It also meant that support from Hill's guns might be less effective than it would otherwise have been.

A third, precise flight landed most of its parachutes in the trees. Many of these carried two-gallon petrol tins tied together in bunches of eight, 'like metal grapes', which all contained water. The Japanese shot holes through most of them, but a high percentage of the medical stores sought by Colonel Young was recovered after dark, together with a very little water. Two Indian gunners were killed outright by the loads from jute parachutes which had malfunctioned. But all patients in the ADS received anti-gas gangrene serum, and morphia where essential. 'The situation was much improved.'

Other drops followed daily, largely successful, though again marred by breakages from jute parachutes, causing further casualties. One Dakota crashed killing the pilot. Extraction of parachutes from the trees remained a desperate business.

Some US airmen had to bail out over an 'unadministered' area of Nagaland, where British administration did not obtain. The head-hunters, who had not been 'reformed', decapitated the Americans and put their heads on posts.

On Supply Hill Coath was astonished at the urgent requests he received from his and Fred Collett's 'D' Company platoon commanders to mount patrols against the enemy. Short of water and ammunition, unshaven, exhausted, hungry, unwashed, thirsty, surrounded by un-buried Japanese dead, British and Indian troops still sought to take the action to the enemy, requests that had to be refused. The priority was overwhelmingly defensive.

The Rajputs were right forward. On 13 April they took the worst of a mortar and anti-tank bombardment on fixed lines straight into their trenches, until Subedar Sultan Singh was forced to withdraw with two platoons, one now consisting of seven men only and the second also savaged and unable to continue. Lieutenant Jack Faulkner was sent from 'A' Company with his platoon to relieve them. He found the Rajput trenches empty except for dead bodies. On the way, however, he had cleared the Japanese off the hill by direct rifle attack from his under-strength unit.

The remainder of 'A' Company followed from their own positions on Kuki. 'C' Company's Commander, Tom Coath, his Company reduced to fourteen men, briefed Major Kenyon. Kenyon ordered Faulkner to take a basha on the hill where Japanese had been seen and heard carelessly talking, as was their insecure practice. Faulkner was armed with a Molotov cocktail (a bottle containing petrol and a fuse) which he lit and threw against the attap basha. It failed to ignite. He picked it up, relit the fuse and dropped the Molotov into the basha, where it exploded almost in his face, burning off his eyebrows.

The Japanese hung on as long as they could in the blazing hut, finally evacuating the position, according to one account 'squealing like pigs and stark naked, carrying their clothes in one hand and weapons in the other,' to be shot down by Faulkner's platoon Bren gunner until his gun jammed. An 'A' Company attack under an unexpectedly weak smoke-screen failed to clear the forward trenches in order to reoccupy them with British troops. The assault had the sole effect of bringing down Japanese fire on Kenyon's own positions.

Lieutenant Peter Doresa's platoon was infiltrated by Japanese using, not bugles and voice-terror, but 'the silent technique', gym-shoes and weaponry wrapped in material. Doresa had ordered that there should be no firing over fifteen yards' range. He did not himself fire, or so instruct his Bren-gunner, a Private Peacock with a brother also in 'D' Company, until the enemy were within five yards of his trench. At the order 'Fire', the whole platoon joined in with tracer and parachute flares until the Japanese withdrew. The platoon stood down on 50% manning.

Peacock's brother, alone in a trench because his companion had been killed by a mortar bomb, fell asleep during a lull to wake up with a Japanese officer beside him. When the Japanese turned, Peacock struggled with him until he broke the officer's neck, then ran him through with his Samurai sword. Elsewhere on the hill, a British soldier shot three Japanese, one after the other, as they leapt into his trench.

At 9 am 'C' Company's battered 14 Platoon had reinforced 'D' Company forward. At 10 o'clock Sergeant Henry Morley and Private Norton, both 14 Platoon, were killed by snipers. At 11 am Norman and Thrussel took the mortar forward and fired 18 smoke bombs at a basha. Although two hit the basha on the left, the right was not damaged. Smoke was ineffective against this snipers' nest. Molotov cocktails were no use either.

The Japanese began voice propaganda in English – 'You are sur-rounded. Surrender or you will all be annihilated' – and in Urdu to the Rajputs who had, by that time, gone back. Lance-Corporal Crabb and Private Gallon were wounded. All was confusion. Norman had no tiffin but – and it is a tribute to Eves and the West Kents – bully beef, fried tomatoes, baked beans and a little tea later on in the middle of that hideous battle.

This day, known as 'The Bad Day' or 'The Black Thirteenth', was no less 'black' on the tennis court. Although the Mountain Batteries' 3.7 inch guns were as accurate as ever, it appeared to 'B' Company that the rate of fire into the Japanese infantry in the dead ground or attacking across the court was slower than before. Perhaps, Winstanley thought, it had been affected by the failure of the airdrop. The mortars too were less plentiful, for the same reason, and also because Sergeant King's mortars were required elsewhere.

The badly reduced 9, 10 and 11 Companies of II Battalion of 58 Regiment continued to assault in waves, supported by grenades and mortars. Although the tennis court and its surroundings were now strewn with enemy corpses, 'B' Company too suffered heavy losses. Sergeant Glyn Williams was wounded in the neck and paralysed on the right side, but, after a visit to the Dressing Station, returned against orders to his platoon. Bren guns jammed in the hands of meticulously trained but exhausted men who could not keep their weapons dry and under cover. A Section was overrun, and a party of Japanese rushed the Club House. Victor King liquidated them with grenades slung through the window.

Attack after attack was defeated with rifle and Bren-gun fire or at the point of the bayonet. The last two assaults inflicted the most extensive casualties of all. The bodies on and around the tennis court included those of the massed ranks of Japanese infantry, but also many West Kents. The last infiltration that night, against the mound, was defeated by a Private Williams and his fellow Bren gunner who, when the gun jammed, felled the leading enemy soldier with a shovel, two others running away.

The West Kents had now lost 150 killed or wounded out of their original establishment of 440. 'D' Company had thirty survivors out of seventy-five, 'C' Company perhaps ten. John Laverty again turned to Hugh Richards for support, this time to relieve Winstanley's 'B' Company, not a request much stressed in demonizing literature about the Garrison Commander.

The latter made his difficult way past the snipers to Colonel Brown who, to avoid the disharmony between the Commanders on Garrison Hill, had moved his own headquarters to Hospital Spur. Brown agreed that a composite force of Assam Regiment and Assam Rifles should relieve the West Kents that day, 14 April.

When Richards returned from the field to his command post, he drafted, in response to a suggestion by Laverty, an Order of the Day which some observers believe to have a Cromwellian ring, or even the authority of the Psalms. One copy was typed for each unit, and handed out to them under fire:

'I wish to acknowledge with pride the magnificent effort which has been made by all officers, NCOs and men and followers (non-combatants) of this Garrison in the successful defence of Kohima.

'By your efforts you have prevented the Japanese from attaining this objective. All his attempts to overrun the Garrison have been frustrated by your determination and devotion to duty. Your efforts have been in accordance with the highest traditions of British arms.

'It seems clear that the enemy has been forced to draw off to meet the threat of the incoming relief force and this in itself has provided us with a measure of relief. His action is now directed to contain us by harassing fire, while he seeks to occupy odd posts under cover of that fire.

'The relief force is on its way and all that is necessary for the Garrison now is to stand firm, hold its fire and beat off any attempt to infiltrate among us.

'By your acts you have shown what you can do. Stand firm, deny him every inch of ground.

'I deplore the sufferings of the wounded: every effort is being made to alleviate them at the first opportunity.

'Put your trust in God and continue to hit the enemy hard wherever he may show himself. If you do that, his defeat is sure.

'I congratulate you on your magnificent effort and am confident that it will be sustained.

Hugh Richards, Colonel
Commander Kohima Garrison
14 April 1944

Men like Williams, Haines, Norman, Tacon, and Brown, and Corporal Richards who manned the Bren gun under the worst of the grenade fire at the most dangerous edge of the tennis court, understood the Colonel.

XVII

THE FIRST ASSAM
TAKE OVER

COLONEL BRUNO Brown now appointed Major Albert Calistan as Commander of the Assam Regiment and Rifles composite company, relieving Winstanley's 'B' Company of the Royal West Kents at the tennis court.

Albert Calistan has already been described. A former other rank in the Brigade of Guards, he and the actor Nigel Stock had married American nurses stationed in Assam. (US nurses were forbidden to marry foreigners when on active service: they were court martialled and sent home.) He was slight with black hair and a moustache. He was 'hard as nails, hot tempered, fastidiously correct and smart, a severe disciplinarian insisting on the meticulous performance of duties under no matter what conditions, and of great personal courage.' After the war he became a successful insurance executive in the US. He and his wife parted.

His earlier experience with the garrison after his splendid defence of Jessami had included the evacuation of the Hospital area and service on Garrison and Supply Hills. He reported Hurricane attacks on 8 and 9 April at Naga Village and Merema Ridge. He also refers in the War Diary to the continual rumours between 10–14 April of early relief by 161 Brigade.

Calistan took over 'B' Company's positions by 3 pm on 15 April. In moving from Hospital Ridge on relief by 'B' Company, a brother officer, Major Askew, had been killed by a sniper close to the Garrison HQ. One NCO and two IORs were also killed and five IORs wounded en route to the tennis court. Their reception by the Japanese was noisy and violent, but Calistan said that his platoons (two Assam Regiment and one Rifle) 'knew the tricks', keeping calm and quiet under the grenades. Peter Steyn commanded the left platoon, Donald Cleland leading the Rifles platoon.

The barrage intensified at dusk, including spring-discharged grenades and LMG and MMG using a high percentage of tracer. Several Japanese, still III Battalion of 58 Regiment, crawled right up to the Assam trenches trying to lob in grenades, met by the Battalion's counter-grenade fire. Assaults usually took place just before first light, at 8.30 am and at dusk. At the slightest movement, Calistan believed in immediate response fire.

He regarded 2″ mortar fire from the shoulder at very high elevation and twenty-five to thirty yards range as the most effective method of keeping the Japanese at bay. On 16 April his company blew the Japanese out of one bunker and set fire to two others.

On 17 April another bunker was taken by four men led by a local naik called Dilhu Angami who charged down from the terrace above the tennis court, clutching grenades with the pins out. Their forty-yard dash was covered by a Bren on the left and another in the Club manned by a Khasi (matriarchal tribe from Shillong), Sepoy Wellington Massar, the 'bad boy of the battalion', who stood on the billiard table with his LMG aimed through a hole in the Club wall.

The attack achieved complete surprise and both the Japanese detachment and the target machine-gun, which were behind Colonel Keene's bungalow and had caused casualties, were destroyed. But in covering the party's successful withdrawal, Wellington Massar was wounded and fell from the billiard table. With great courage, he climbed back and fired until his colleagues were safely back. He refused to go to the ADS and had his wounds dressed in Calistan's HQ. He died later in Dimapur hospital of gangrene. As a hill man he had refused amputation. It was on this occasion that the raiding party returned with seven rifles and bayonets, one sword, two grenades and some signal equipment. Calistan was meticulous in noting, that after every attack on their position, the Japanese returned to repair and dig in. (His, and Colonel Richards', comments on Japanese tactics are at Appendix A.)

The disciplined, aggressive conduct of the Assamese led to Allied supremacy at the tennis court for five days, longer than any other formation. Although there was further bombardment, Calistan's vigilance, with mortars, Brens and rifle fire, ensured that there were no more completed attacks across the court. So dominant did this Company become that, on the last night of the Siege, the Japanese attacked Supply Hill rather than the tennis court, feeling a weakness in the gallant stand mounted on the hill by Rawlley and Kuriyan.

At 4 pm on 19 April Calistan was relieved by a Company of the 1/1 Punjabis. Unfortunately, pointed by a lot of noise from their Brens and LMGs, the Japanese attacked the tennis court with grenades and gelignite, accounting for 23 casualties in one Punjabi platoon alone: the Indians were saved by DF fire from Jotsoma called up by Major Gavin Dannett, their Company Commander. They lost the position so recently vacated by the 1st Assam and it had to be reoccupied in a determined effort by another Punjabi platoon.

Elsewhere, a curious incident occurred in a 'thick white pall' near the dropping zone, formed by Japanese smoke bombs mixed with mortar HE. (This mixture, and rifle fire, caused casualties among Barratt's

Indians.) One of the officers from HQ was approached by a Lance-Corporal who claimed to have been invited ('Come over 'ere') by four Japanese in a bunker between 'A' and 'D' Company, gossiping happily and handing out a packet of rice as inducement. On instructions from Laverty's command post, the Lance-Corporal took his Bren and his patrol and shot them.

On 14 April an officer patrol of 4/7 Rajputs led by a Lieutenant Johnson stealthily entered the garrison from Brigade. He reported that 161 Brigade were still in the Jotsoma Box, although an advance had been made to Punjabi Ridge where the garrison had already seen fighting. The Second British Division from Dimapur was held up by road blocks two miles from Jotsoma. Warren still thought it inadvisable to leave the guns without the security that the Division's force would provide.

Laverty told him, in a message repeated to Warren later by Richards, that, unless help arrived within forty-eight hours, Kohima would fall. 'The men's spirits are all right, but there aren't many of us left.' Johnson reported this to Brigade on return, adding that the garrison was 'utterly exhausted'.

In fact it was on 15 April that 5 Brigade destroyed the last road block and met 161 Brigade. Brigadier Warren moved the 1/1 Punjabis forward, now commanded by Colonel Harry Grimshaw, today a retired General in Colchester. Heavy fighting was visible on Punjabi Ridge under the 2nd Division's 25-pounders, but the relief promised for the following day did not materialize and the projected evacuation of the wounded did not take place that night.

What had happened was that Major-General Grover had disapproved Brigadier Warren's plan for the relief on grounds of probable insecurity to the right flank and of inadequate time for reconnaissance by Brigadier Shapland's 6 Brigade. There also existed new intelligence that General Sato, commanding 31 Division, intended to take the Ridge line Merema-Cheswema north of Kohima: Japanese artillery would then have commanded 2nd Division's main communication on the Zubza-Kohima road. Relief was therefore postponed until 17 April.

Meanwhile on Supply, 'C' Company had relieved 'D' Company in their forward positions. At 4.30 pm Corporal Norman, Privates Thrussell, Johnson and a Staff Sergeant went forward of 'D' and, under sniper fire, blew up three enemy bashas behind Japanese lines. A Royal West Kent Corporal was on water fatigue that night and walked one and a half miles to the water point on Garrison Hill where he had to wait two and a half hours to fill his container from the pipe. The Dressing Station was on the way. He found this sight, with 250 wounded inside the perimeter, a terrifying and heart-breaking experience. 'We kept falling over dead bodies, black and decaying because there was limited movement in these daylight hours when they could be buried. The smell was overpowering. Hundreds of wounded were lying in open pits. The area was continually mortared and shelled day and night. The wounded were wounded again, rewounded, killed or dying.'

The water party returned to Supply Hill later that night. They described it as 'fairly active', i.e. the Japanese did not actually attack, only fired machine guns and grenades. The weather was now 'mild'.

On Saturday 'C' Company, or what was left, was absorbed by 'A'. Their cook house was mortared and a Corporal and Cook injured. Water and medical supplies were successfully dropped by the RAF. Only five parachute loads out of 78 were lost. At 2 pm a grenade attack by four Gurkhas and their British officer against Japanese digging-in failed in the face of mortar fire.

The enemy fired machine guns and discharged cap grenades all through the night, but did not advance. 'A' Company learned that 'they definitely would be relieved next day'. Sergeant Boxall, Privates Foord and Crosby were killed.

'A' Company saw a platoon of Rajputs who confirmed that 161 and 5 Brigade had met at Jotsoma. At 3 pm other Rajputs were observed to occupy a 'village' without Japanese opposition. Many trucks, despatch riders etc were seen at 161 Brigade HQ two miles away. It was then clear that relief might not be far distant. There was plenty of grenade and machine-gun fire, but 'nothing else exciting' on Supply during the day, although Private Calton, wounded earlier, was killed. The Indian National Flag was observed flying on one of the hills.

The Assam Company's actions on the tennis court had eased the tension and disappointment a little. But in the darkness that night of 16 April the Japanese 7 Company under Lieutenant Ishida of II Battalion attacked in strength against 'A' and 'C' Companies of the Royal West Kents on the southern tip of Supply Hill. Many of the British had been wounded at least once and all of them were exhausted. In the blackness, completely out-numbered, they fell back after vicious hand-to-hand fighting. Colonel Laverty had no sound units available to reinforce them and again sought Colonel Richards' help. He, after consulting Bruno Brown, sent forward two somewhat untested platoons of the Rifles and 17 mule drivers from the Regiment's Transport Platoon, who had had only the most exiguous practice in weaponry. None possessed automatics. They eventually withdrew with the West Kents to Kuki Piquet and Garrison Hill.

Then the remarkable Naveen Rawlley regained all these lost positions, twice lost them and twice regained them. According to the citation for his MC, on three occasions he personally led his Indian troops back into vacated positions.

On Hospital Spur the Assam Rifles drove off another attack, retaining their position and killing twenty-four Japanese. The 'putrid accumulation' here of enemy corpses over the past weeks was evidence of the skill and valour with which this paramilitary police unit had defended the garrison.

The 1/1 Punjabis could now be seen on Piquet Hill only half a mile away. Another assurance of relief from 161 Brigade, this time for 18 April, referred specifically to plans for the evacuation of wounded and to heavy artillery cover for the surrounding features during this projected operation.

Japanese phosphorus bombs and grenades were now directed at Kuki Piquet followed by a screaming infantry assault through the blazing bashas against 'D' Company under Fred Collett, now reduced to forty men. Between Kuki Piquet and Garrison Hill were the remaining seventy men of 'A' and 'C' Companies. There were also Rajputs on both positions. The Assam Company was still at the tennis court and defeated one more determined attack on the evening of 17 April. Bombardment of both Garrison Hill and Supply Hill began and lasted for five hours, particularly heavy in the West Kents and Garrison command post areas. Summer House Hill was a wracked inferno of flame and destruction, covered in rubbish, the bare trees hung with parachutes.

The bombardment of Supply ended at 9.30 pm. Rawlley and two men left their trench to warn Lieutenant Kuriyan and any Assamese left that an attack might be imminent. When he got down to his Company's trenches, all of them were empty. (He did not, however, even get to Kuriyan's position). Instead came 'shoulder to shoulder, a solid phalanx of Japanese, advancing up the hill' followed by two more waves. Major Rawlley and his escort just managed to get away ahead of them, challenged by 'D' Company of the West Kents on Kuki Piquet who refused to believe them. They then lay thirty minutes in the cross-fire until 'admitted' by Fred Collett and finally reached Richards at the command post.

Kuriyan, too, on the other southern slope of Supply realized that his platoon had been bypassed and that he was cut off. Only then did he withdraw, after a most gallant fourteen days' fighting.

Colonel Grimshaw had sent Gavin Dunnett and his 1/1 Punjabis forward precisely to seize Kuki Piquet, and to ensure that 31 Division could not capture Kohima Ridge before 161 Brigade broke out of the Jotsoma Box. If Sato could take the Ridge now, he could be rapidly and substantially supported from Imphal which he could still assume would soon be in Japanese hands. The 'mountain fastness' would then be truly impregnable.

Dunnett was too late. At 2.30 in the morning of 18 April phosphorous bombardment of the bashas on Kuki Piquet opened the way for another howling infantry assault with grenades and machine guns. The hill shook under Japanese 3″ mortar bombs and, later, under the shells of 3.7 inch howitzers in defensive fire brought down by Major Yeo from 24th Indian Mountain Regiment. 'D' Company fought bravely, Collett moving his sections correctly from one gap in the line to another. But, their trenches penetrated and with heavy losses, only twenty-five fit men now broke back in the end to Garrison Hill. It had needed a battalion to out-manoeuvre them. There were Japanese everywhere, in all the trenches, in the bashas, behind trees, preparing to advance down the reverse slope and up to Garrison Hill. The blinded Company Sergeant-Major Haines with his escorting private soldier, rallying, advising, encouraging all his men, was at last brought down. At this desperate moment Laverty ordered forward Thomas Hogg and the three survivors of 10 Platoon to Kuki Piquet, just vacated by 'D' Company.

Sergeant King's mortar section, the very last defence of Kohima, was now moved to a site from which it could strike Kuki Piquet. He began a bombardment which held, or seemed momentarily to hold, the Japanese. King's jaw had been smashed by shrapnel or a shell splinter. He had to hold it up with his hand and his mouth dribbled blood. He did not go to the Dressing Station until he saw his shells landing on the target. When he did go, he was knocked unconscious by a near miss, and only then did the doctors begin to operate.

No one knows today why General Miyazaki, or whoever was in tactical command of the regiments at Kohima, did not that very night fling his overwhelming mass of men into a final, annihilating assault on Garrison Hill. Its battered defenders were certain, however, that he would do so in irresistible force at dawn. When they did so, there could be no successful resistance. All would be swept away. (It was during that fateful night that a very young private soldier asked the Garrison Commander: 'Sir, may I ask you a question?' 'Of course, what is it?' 'When we die, Sir, is that the end or do we go on?') When Colonel Richards left his command post later that morning after the most severe bombardment in the Siege, he could not comprehend how his own headquarters and that of Laverty had survived. He found 'trench after trench filled with British and Indian dead and knew, without any shadow of doubt, that unless relief came within twelve hours, it would come too late.'

As Jimmy Patrick said in the 7th Gurkha Regimental Journal of December, 1946: 'The size of the (Japanese) force rather shook us. Had they tried a little harder, they could easily have wiped us from the face of the earth.' It may be, as has been said, that no battalion-scale assault could have been mounted in that mountainous terrain.

They tried, nevertheless, quite hard. Around Patrick that night, after very heavy shelling, mortaring, grenades and small arms fire, the Japs came in. All was confusion. The phosphorous shells were frightening, much more demoralizing than HE. The remaining bashas caught fire, and it became impossible to see what was going on or distinguish friend from foe in the smoke and uneven glare of flames. He did his best to keep control, but could see only to his immediate front. He did not himself fire, too busy trying to see what was happening. There were Japs all round. The left and right flanks had broken. There was a flash and a loud explosion. He fell backwards into a slit trench. He could not see. He began to stumble slowly back. After a time he reached a Nissen hut and went inside. There were men in it, some of them European. They were amazed that he had come through alone.

They wiped away some of the blood streaming down his face and put a field dressing over his lost eye. He went back to Garrison HQ and was taken to an aid post where they dressed the eye and a chest wound from grenade fragments. He was taken back to HQ, reported and was put to bed, in *sheets*, he believes to this day.

There was now nothing left, except Garrison Hill, of the perimeter occupied on 5 April. Hundreds of exhausted men, many wounded, were crammed into an area about a fifth of the original, held in a coming disaster that seemed for some too huge to comprehend. The ox-borne 4 Company of I Battalion of 58 Regiment had even made progress on Hospital Spur where, fortunately, the ground was almost solid rock and the men could not dig in. Concentrated artillery fire next day brought, in the Japanese phrase, 'blood and death', when the order was given to retreat, only fifteen men led by a Sergeant returned. The Japanese War Memorial is now on this spot, initiated in a ceremony in 1991 where the Company Commander's (Yamamura from Migata Prefecture) batman, Sato, gave a moving demonstration of his personal grief.

It seems to have been at this extraordinary moment that General Sato decided to move from the offensive to the defensive, but not before mounting an unsuccessful attack with 138 Regiment and a depleted 58 Regiment, four of whose Companies had been completely annihilated. Thereafter, 138 Regiment, as the main force, 'Right District Command', held the hills north of Kohima. The Central area was under the Mountain Artillery Regiment Commander, one battalion each of 124 and 138 regiments defending Point 5120, 58 Regiment to the left.

XVIII

THE GARRISON RELIEVED

THAT MORNING the Japanese were one hundred yards from the ADS which, according to one account, now held six hundred casualties. The perimeter, including tennis court and the desolate, filthy Garrison Hill, had shrunk to only three hundred and fifty yards square. The chaos and stench of the Dressing Station were compounded by a rush of useless and terrorized non-combatants milling about, the consciousness that there might be no ultimate escape heightening their panic further.

The mist lifted and the sun rose over the hills. Still no final attack had been mounted, no knockout blow. Richards saw Gavin Dunnett's Company of Punjabis only 800 yards away moving on Piquet Hill. Up the winding Dimapur-Kohima road came eight Stuart tanks in two troops, slowly, since the khud, the woods and the precipitous mountains prevented movement off the road. Following them, as the armour fired on enemy artillery at Merema, came Major Tom Ware's Company of 1/1 Punjabi, last met near Jock Young's Kharasom just before the Siege, moving up from Ms44 to Bare Hill. The tanks were stopped for an hour by a road block at Ms45, destroyed it and moved on with the infantry to the foot of IGH Spur.

In the course of their advance they disposed of an enemy gun which at 11 o'clock had created havoc amongst patients on the road, killing Captain Topham and a large number of walking wounded in the process of evacuation. Corporal Norman saw torsos without arms or legs, the heads blown off, heard the screams of the injured. But by that time the major shoot which had begun from 2nd Division at 8 am had got into its stride against the Japanese batteries. 25-pounders from Zubza now joined the 3.7 inch from Jotsoma against Kuki, Supply, Detail, Jail and Garrison Hills, and against enemy positions on the tennis court. All were directed by Yeo and by his successor, Major T. N. H. Harrison, 2 i/c 24 Mountain Regiment, an appointment which Yeo then assumed. (When the 2nd Division moved from Dimapur to Kohima, the only positions available for the guns were at the side of the only road, which had steep slopes on each side; the guns were lined up one behind the other, 3.7 inch, 25-pounders and 5.5 inch. Artillery from other Divisions whose infantry had already joined the battle were ordered to return to India because there was no room for them.) Additionally, Hurribombers and other aircraft from 221 Group had now achieved complete air superiority.

161 Brigade had already planned the evacuation of 320 wounded, which did not include those with light injuries. Colonel Young personally monitored their departure from his Dressing Station. All of the men received half a grain of morphia before limping or, for 140 of them, being carried down the hill on stretchers by Barratt's Indian composite company and other more disciplined non-combatants.

Major Richard Pilcher, Young's 2 i/c outside the garrison, had assembled ten three-ton lorries and thirty ambulances at Ms42 under Colonel George Collingwood, Brigadier Warren's second-in-command. These two officers then moved ahead in Bren carriers to a point at the foot of Hospital Spur where vehicles could turn and where Pilcher set up an emergency dressing station. Tanks guarded the position, helping the artillery to deal with such enemy guns as those described by Norman. Many of the wounded were killed and eleven out of fourteen in the loading party, including Pilcher, were killed or wounded by a Japanese 75 mm gun deliberately targeting larger groups of wounded.

Four hours elapsed, under sniper and mortar fire, between the departure of the first patient from Garrison Hill and that of the last ambulance for Dimapur, but the evacuation was not greatly hindered and certainly not stopped by enemy action. Pilcher's plan, which worked, had been to station himself near the mortuary of 53rd Indian General Hospital on the eponymous Spur, calling up vehicles two by two from Ms42. The loading party in their 'clean and starched uniforms watched the thin, bearded and bandaged scarecrows, some on foot and some on stretchers, come painfully but cheerfully down the long slope past the ruined buildings to the background of the continual trumpeting of the guns'. On the ambulance train from Dimapur, when a Gurkha officer asked the Bengali doctor for 'bread and cheese and pickles, and beer', that is what he got.

Lieutenant-Colonel Grimshaw, commanding the 1/1 Punjabis, sent Dunnett's platoon to the tennis court where, as has been said, they relieved Calistan and his Assamese. They sustained, under mortar and slab (gelignite) explosive, the heavy casualties referred to earlier. Richards, nevertheless, had been right in recommending, despite the dangers, that the tennis court continue to be held. A dangerous situation was averted, as so often, by the Jotsoma guns. Another assault that night was beaten off by the Punjabis who, at daylight next day, in a brilliant attack by Jemadar Mohammed Rafiq who had lost three section commanders, led a platoon to recapture the trenches taken in the previous night's grenade action. Sixteen Japanese were counted dead. A Japanese 37 mm mortar bombardment was launched that night, the last ever on Colonel Richards' command post.

Earlier in the morning of 19 April 'A' Company under Major Tommy Kenyon found that State troops had abandoned bunkers twenty yards from 'A's weapon pits and about the same distance from Laverty and Grimshaw's command posts. The bunkers were occupied, or being occupied, by 58th Regiment troops infiltrated through the bushes in the darkness. A series of deadly individual fights then took place, 'a game of hide and seek'. Covering fire with smoke from 'A' Company later enabled a Punjabi platoon to assault the bunkers at dawn, driving out the enemy. Twenty Japanese were killed, some burned alive when kerosene in a bunker set fire to their phosphorous bombs, their clothing and themselves. 'D' Company, 4th Rajputs, however, were driven off Terrace Hill.

So as to deploy more troops, an expansion of the perimeter was required. All seventy-two guns of 2nd Division put down a bombardment at first light on Kuki Piquet, followed by a Punjabi attack under Tom Ware. Richards supposed that nothing could have survived this rain of shells, but when the Punjabis reached the summit, 'the bunkers came alive', aided by machine-gun fire from Jail Hill and Transport Ridge. The platoon was forced to withdraw. These were the same conditions which had made so difficult the lives of the Royal West Kents, the Assam units, the 4/7 Rajputs, and Major Rawlley and Lieutenant Kenyon's Indians over the past fifteen days. They would be repeated over and over again in the second phase of the battle for Kohima.

Although still under fire and still in trenches, the hard core of the garrison knew that they had come through and that, within hours, the ordeal would be ended. Still they stood to all night, waiting for the final relief. This came at dawn on 20 April when the Royal Berkshires marched in under Lieutenant-Colonel Wilbur Bickford from Shapland's 6th Brigade, immaculate advance guard of the 2nd Division.

Bickford and others were horrified by the desolation of Kohima Ridge. 'The stench of festering corpses . . . the earth ploughed by shell-fire . . . human remains lay rotting as the battle raged over them . . . flies swarmed everywhere and multiplied with incredible speed . . . Men retched as they dug in . . . the stink hung in the air and permeated clothes and hair . . . We were profoundly shocked by the conditions on Garrison Hill.' Jawans of the Assam Regiment 'took a last glance at the battle-scarred hill festooned with dangling parachutes caught up on blackened and blasted trees, and wondered by what miracle they had been spared.'

The Fourth Battalion of the Royal West Kents went down the hill in twos and threes. Some had to march for as much as four miles before finding transport down the mortared road, on which snipers were said to lurk as far back as Ms18. Others got lifts on trucks almost at once. At Ms30 they were given biscuits, tea, mixed fruit, sausages, fags, matches and chewing-gum. At Ms8 they turned off the main road to their camp. Here they had 'a lovely cup of tea and a lovely hot bath and shave'. They felt better for that. For dinner at 6 pm they had bully beef rissoles, potatoes, fried tomatoes, gravy, treacle duff and tea. They slept in bashas with lamps. Next day they visited their wounded friends in the Military Hospital at Dimapur. Conditions there were bad. The West Kents had not had their wounds dressed, their sheets changed, or been bathed. Complaints had been sent to GHQ.

In the evening they saw Brian Donlevy in *South of Tahiti*. Next day Brigadier Warren addressed them: 'This is the first time in history that one battalion has stopped an enemy division, and not only stopped it, but split one brigade' (presumably 58th Regiment) 'so badly that all the King's horses and all the King's men couldn't put it togther again.' Corporal H. F. Norman sent his 222nd Air Mail Letter Card to his mother, father and Sheila.

According to their War Diary, the Royal West Kents at Kohima sustained 199 serious casualties out of an original 444 men, of whom 61 were killed. The *Garrison* War Diary records 600 casualties, 250 assumed dead, not including the West Kents or the Assamese. 260 out of about 800 men of the Assam Regiment reached Kohima from the battles at the outposts, and Peter Steyn's Official History records the deaths of two officers and thirteen other ranks, three officers and eighteen other ranks wounded during the Siege. There is a reference, in the private diary of an other rank in the West Kents, to a Fourth Battalion strength on 22 April (i.e. immediately after the Siege) of only 90 men and the consequent necessity to form a composite Company of 'B' and 'D' Companies, then sent to reinforce the 4/7 Rajputs on guard duty at Ms32.

Kohima was described by a left-wing anglophobe Indian commentator as the 'Stalingrad of Burma'. Slim said, in *Defeat into Victory*: 'Sieges have been longer, but few have been more intense, and in none have the defenders deserved greater honour than the garrison of Kohima.' Lord Mountbatten's remarks have already been recorded. The official historian of the Cabinet Office, Major-General S. Woodburn Kirby's verdict was that 'the heroic defence put up by Richards and his small garrison against overwhelming odds thus played a vital part in the defeat of the Japanese'. Richards himself, in his modest way, said only that, until Supply Hill and Kuki Piquet, he 'had always thought that we should be able to hold out. I think this feeling was largely shared. There was certainly no atmosphere of gloom and despondence.' After those comments, however, he concluded, 'Had the Jap followed up his capture of Kuki Piquet on

17 April with a further attack in strength on Summer House Hill, I think it is almost certain that we should have been overrun.'

But some of the West Kents, perhaps all of them, in their strength, experience and faith in Warren, even then never doubted that they would 'win'. Some of them, however, might attribute that extraordinary confidence to delusion born of absolute exhaustion and, after all, the Punjabis had nearly reached them.

Kohima really was the turning point of the Burma campaign. If the Ridge had been lost, the consequences for IV Corps and the Imphal battle, for Ledo, Stilwell and the Chinese, even for India through Dimapur, would have been incalculable. XXXIII Corps under General Stopford, furthermore, could not have beaten Sato and 31 Division for many more months than were in fact required. Because Kohima was denied to the Japanese, they could not prevent the detraining of reinforcements at Dimapur or cut the link to US/China forces.

Colonel Richards' decision to concentrate on the Ridge and not on the Boxes was the correct tactical plan, except for the Box at Workshop. He had little Intelligence, few sensible instructions other than a general permission to abandon Kohima at his own judgement, continual arbitrary removal of resources and, outside the remarkable Assam units, no coherent or trained fighting formations until the last-minute arrival of the Royal West Kents. (Exceptions included the leadership provided by Major Naveen Rawlley, MC, Indian Army; Captain Jimmy Patrick, 1/7 Gurkhas; the unidentified Lieutenant Kuriyan; Lieutenant John Wright, and Lieutenant James Barratt, 1/17 Dogras.) His other contributions were inspirational leadership in the field and, also, the prior provision and distribution of food, ammunition and, to the best of his ability in the administrative shambles, medical care and water.

Without the presence, skill, courage and experience of Lieutenant-Colonel John Laverty and the officers and men of the Fourth Battalion, Royal West Kents, the Siege would not have endured beyond 6 April or 7 at the latest. This trained, united and magnificently British Battalion transformed inevitable defeat into something like victory. Short of sleep, at a numerical disadvantage of between twenty and thirty to one, without much food, always short of water, in continual close combat against an incomprehensible and brutal enemy, thousands of miles from home or any of its joys, the band of Kentish and Welsh men held the pass. Those who held it were junior officers, NCOs and other ranks, most wounded and many killed, who did not give a personal damn for Empire. 'It was a private's battle.' As for casualties, 'D' lost fifty men out of an under-strength seventy-five; one platoon was reduced by the end to only one young private who, with a broad grin, asked his Company Commander if he might put up his 'pip'. Sergeant King's mortars made a priceless and consistent contribution. Major Yeo's direction from his OPs of defensive fire from the 3.7 inch and 25-pounders at Jotsoma and Zubza was as crucial for the garrison's survival as the conduct of the infantrymen. Captain Hirakubo said that the *later* British shelling by up to one hundred guns at a time, 11,500 rounds in a two-day period, was almost unendurable, like a series of 'terrible, thunderous, drum-rolls, switching unpredictably from selected target to target, made even more distracting by accurate aerial bombing'. He has made the additional point that the arrival on the battlefield of British tanks was perhaps as decisive a factor in damaging morale. The Japanese could only encounter the Lee/Stuarts with Molotov cocktails and dynamite.

As for the others, the Assam Regiment's performance at Jessami, Kharasom and Phek caused damaging tactical delay to 31 Division's assault on Kohima, as did that of 50 Indian Parachute Brigade at Sangshak. Filleted by these actions and by the retreat, this young regiment, in particular under Major Calistan at the tennis court, where it behaved with incomparable aggression, conducted itself with honour. On Hospital Spur, the gallant Assam Rifles held the back door throughout the Siege.

All casualties had been considerable, but General Sato's had been the worst. A Burman living on the Chindwin during the Japanese retreat – later a rout – southward, said that when the 15th Army crossed that river, if the word 'Kohima' were mentioned, 'They would say nothing, only shake their heads'. The logistics had turned against Sato and Mutaguchi. The gate swung slowly open on the Hinge of Fate.

XIX

MEANWHILE, OUTSIDE . . .

FROM 5 to 18 APRIL when reinforced by Tom Ware and Gavin Dunnett's Companies of 1/1 Punjabis under their new Battalion Commander, Henry Grimshaw, one pitifully understrength battalion each of a British (Royal West Kent) and an Indian Regiment (1st Assam), plus platoons of 4/7 Rajputs Regiment (Jack Cargill) and tiny Indo/British composite units, had thus held Kohima. Artillery support by 24th Indian Mountain Regiment (Humphrey Hill) from Jotsoma, the HQ of 161 Brigade, ex-Arakan, (Brigadier Warren), of which the RWKs, 1/1 and 4/7 were the component battalions, ensured their survival. Harold Briggs' 5th Division, to which they belonged, was very proud of them.

Another division and other brigades had meanwhile arrived in the north-east and were moving, terribly slowly, to relieve the garrison and 161 Brigade itself. At the cost of a little repetition, it is worth outlining what was going on all this time *outside* the Ridge.

In April, 1942, because of near-anarchy in India, caused by the Civil Disobedience (Satyagraha) movement of Gandhi, Nehru and the Congress Party, Major-General John Grover's Second British Division was diverted at sea to Bombay from its destination in North Africa where it was to join the 8th Army. Once in India, engaged initially in combined operation training, the Division's low opinion of the Indian Army, until they fought beside them in Assam and after, based largely on Indian *administrative* units, was matched by that Army's resentment of this cuckoo-in-the-nest, and the dislike, on expenditure and other grounds, felt by civilians, babus or Congress.

It, one of the two regular Divisions of the British Army, was scattered all over the sub-continent. It had served under Wellington in Spain, in the Crimean War, in France throughout the Great War. The 2nd Division comprised battalions of some of the great County Regiments of the British Army, whose names echo down the centuries, Royal Berkshire, Queen's Own Cameron Highlanders, Dorsetshire, Durham Light Infantry, Royal Norfolk, Lancashire Fusiliers, Royal Scots, Royal Welch Fusiliers, Worcestershire and Manchester Regiments. Its Commander, John Grover, only forty-seven, was a devoted, professional officer of remorseless dedication to detail, who yet seized the allegiance of his officers and men, doubtless through a similar dedication to their welfare, equalled, as one historian said, only by Lord Hill who introduced regimental schools and sergeants' messes. Grover had been in the Shropshire Light Infantry (of which he was later Colonel of the Regiment) in the Great War when he was wounded three times and won the MC. He fought too in the B.E.F. before the evacuation of the British Expeditionary Force in 1940 at Dunkirk. After Kohima, he became Director of Army Welfare and, on retirement, General Secretary of the Officers Association.

In India, 2 Div as it was known, was until 1944 the only Division under Lieutenant-Colonel Montagu Stopford's 33 Corps whose function was the conduct of Combined Operations, then thought to be the most viable, perhaps only, method of retaking Burma. Stopford had been an officer in the Rifle Brigade with which he had fought in the Great War. In World War II, he commanded a Brigade in France, then a division in the UK before becoming Commandant of the Staff College. He later led 12 Corps for a time, followed by his present posting.

His mind was clear and rapid, his gait calm, even slow, his intentions both deep and wide-ranging. He was brave and retained the confidence of his subordinate commanders, although, in his later dismissal of Grover, criticized for inability to delegate and for excessive compliance with his superior's demands.

On 18 March, 1944, Grover, whose Division had just completed jungle training, sought an interview with General Sir George Giffard, GOC 11th Army Group, the superior formation to Lieutenant-General Slim's XIV Army, to discuss projected reductions in his Division as drafts for XIV Army. (By this time, combined operations were on the back burner, the landing craft needed in Europe.) He asked Giffard whether 2 Div could help to meet the Japanese advance across the Chindwin. Giffard replied that it could not, since it could not be maintained in the XIV Army area. It could therefore go on leave.

Five days later, however, Stopford was ordered to proceed to Slim's XIV Army HQ at Comilla, and 2 Div was told to start moving on 24 March by road and rail to the Burma front.

On 1 April 5 Brigade, as 2 Div's first formation to move on Kohima, began to arrive at Dimapur railway station, preceded by its Brigadier, Victor Hawkins, who had decided to concentrate the Brigade at Bokajan north of Dimapur, an especially vile piece of jungle. If the Battalions – 1 Camerons, 2 Dorsets and 7 Worcesters – hated Bokajan, where they only stayed a few days, they despised the panic and chaos of Dimapur even more. The base was filled with refugees, coolies, men unable to rejoin their units down the blocked road to Imphal and, worse, a mentality among base-wallahs unhelpful, even hostile to the prosecution of war and to the acquisition of legitimate transport and other arms and equipment.

By 10 April nevertheless, Warren was able to wireless the garrison that 5th Brigade were forming up at Dimapur for the advance on Kohima. After 5 and 161 met, Warren would be able to relieve the garrison. Unfortunately, this took no account of the road block met by Hawkins at Ms32 on 11 April and the many road blocks thereafter, which prevented the early junction hoped for between the two Brigades. At least 2 Div had been able to acquire the equipment it needed: at least Grover had taken over from Ranking and had ordered Hawkins forward.

On 11 April, after looking at the enormous heights and distances of the terrain, Grover realized that, although Brigadiers Hawkins and Warren should still try to join hands, they must thereafter attempt to operate jointly. In the meanwhile, because he believed that 31 Division had given up frontal attacks on Kohima in favour of infiltration or flank action, the aim should be to protect Dimapur from static and mobile positions while getting as large a force as possible forward to Kohima. 161 Brigade had been unable to take the road block at Ms32 and the Worcesters moved forward, eventually to Zubza where they formed a box and, with artillery support, succeeded in destroying a Japanese platoon. The Camerons were at Ms32 itself, about four miles west of Zubza, overlooked by Japanese in Khabvuma village and, it emerged, by a 75 mm gun in Merema.

This was the day, inside Kohima, when there were so many patients that their trenches in the Advanced Dressing Station were now within 200 yards of the tennis court.

On 12 April the Camerons occupied Sachema, a Naga village south of Zubza, a patrol under Lieutenant W. J. McKillop ambushing 19 Japanese the following day. 10th Field Regiment's twenty-four guns began defensive fire against the Japanese position on Bunker Hill (Merema) which contained a 75 mm gun, the Camerons moving next day on the other side of the hill behind that position. The white houses of Kohima in their towering mountains were visible from the box. So was the main Japanese bunker, only 500 yards away. Everything seemed very peaceful, with the Camerons eating in the open from their mess tins.

On 13 April a patrol reported that Bunker Hill was deserted. This information was refuted when a small reconnaissance patrol was allowed on the hill unmolested but shortly put under very heavy fire from hitherto apparently unoccupied bunkers. These may have contained as much as a Japanese company. Another company from 138 Regiment intending to occupy Zubza found it full of British troops 2 Div was quickly identified as 'from Yorkshire', but although the 'Cross Keys' are the Keys of York, the Division contained no Yorkshire regiments. The

Japanese achieved surprise, but crews of the 149th Royal Armoured Corps scrambled into their tanks just in time to fire their 75 mm cannon point-blank. Only two out of one hundred Japanese survived that skirmish or the Worcesters' later duck-shoot against their bashas.

In Kohima, it was 'The Black 13th', black on Supply Hill, black because of the failed airdrop with supplies to the Japanese or to the wrong British units, black on the tennis court. Next day Richards heard Laverty tell Warren that 'unless relief came soon, it will be too late'. 5th Brigade was eight miles away but did not overcome the last road block until 15 April when Hawkins met Warren who, at last, was able to send forward the Punjabis.

The Manchester Regiment's MMGs, the Camerons, the tanks, the mortars and the twenty-four 25-pounders of 10 Field Regiment, firing during the action sixty rounds apiece, came up to their positions at noon on 14 April for the planned 5 Brigade attack on Bunker Hill. The rain was heavy and Brigadier Hawkins feared that that might cause the tanks to slip over the khud. The Jocks went forward, supported by armour firing over open sights against opposition from the crest. Company Sergeant Major Cook, who had boxed for the Army, took a sword from a Japanese officer and, after killing him, used it against all-comers. Seeing a Japanese soldier throw a grenade, a Company Commander, Captain David Graham, flung himself on the earth whereupon a Jock threw himself in turn on top of him. 'It's OK, Sir,' said the Jock when both noticed that the grenade was dud.

By 2 pm the Camerons had, according to a subsequent Japanese report, annihilated an entire Company. They had taken Bunker Hill. The position was then relieved by the Royal Welch, and the Battalion, less 'A' and 'B' Companies, moved back to Zubza.

There were no major actions in Kohima on 14 April, only an unsuccessful attack by forty Japanese using gelignite.

Very useful intelligence was acquired by 208 Field Company from the bodies next day, together with pay-books, phrase books and some fairly old-world 'dirty postcard' material. It was also determined that the defenders were from 1st Battalion, 138 Regiment, recruited in Hokkaido where the men are considerably taller than elsewhere in the Japanese islands. The Dorsets, then under Colonel Jock McNaught and relieved from picket on the Dimapur road, met Brigadier Warren at 11 am, while the Berkshires, DLI and Royal Norfolks moved up to Zubza where they joined the Royal Welch Fusiliers of 6 Brigade. The latter were to have relieved the garrison on 16 April with the Punjabis under Warren's command, but Grover did not approve of Warren's plan and the operation had to be postponed until 17 April, the garrison apparently being informed.

This news was serious for the garrison. The tension on the night of 15 April was only relieved by Calistan's brilliant attack across the tennis court, and the gallantry of Sepoy Wellington Massar.

On 16 April two sections of the Royal Welch Fusiliers were overrun by Japanese on the road south of Lancaster Gate at Lone Tree Hill. Prisoners were taken, but a counter-attack led by a Lieutenant T. H. Callaghan of 9 Platoon killed all the enemy and brought about the escape and return to their unit of the RWF prisoners. 161 Brigade, however, decided not to mount the main attack on Kohima, putting it off again until 18 April, yet another day.

In Kohima on 17 April the men were exhausted by nearly two weeks of hand-to-hand fighting, mortar and artillery shelling, lack of sleep and water. Even the bravest began to fear. Supply Hill and Kuki Piquet fell. As we have seen, had the enemy pressed home its attack that night, Kohima would probably have fallen.

On 18 April, with Hurribomber and massive 3.7 and 25-pounder artillery support, the 1/1 Punjabis came into the perimeter at IGH Spur from the road, followed by the ambulances and other transport for the hundreds of wounded. The garrison took on a new lease of life, a renewal created by the arrival of friends and the news of friends to come, and by the certainty that the end was more than in sight. Courage and endurance were stiffened, even reborn.

Generals Stopford and Grover met at the latter's HQ to plan the future, in particular the seizure of Merema Ridge and the battle ahead for Kohima itself. On 19 April Brigadier Warren, whose 161 Brigade was intended to relieve the garrison, determined that on account of the past fortnight's fighting it was too tired to continue for the time being. He sought General Grover's permission to retire. Grover agreed that those soldiers who had actually taken part in the Siege should go back to Dimapur. Unfortunately, in the meanwhile, the Rajputs were very badly cut up on Terrace Hill, including the gunner officer, Lieutenant Loudon, who shot eight Japanese before being grenaded.

Grover decided that this feature must be retaken. The Durham Light Infantry were called upon and seized it after an artillery shoot with bayonet and grenade. Fifty Japanese were killed and some thirty of the DLI, including the Company Commander, Robert Allen, who with his last breath congratulated the men of this magnificent Company. At the same time the Royal Berkshires moved up to take over in Kohima from the Royal West Kents, the 1st Assam Regiment and all others of that remarkable band.

6 Brigade had taken over responsibility for re-establishing the Kohima area on 15 April. All its regiments, Berkshire, Durham Light Infantry and Royal Welch Fusiliers, had fought nobly along the road from Zubza

against an enemy which held its bunkers to the last man. Lessons were learned, and Japanese killed, including the Commander of I Battalion 58 Regiment by the Royal Scots. On 14 April 18 Platoon of the Royal Norfolks under Sergeant Hazell killed thirty Japanese out of a force of one hundred attacking a tank laager. Another unit at Ms32 repulsed a Japanese platoon. It was now that troops came across the Japanese habit of decapitating the dead.

The guns of Zubza and Jotsoma and the Hurribombers attacked Jail and GPT at 0900 on 20 April. At 9 am the tanks, followed by the Royal Berkshires, came into Kohima at Indian General Hospital Spur.

'The filthy, bearded, bedraggled scarecrows' of the Royal West Kents Regiment, and the little jawans of the 1st Assam Regiment went down the hill to rest for a while. The second phase of Kohima would begin, no more naked, unbelievable glory, but still British and Indian courage and endurance against Japanese tenacity. On the Hill itself the leafless stumps of trees were hung with parachutes, some still carrying their loads. The ground was pitted with fox-holes; corpses lay everywhere, the stench of rotting bodies . . .

> 'O little mighty band that stood for England
> That with your bodies for a living shield
> Guarded her slow awaking.'

XX

THE OUTLOOK FOR
GENERAL SATO

BEFORE THE battle, the Commander of 31 Division's 124th Regiment had addressed his men as follows:

'Since I took over the Regiment and until the unit arrived in Burma, we have done a marvellous job. Today we are on the eve of a great battle which will decide the fate of Burma, India and the Greater East Asia Co-prosperity Sphere. Respect and obey your senior officers unquestioningly and always remember you are fighting for the Emperor. Keep in contact and on friendly terms with other troops.'

That was in early April. A diary found on a Japanese corpse in the Kohima area on 2 May read: 'Even here the confusion and the contradictions in our operational work are enough to make one weep.'

It is not possible to ascribe that comment to particular events and, indeed, a month of brilliant resistance would pass before the Japanese left Kohima. They had, nevertheless, failed to take the Ridge, Sato's main objective in controlling access to the great British storehouses at Dimapur and Imphal. They had suffered casualties. They had lost valuable equipment. Ammunition, especially for the mountain guns, was tight at six shells per diem. There was no chance of reinforcement, as opposed to the arrival of an 'allied battalion every day' with armour and artillery. They had no air cover worth the name, against regular waves of British bombers and fighters. Food was getting scarcer and there was little hope of resupply through the difficult Somra Hills, whereas the British were resupplying with 6,500lb supply drops from DC3s and C67s, unimpeded by the enemy's 5th Air Division.

The Japanese *could* live on very little: rice, salt, sesame seeds, salt fish. Their endurance was remarkable. Many of them did not dislike the jungle, regarding it not as a frightening but as a friendly, dark place where 'one could cover oneself up'. They could, if necessary, live on the jungle, eating bamboo shoots, 'what the monkeys ate', rats, snakes and lizards cooked with pepper. But these were for emergency, although one which was to come sooner than they had planned.

They had come up from the Chindwin, carrying 50lb packs with rice, beans, canned fish, biscuit, as well as ammunition. The rations to get 15 Division to 'Mission', where they cut the Kohima-Imphal road, were intended to last ten days, over a journey of some 300 kms in the mountains with little rest or sleep. Thereafter they were supposed to live off British dumps and warehouses, organized by their Battalion Supply Officers ('Supply Colonels') whose duty was to supply and cook food for 1,000 men each. The main items of diet were rice cakes – two pieces per man pressed by hand – salt, and pork when available. The cookhouses were usually on reverse slopes near Battalion HQ.

No rice was to be delivered to the Division from the rear. It was fortunate, therefore, that the Japanese discovered sacks of rice and salt, enough for two years' consumption, at the foot of Treasury Hill. One of 58 Regiment's Supply Officers worked through the night to collect as much as possible, in fact three months' stocks for one battalion. But the British bombed the store next day. The rest was destroyed before supplies could be decentralized, and other battalions had no alternative sources.

Pork from the pig collection area 10 kms from Kohima had to be brought into the battle area on stretchers returning from the dressing stations. About a third of the cattle – beef-on-the-hoof – had died or been killed on the march from the Chindwin. There was malaria, dysentery, much beri-beri, possibly from polished rice or lack of vitamins. There was little quinine and, if malaria and dysentery struck together, death followed in three days. Some supplies were captured at Sangshak, but none at Kangpokpi (Mission): the men were starting to eat mules.

The journey through the Naga Hills, however heroic, and subsequent fighting in the rains, caused equipment to become mouldy and fall to pieces. Leeches were a scourge, tropical ulcers proliferated, the animals sank in the mud and died, weapons had to be transported by hand, the monsoon reduced air support even further, the lines of communication were cut.

The entry in the diary of one Japanese regimental commander would, by late April, not have been ratified with enthusiasm. 'The enemy is defending her national frontiers with full force, but it is useless to defend it against the Son of Heaven. For deep in the souls of the warriors of the Rising Sun is the peerless spirit of Yamoto Damashi', The Spirit of Japan.

And southwards near Imphal, the Japanese (15 and 33 Division) were, for the first time, failing to destroy equivalent British units such as 17 and 20 Divisions, while demonstrating strategic error and all the signs of weakness and eventual defeat. Here, and under Wingate's Chindits, the British were showing skill and courage to match that of the enemy. Above all, at Kohima an entire Japanese Division had lost momentum, *held* for sixteen days by about 800 British and Indian fighting men. Our generalship, too, was becoming as formidable to the Japanese Divisional

Commanders, Sato, Yamauchi and Yanagida, as their own Army Commander's was suspect.

Yet, by preference in multiple bunkers rather than in the open, 'the warriors of the Rising Sun' defied their enemy and fought on with stubborn valour. The relations of mistrust and dislike between their Army and Divisional Commanders do not seem to have adversely affected their morale or fighting spirit.

In the 1930s Mutaguchi and Sato were respectively members of the Imperial Way and Control Factions, both dedicated to the overthrow of Parliament, the Imperial Way more willing to adopt such means as assassination and with a loathing of the Soviets. Sato himself, incidentally, had fought against the Russians. Mutaguchi's misty and self-serving ambitions were known and repellent to Sato who rejected the Army Commander's wish that 31 Division should advance to Dimapur, as did Kawabe. XV Army's promise of ten tons of food a day after leaving Homine and 250 tons by 31 March was not fulfilled. The rations carried from the Chindwin were soon exhausted and, although foraging helped 58 Regiment and 138 Regiment, 124 Regiment and Divisional HQ were in a bad way.

As for ammunition, the Japanese mountain guns of which there were seventeen, were allotted 180 shells each. By the end of May they had no more to fire at a time when the British not only had air superiority but had used 11,500 artillery rounds in two days, against six a day for each Japanese piece.

Mutaguchi was aware that Sato had not completed the capture of Kohima, but regarded that as merely a question of time. In the meanwhile, he sought a contribution from 31 Division on the Imphal front. Ordering Sato to 'take Kohima by 29 April', on 17 April he required him to send a Brigade group to the aid of 15 Division on the north side of the Imphal perimeter. The forces were infantry (138 and 124), and one mountain artillery battalion (31), all to be commanded by Miyazaki who was at that moment in charge of a raging battle on the Ridge.

Sato accordingly 'instructed' Miyazaki to concentrate these units on the Aradura Spur, but it is unclear whether he ever had any intention of obeying Mutaguchi's order. Simultaneously, he ordered the continued deployment of most of 138 on the Cheswema-Merema Ridge, of 58 on Garrison Hill and of a Battalion of 124 in Naga Village as well as that on Aradura. On 19 April Sato stalled by asking for transport for the reinforcements to Imphal. He was told to use captured British lorries. Among his other objections to the Army Commander's proposal was his certainty that troops would be inadequately supplied by the staff of XV Army, regarded by him as incompetent and indifferent to the men's needs. Fighting and constant scavenging for food to keep alive were to him incompatible. On 20 April a copy of the Army Commander's order to Sato was captured on the Imphal plain. On that day or the next, the subaltern Carbonell of the Royal Cameron Highlanders shot dead a sergeant-major on a bicycle near Merema who was carrying another copy. Commander XIV Army's consequent orders that maximum pressure on Kohima should be exercised to ensure that Sato could not comply with Mutaguchi's orders had the ironic effect of meeting Sato's personal wishes, as well as contributing to the survival of Imphal.

Generals Slim and Stopford, until the arrival in May of 7 Division under Messervy with Loftus-Tottenham's 33 Brigade, chiefly depended on Major-General John Grover's 2nd British Division. The three Brigades of this Division were the 4th under Willie Goschen of the Grenadier Guards, with battalions of the Royal Scots (McKenzie-Kennedy), Royal Norfolks (Robert Scott), Lancashire Fusiliers (Billy West); 5th under Victor Hawkins, with the Worcesters (Jack Stocker, then Irvine), Dorsets (McNaught, later Geoffrey White), and Camerons (Peter Saunders); 6th under J. D. Shapland with Royal Welch Fusiliers (Lt-Col Braithwaite, later Stocker), Royal Berkshires (Wilbur Bickford) and the Durham Light Infantry (H. I. Brown).

Even these, like the Queen's Royal Regiment, 4/15 Punjabis and 4/1 Gurkhas of 33 Brigade who had learned in the Arakan to respect the Japanese and to understand and fear the climate and the ground, would not have predicted the events of the weeks ahead. A sick, half-starved and under-equipped enemy on the defensive proved as hard to defeat as that same military race in health and strength on arrogant offensive, at least until the May breakthrough when Sato finally admitted the impossibility of holding Kohima.

Slim did not like but did respect the Japanese. He believed that, even in the last terrible days of their retreat, no Army could have excelled their conduct. He went so far, in an address in Tokyo, as to say that in any future conflict in which Japan was not the aggressor, he would prefer to have them on 'his side' rather than against him.

XXI

THE RIDGE

WE HAVE seen that Second British Division (2 Div) arrived in India in April, 1942. It then underwent lengthy training in combined operations, until it became plain that seaborne resources were almost monopolised by the European Theatre. The Division was about to disperse on leave when in mid-March, 1944, it was ordered to make for the Burma Front under XXXIII Corps and XIV Army.

During the operations that followed, circumstances produced in this Division an almost unparalleled intensity of camaraderie between its individuals, battalions and brigades. The men, so long 'idle', now confronting their first chance of battle – for they had all, Regulars, Territorials and Hostilities Only, joined to *fight* – had a sharp sense of attack in their spirit, as well as considerable interdependence. They were united by hatred of an enemy whom, nevertheless, they neither knew nor understood, in a war that lacked cause, certainly not the cause 'Empire' or of Burma. It was a 'clean, pure war' in the sense that civilians (except the Nagas, their allies) were not involved, in a piece of territory that was as emotionally meaningless to them as it was to the Japanese. Above all, the British were joined by an unanimous desire to go home, symbolized in the ubiquitous phrase 'Repat' or 'Repatriation'.

Besides these attributes, the divisive factors, social and geographic, had minor significance, no greater in kind than differences in the Japanese Army between men from Honshu and Hokkaido, although the 'Regulars, Territorial, Hostilities Only' syndrome was perhaps more marked, because more 'fixed', in 2 Div.

Soldiers must revere their General. John Grover, sometimes known as 'Blackjack', was exacting, demanding, but their 'father', acquiring every man's personal allegiance, even devotion, binding them in fellowship by close contact and discipline. (As Colonel of the King's Shropshire Light Infantry after the war, he knew every detail of the lives of the officers of that Regiment.) This relationship was unique, because the Division had been preserved in over two years together without great casualties or even changes in the cultural and social make-up of its Regiments, in aspic as it were. Now that it is all over, 2 Div, while explaining that theirs was a private soldiers' war, almost a mediaeval campaign, admit that they were not as good soldiers as the Japanese in defence, where the latter were incomparable, but less rigid and stupid than the Japanese in attack and commanding a courage which enabled them to go on and on. And, as time went by, they learned the secrets of reverse slopes, of getting above the enemy; they lost their innocence, and learned technique to add to their own bravery.

Love of country, unimaginable adversity, distaste for enemy and battlefield, distance from home plus character, training and leadership produced not just a victorious Army but, even today, groups of men who, at their reunions, manifest a heart-breaking regard for each other and for the values which kept them upright for so long.

It is sad therefore to have to observe that two weeks of action in France earned the Dorsets, one battalion of the Second Division, 'more medals for bravery than did the months in Assam and Burma. Was this one more manifestation of those at Delhi denigrating 2 Div?' Norman Havers' suggestion in *March On* is supported by Arthur Swinson's *Kohima*.

Before General Grover was replaced on the Kohima/Imphal road, having won the battle, David Wilson of the 8th Argylls, then Brigade Major of 6 Brigade, was with him in his dug-out when Grover received the news by telephone of the death in Naga Village of Ian Thorburn, Brigade Major of 5 Brigade. For about thirty seconds he seemed to have been 'knocked cold', before continuing to talk as if nothing had happened. Ian Thorburn was a Wykehamist, 'the Wykehamist Mafia', but, multiplied by many other deaths, the strain on the Divisional Commander may have been greater than anyone realized at the time. And it may be that his Great War, direct, confrontational methods were in part behind Slim's comment that 'the Second Division was *too* damned brave.'

He was held in the highest regard by the Division whose resentment, even disgust, at his removal from the battle was expressed to the highest level. Whether or not as a result, he was honoured with a CB very quickly indeed. His ADC, later Sir Gilbert Longden MP, has described him as an officer whose first consideration was invariably the morale of the men under his command.

Grover was succeeded by Major-General Cam Nicholson, a first-class officer who, nevertheless, lacked Grover's personal appeal to his battered but rusé men. In Nicholson's presence, Archie Wavell, then Viceroy of India, presented at Maram the Immediate Awards for Kohima. Wavell had commanded both 6 Brigade and the Division at Aldershot, and 6 Brigade mounted the Guard of Honour on this occasion, with the same three Battalions – Royal Berkshires, Royal Welch Fusiliers and Durham Light Infantry – as he had had under his command ten years before.

The Field Marshal was an extremely taciturn man. He said that he would make no exaggeratedly laudatory remarks: the troops had done well, but that was only what he expected from his old Division. The Japanese were beaten, they would surrender, and 'we would all go home'. A lot had changed in Britain; it was not the same as it had been in 1939. The Division might wonder what they had been fighting for. Peace would be hard; it would need training and discipline.

The men looked as if they had come out of a cold shower. They wouldn't have taken it from anyone other than a member of the Second Division family, and they knew that Wavell would never 'flannel' them.

General Mutaguchi was at odds with Sato, as he was with both his other Divisional Commanders, just as relations between Stopford in XXXIII Corps and Grover at 2nd Division were, though more impersonal, becoming critical. Admiral Mountbatten, the Supreme Allied Commander South East Asia (SACSEA), was under military and political pressure to return the aircraft he had 'borrowed' for the move of 5 and 7 Indian Divisions from Arakan to Assam and for the lift to supply IV Corps at Imphal.

This pressure from the Chiefs of Staff became so acute by 1 May that SACSEA was obliged to point out to London and Washington that he had only two options, to keep the aircraft and win the Battle of Imphal, or return them and thereby abandon General Stilwell, the Chinese and the Ledo road, and withdraw both the Chindits and IV Corps. The second alternative would lead to an overwhelming, perhaps total, Allied defeat. In response to a further demand from the Middle East for the return of eighty aircraft, Churchill intervened: 'Let nothing go from the battle that you need for victory. I will not accept denial of this from any quarter.' It is for this tenacity, and for his brilliance as a 'co-ordinator', that Lord Mountbatten should be remembered.

In the meanwhile he urged on Slim, who drove Stopford, who harried the deliberate but professional Grover to a speed that that officer rightly could not always approve. Grover, nevertheless, was not himself unaffected by the urgency of his superiors, advising courses which his Brigade Commanders sometimes considered premature, even unwise and wasteful. Much as he was admired by his men, the sobriquet 'Butcher' Grover was heard more than once. At the same time, Generalissimo Chiang Kai Shek and Washington made known that they also believed that the British were moving too slowly, with too great a dependence on the borrowed aircraft and not enough on reopening the Kohima-Imphal road. On 20 April the Army Commander himself advised General Stopford that 2 Div's plans were 'too methodical', an assessment doubtless strengthened by Mutaguchi's captured order to General Sato and the imperative need to prevent the latter reinforcing the northern Imphal front from 31 Division at Kohima.

Uninformed critics, or rather those only familiar with the deserts of North Africa and the plains of Central Europe, could not imagine the drenching monsoons, the wet heat, the jungles and mountains of Burma where, as David Rooney remarks in *Burma Victory*, 'terrain dictated attacks by platoon or company, rarely by an entire battalion, let alone a division. Critics of Second Division were slow to learn the lesson that in the hills of Nagaland, one depleted battalion – The Royal West Kents – had been able to hold up an entire Japanese division.' Stopford was under the further misapprehension that 2 Div confronted only five battalions, not the nine actually in the field.

Grover, nevertheless, since he commanded a division, had a divisional or at least a co-ordinated plan for the capture of Kohima and the opening of the road to Imphal by his three Brigades.

4 Brigade under Willie Goschen (Royal Scots, Royal Norfolk, and Lancashire Fusiliers when they were not detached to 5 Brigade) were to move in a great sweep from Jotsoma south-west through Khonoma (once the stronghold of Anglophobe Nagas, won over by Pawsey), to Mount Pulebadze. They would then occupy Aradura Spur to the east close to the Imphal road, held by 124 Regiment under Miyazaki.

5 Brigade under Victor Hawkins (Camerons, Dorsets and Worcesters) were to make a left hook from Zubza via Merema at 138 Regiment and Sato's HQ at Naga Village; to open the road to Kohima, contact 161 Brigade and, with Warren, take Kohima.

6 Brigade under J. D. Shapland (Berkshires, Royal Welch Fusiliers, Durham Light Infantry) were to attack the DC's Bungalow and Supply Hill with artillery, mortar and tank support.

With the arrival in Assam from Arakan of General Messervy's 7th Indian Division, 33 Brigade under Loftus-Tottenham (1st Queens, 4/15 Punjab and 4/1 Gurkhas, the latter already on Congress Hill under 161 Brigade), would come forward on 5 May under Messervy's command and, to Grover's relief, the battle would become two-divisional. Messervy, incidentally, had not only been captured by the Germans in the Western Desert and escaped, but had been sacked as a Divisional Commander by the Commander of 8th Army, then Ritchie.

By no means all these plans became actual or remained unaltered. As an indication of the unreality even at 2 Div HQ, Grover's first programme – considered too *slow* by Stopford – envisaged clearance of the Bungalow area by 24 April, of Supply Hill two days later and the 'first part' of Garrison Relief on 27 April, 'before starting major operations'.

In the 6 Brigade area, the Berkshires on 21 April, amid the squalor of Summer House Hill, found things little better than they had been under Richards and Laverty. But there lacked at first the unremitting Japanese offensives which the Royal West Kents and their comrades had had to endure. The first part of Grover's instructions (DC's Bungalow) was tried on 23 April by a platoon of 'C' Company of the Royal Berkshires with support from 149 Royal Armoured Corps one of whose Grant/Lee tanks was supposed to get up a drive to the Bungalow. The road was blocked, the drive was too steep and, unfortunately, the artillery support landed among the AFVs without, however, causing serious damage. The armour and the infantry succeeded in blasting several bunkers – all the Japanese in four of the bunkers were killed – but not the main bunker. They withdrew for the time being.

The drive, incidentally, was built by the Nagas for Charles Pawsey at his own expense, but even a private car could not manage it without backing and filling. A great deal of time and thought was devoted in the coming days to finding a method of driving a tank into a position where it could dominate poor Mr Pawsey's now ruined residence and garden.

The Royal Welch Fusiliers under Braithwaite were unsuccessful that day in taking high ground to the right of the road from Jotsoma. In Kohima itself, seven hundred feet above the road, the Berkshires held the perimeter to the north and east and the Durhams to the south and west. Most supplies continued to be flown in, at least of food and water. Water was still rationed to half a bottle, two pints for tea. Shaving and washing were forbidden. Some supplies were humped up, with effort, from the Dimapur road.

On the same night as the attack on the bungalow, a heavy Japanese mortar and spring-grenade bombardment preceded an attack by fifteen Japanese who entered the perimeter and whose snipers killed and wounded men of the Berkshires before being wiped out by 1 Platoon. At least one hundred Japanese were killed by 'B' Company when they attacked up the cliff from the road on scaling ladders. As they appeared on the ladders they were eliminated. None escaped from the Berkshires' fire. ('A' Company faced Kuki Piquet and 'D' was in reserve behind 'A'.)

The Royal Welch Fusiliers had not been heavily engaged since their heavy casualties in Arakan, except during the enemy over-run of 9 Platoon 'A' Company on 16 April, reversed by Lieutenant Callaghan's counter-attack. After an artillery shoot in the Jotsoma area, however, the Battalion lost twelve killed and forty-seven wounded, with seventy sick by the time it relieved the Durhams on 29 April.

On 22 April the DLI were dispersed in open holes. Privates Battle and Daglish were killed by 75 mm shells. The Durhams were to attack Kuki Piquet on 23 April. Their positions were connected by crawl trenches. Eyes got tired, ears cocked for the click of the Japanese spring-grenade dischargers. 'D' Company, under Major 'Tank' Waterhouse, had gone forward the previous day under a smoke screen, followed at various levels on Garrison Hill by 'A'. 'B' and 'C' Companies. The night was moonless, the parachutes in the branches, swayed by the breeze, looked like ectoplasm or cartoon ghosts. Waterhouse, asleep at one o'clock in the morning, thought that a Japanese mortar and grenade assault at that time was not, in the naval phrase, his part of ship. He went back to sleep again. But the Japanese attack from Kuki Piquet, directed at a platoon of 'C' Company, became extremely aggressive with considerable losses in killed and wounded among the Durham's light machine-gunners and other infantrymen.

A complete battalion of 138 Regiment 'came up the slope, shouting "Banzai", shoulder-to-shoulder, with those in front wearing gas-masks and throwing phosphorous grenades.' As they fell to the platoon's automatics, they were almost instantly replaced. At 3.30 am they broke through the Dorsets' 'C' Company. Elsewhere on the hill, an ammunition dump exploded. 'The place looked like Blackpool on a summer night, plus a firework display.' A food store was on fire and even the pine trees were ablaze. The battlefield seemed to be flaming, with a hideous din from exploding shells, projectiles, Japanese yelling, the thud and crackle of weapons, the bursting of bully-beef cans. All the DLI Battalion's communications had gone. The gunner on the OP was dead. No defensive fire could be called down for some hours.

'C' and 'D' Companies formed a defensive line and, themselves now shoulder to shoulder under heavy and damaging grenade assault, held the Japanese waves, although losing men fast. There was no reserve, but at 4 am they counter-attacked. Waterhouse's second-in-command, Willie Lockhart, was killed. Bill Watson of 'D' Company was last seen before his own death clubbing Japanese with the butt of a Bren gun. A bullet broke Lieutenant Pat Rome's arm, which he then hung in a rifle sling, just after he had rescued a blinded Corporal named Worthy. One of the batmen, 'Snowball', had both his legs broken. An infantryman, Private Edwards, hit in the stomach, died slowly, crying and cursing in agony beside Pat Rome. Major Roger Stock, commanding 'C' Company, after talking to Waterhouse about their next leave in Teesdale, was never seen again. A Bren gunner had his hair parted by an LMG bullet. He said, 'My God, I've got a bloody headache.'

At 5 am the DLI Battalion Commander, Colonel John Brown, launched 1 Platoon of 'A' Company under Sean Kelly with fixed bayonets into battle. Many of the bodies, friend or foe, which littered that grisly landscape had been carbonized by the flames from the ammunition dump, lying on top of one another without distinction of rank or race. The platoon attacked with grenades as well as rifles to clear the enemy out of the original trenches, Corporal Arthur Breden's section using stens. Captain Kelly and Breden 'bowled' grenades into a Japanese bunker. A Scottish Bren gunner called McLellan got his backside jammed in a foxhole and had to be extracted.

The platoon, despite serious wounds to Breden's legs, reoccupied the trenches. Breden was wounded again in the chest and shoulder, but continued to direct his section sitting down until a mortar burst killed him. Kelly was also wounded. The second platoon, under Peter Stockton, almost instantly killed with his batman George Mathers, his Sergeant and two section commanders, was wiped out by automatic fire from Kuki Piquet while mounting a gallant daylight attack on Japanese trenches.

Sniping, during work on improvements to the dug-outs, now took a further toll. 'It was difficult to stop the snipers,' said Captain Kelly. 'But the stretcher-bearers, particularly Lance-Corporals Spencer and Stokell, worked without ceasing from 3 am. What cold-blooded courage! If ever there were heroes . . . It's nothing to charge in cold blood, but to kneel and do your job where a man has just been hit and where you must be hit too, if another comes, is the bravest thing I know.'

Only four officers were left from the fifteen in 'A', 'C' and 'D' Companies. Only sixty men survived from the original 136 in 'A'. Pioneer and carrier companies also lost many killed and wounded. The difficulties in evacuating wounded to the road were acute. Colonel Theobalds, formerly Oxfordshire and Buckinghamshire Light Infantry, the Garrison Commander, killed with his own weapon a section of Japanese whom he had found digging-in only five yards from his dug-out. Elsewhere, a little Japanese lay on the ground crying 'Tojo, Tojo': A DLI sten jammed and they finished him off with a rifle. 'It made one think of shooting rats.'

138 Regiment renewed their assault on 27 April, this time against a platoon of 'A' Company with similar massed tactics to those employed four days before against 'C'. The two Japanese infantry companies conquered by weight of numbers and extensive use of grenades. The Durhams' 'A' Company platoon was overrun by Captain Watazi's Battalion of 138. On the summit the enemy celebrated the Prime Minister's birthday with shouts of 'Tojo'; a dawn attack next day by the Battle Patrol led by Francis Grenfell blowing a hunting horn, and by Tony Shuttle's composite force, drove them off it. Although the enemy escaped under smoke, the DLI had temporarily recaptured the position. They were relieved, again under smoke, for forty-eight hours on 29 April by the Royal Welch Fusiliers. Before leaving they established a cemetery which they called 'New Gateshead'.

The splendid Welshmen found the circumstances unattractive, strewn with debris, tins, ammunition boxes, discarded equipment, cartridge cases. Dug-outs, latrines, cook-houses and graves were hugga-mugga.

Digging usually uncovered either a latrine, or bodies, or a grave. Rotting Japanese bodies themselves formed, in some slit trenches, the protective parapets. Men could only move through muddy, shallow communication trenches. The smell was nauseating.

Two Curtiss Commandos dropped water and rations to the Royal Welch Fusiliers in a reasonably accurate parachute drop through thick mist and also through an artillery, mortar, machine-gun, grenade and phosphorus shell barrage against Garrison Hill. The parachutes were of various colours and often hung up in the trees, to be shot down through the cords or by breaking the branches. They had other uses, being as warm as a blanket, soft as a mattress, and provided admirable insulation for the doors, walls and roofs of dug-outs.

On 24 April the Japanese had blown up two fixed weapon pits in the Berkshire area and, in a fierce battle, captured the final bay in a long trench system on Garrison Hill.

Two days later the Dorsets, under Lieutenant-Colonel Jock McNaught, were ordered to take two companies to the 'sniper-infested sides' of Garrison Hill as reinforcements, but also in order to pass a troop of medium tanks through to 5 Brigade. To do so, it was essential to control the Deputy Commissioner's Bungalow which dominated the road junction up which the tanks must pass. As we have seen, the Bungalow which had been held by the Japanese since early April, was on a spur of four terraces, each separated by a steep bank between two and forty feet high. At the top was the Club Square with a small mound to the south, the tennis court ten feet below that, bounded by a large iron water tank and the servants' quarters. Forty feet below, on the lowest terrace, were the ruins of the Bungalow gardens. The fall from the Club to the road was about 100 feet and very steep. Nothing whatever, as has been said, could be seen from any one terrace to that below. It was not until early May that an Assam Rifles officer pointed out to the Dorsets that the tennis court was where it was, and not on the top terrace or Club Square.

On April 26 the Royal Berkshires were to clear Club Square and the Mound, 'C' Company of the Dorsets to deal with the tennis court or 'centre terrace' as it was then known, and 'A' to establish itself above the road junction. At 3 am 'A' Company's attack under John Bowles had 'set off' the interrelated Japanese strong-points. Hand-to-hand fighting with the bayonet began. Lieutenant Jock Murrill's platoon commanded the road junction, and a section 'mopped up' some Japanese dug into bunkers on the side of the road. Two other platoons took the Bungalow, but had to withdraw under heavy fire from the bank below the tennis court. John Bowles and the rest of 'A' hung on beyond the bungalow by

1. Kohima : Garrison Hill in foreground with hospital on lower slopes, looking toward Treasury Hill (right middle distance) and Naga Village on skyline left.

2. Kohima : 1.Deputy Commissioner's Bungalow & Tennis Court. 2.Garrison Hill. 3.Kuki Piquet. 4.F.S.D. (Field Supply Depot) 5. D.I.S. (Detail Issue Section) 6.Jail Hill. 7.Road to Imphal. 8.'Pimple' 9.'Congress Hill'. 10.G.P.T. (General Purposes Transport) 11.Norfolk Ridge. 12.Rifle Range. 13.Two Tree Hill. 14.Jotsoma Track. 15. Pulebadze Peak. (7532ft.) 16.South end of the Pulebadze Ridge. 17. Top End of the Aradura Spur. 18.Japvo Peak. (9890ft.)

3. A section of the Garrison Hill battlefield.
4. Jail Hill, where the Japanese held out for several days.

5. The Naga Village battlefield.
6. The main street at Kohima after the battle.

7. Kohima: trenches on D.I.S. Ridge looking towards DC's bungalow. In the right distance is Kohima Town and beginning of Naga Village.

8. 2nd Division reinforcements moving up the Dimapur Road to Kohima.

9. Gunners of the 2nd Division manhandling a gun on the road down to Imphal from Kohima.

10. The Supreme Commander congratulates Jemadar Asghar Ali, MC.
11. Remains of the DC's bungalow taken from the tennis court area.

12. Padre Randolph (see p.72) and Sir Charles Pawsey (see p.28) with men of the Royal West Kents and the Assam Regiment at 161 Brigade Memorial bearing the words: "At Kohima in April 1944, the Japanese invasion of India was halted."

13. The Kohima War Cemetery : the tennis court is seen below and to the left of the white cross.

14. The 2nd Division War Memorial.

the road junction, thirty yards below the Japanese on the terrace above them.

'C' Company had lost a number of officers and men killed and wounded. Next day it destroyed a bunker on the tennis court and took out a Japanese sniper position. The Company was reorganized, after the death of its commander, Dick Castle, by Captain Michael Morice on Club Square and the Mound, together with the Berkshires who had cleared the Japanese off the Mound but had not penetrated the Club building. Japanese grenade-dischargers inflicted seventeen casualties on the Berkshires, who, with the Dorsets, were now facing the enemy at a range of only fifteen yards.

Notwithstanding, the main object of this action, to pass through to 5 Brigade the Lees and Stuarts of 149 RAC and 45 Cavalry[1], had been achieved, thanks in particular to the endurance of 'A' Company of the Dorsets. The tanks will be seen in the next chapter, which describes the advance of 5 Brigade, the Camerons, Worcesters and Lancashire Fusiliers to Naga Village. A Japanese 'banzai' attack on the summit of Garrison Hill was driven off and an attack endured from three-inch mortars dropped earlier in error by the RAF to the Japanese. Next day was spent in constructing head cover and in the Dorsets' second unsuccessful attempt to get a tank up the DC's drive, this time assisted by Colonel John Garwood, the CRE. On this occasion the tank was towed by a bulldozer driven by a Sapper who momentarily left his vehicle. The tank went into reverse and pulled the bulldozer back on top of it, both crashing down the slope.

A Dorset officer, who then visited Garrison Hill for the first time, said, 'Heavy fighting had taken place on these slopes for nearly a month. So close had been, and still was, the fighting, and so heavy the sniping, that it had been impossible to collect the dead . . . after a banzai attack, the Japanese dead lay where they had fallen . . . Not forty yards from the Club Square were piled high the bodies of about one hundred and fifty of the enemy who had perished in a suicidal attack against the Berkshires . . . Our first greeting was from the outstretched arm of a long-dead Jap slaughtered in an attempt to get in amongst the wounded in the Garrison Dressing Station.'

At midnight on 28 April, three companies from Colonel Fukunaga's 58th Regiment infiltrated onto Summer House Hill where close, brutal and confused hand-to-hand fighting with generous use of grenades and bayonets took place between 58 Regiment and the Berkshires. The Regimental Aid Post was saved by the Berkshires' Doctor himself, but all the men in one Company HQ had been wounded by 28 April except for the signaller and the Company Commander. The telephone exchange was knocked out by artillery and mortar. The casualties were extremely severe – eleven officers and two hundred other ranks in this battalion since they had relieved the Royal West Kent – but the Japanese also suffered badly, losing ninety to the Berkshires alone. There were very few of them left, either there or in the Durhams' area.

HQ, 'A' and 'B' Companies of the Berkshires were relieved on 30 April. They returned to Piquet Hill, as distinct from Kuki Piquet, where they could shave and have hot baths for the first time in ten days. They had not had their boots off for twenty days. A detailed account of the action involving the Dorsets and Berkshires is at Appendix B.

In the first three days of these actions 6 Brigade lost 453 men. Because of the shape of Garrison Hill and the steep gradients towards the main road below, defence posts were mainly sited on forward slopes exposed to the enemy. Few had wire obstacles in front. It was not tank country. No one stirred without being shot at and, whenever they did move, men crouched and ran swiftly from cover to cover. Even so, well trained and sited Japanese snipers took a heavy toll. As the road back to Dimapur remained closed except for the occasional convoy which came in at night, under heavy escort, to deliver supplies and evacuate the wounded, most supplies came by air and, because of the very small DZ, a fair proportion of the parachuted containers continued to fall into Japanese hands. The Japanese also still held the main water supply points, so even water had to be dropped in. It was still rationed to between half a pint and two pints per man per day for all purposes, very little in a hot climate. Shaving was forbidden. Throughout the period no one enjoyed more than two consecutive hours' sleep. The give and take of positional warfare continued unabated. By day much gun and mortar shelling was undertaken by both sides and a series of limited attacks were made by and through 'C' Company in the areas of the DC's Bungalow and tennis court. Although casualties were inflicted, the Japanese held out. Every night, one or more of the Royal Berkshires companies were attacked, sometimes twice in the same night. The action was intense, the Japanese advancing in apparently endless waves after gun and mortar bombardment. Sheer numbers enabled the Japanese sometimes to penetrate the battalion position, but by mounting quick counter-attacks and with some fierce hand-to-hand fighting, they were always repelled before they could cause too much damage.

As for the enemy, seven Japanese companies had taken part in the two operations against the DLI, the Berkshires and the Dorsets. Four companies were destroyed, including two under Major Shimanoe of III Battalion. No advance had been made or ground gained against Summer House. These losses had a decisive effect on Sato's eventual response to General Mutaguchi's requirement for the despatch of 31 Division's reinforcements to Imphal. For the time being, Sato only ordered that night assaults be abandoned. 'We're losing so many troops this way, before long we'll be too thin on the ground to achieve anything,' he remarked to General Miyazaki. All three Regiments, 58, 124 and 138, which had accomplished such wonders in the epic march from the Chindwin through the Naga and Somra Hills, were now savagely diminished. No supplies or reinforcements were in view. Arthur Swinson in *Kohima* drew attention to the reduction of the Japanese offensive after 23 April, the date of the Durhams' action, in favour of defence, and to the ending at Imphal of 15 Division attacks. He concluded that Mutaguchi must have been awaiting reinforcements from 31 Division for Miyazaki.

58 Regiment of 31 Division was the Japanese regiment most seriously involved in battle.

I Battalion of 58 Regiment under Morimoto left Maram on April 4, reaching Pulomi on 6 April. They were not in W/T contact with Miyazaki's HQ and, thereafter, continually but unsuccessfully attacked Jotsoma. On 7 May the battalion moved to Miyazaki's HQ when 2 and 4 Companies rejoined the battalion where all remained until 13 May before withdrawing to Garage Spur and Cuckoo Spur. Here they held the line until 3 June.

II Battalion 58 Regiment seized Aradura on 5 April, and DIS – where the commander, Major Nagaya, was killed – on 6 April. From then on, supported by 2 Mountain Artillery Battery, they attacked Garrison Hill without success until the end of April. The Ariga unit (I Battalion, 138 Regiment, under Colonel Fukunaga) was with them from 22 April to end May. Together they held a defensive position under Miyazaki, who had no reserves, on Pimple Hill until 13 May, when Miyazaki withdrew to Mile 50, Fukunaga with one battalion moving to Mile 49, with II/58 on Big Tree Hill. 11/58 and I/38 were under Fukunaga's command from 14 May to 3 June, Fukunaga and I/124 coming under Miyazaki's overall control.

III/58 under Shimanoe left Mao on 4 April, occupied Naga Village in the morning of 5 April and, because Major-General Miyazaki thought it had already taken Garrison Hill, was despatched to Cheswema on 6 April.

'The most serious mistake of my life,' said Miyazaki after recalling them. They returned to Kohima as I/138 arrived, when unco-ordinated attacks were made against Garrison and Jail. Had they not left for Cheswema, they might *really* have seized Garrison and won the Kohima battle. I/138 returned to the Regiment on 10 April. III/58, with 10 Coy/124, went on attacking until April 15. III/58 withdrew south of Naga Village on 14 May, transferring from Miyazaki's command to that of

Colonel Shiraishi, commanding Central Defence Unit, and retiring to Kharasom on 31 May.

124 Regiment, for their part, under Miyamoto reached Chakabama about 10 April, went to Cheswema on 13 April and was sent to Aradura (less 3 Battalion, 1 and 5 Companies to Naga Village) by the night of 23/24 April. From 14 May to 1 June they (I and II Battalions) under Miyazaki's command defended at Aradura, while one battalion was sent to Kigwema on 31 May to cover the Japanese retreat, the main body withdrawing on 1 June.

The Masuda Battalion (II/124) advanced towards Terrace Hill and held there on the east-west line of the hill with 31 Mountain Artillery Battery, withdrawing on 1 June. The Suzuki Battalion, told to help resecure Naga Village on 13 April, later came under Colonel Shiraishi's Central Defence Unit, defending until the end of May when they withdrew to Kozoma, Mao and Ukhrul until 5 June.

Sato's orders to Miyazaki for the reinforcement of 15 Div and Imphal, in response to Mutaguchi's instructions, had included the move of 124 Regiment (less II Battalion, 1 and 2 Companies), I Battalion/138 and 3 Battalion 31 Mountain Artillery Regiment to a sector south-east of Aradura.

The Right Raiding Column, 138 Infantry Regiment (less one battalion), one Mountain Artillery Battery, 1 engineer platoon and medical company were to take up a defensive position on a line Merema-Cheswema-Chechama, and also to harass enemy traffic on the Kohima-Dimapur road. The Left Raiding Column, 31 Infantry Group HQ, 2/31 Mountain Artillery Regiment, and a 58 Infantry battalion, would continue to attack Garrison Hill.

The Centre Defence Unit, HQ of Colonel Shiraishi, 31 Mountain Artillery, III/124 Regiment and an engineer platoon under the 31 Mountain Artillery Regiment would defend Kohima.

The whole move was conditional on the continued security of 31 Division and that, in turn, depended on the Left Column seizing Garrison Hill. When therefore, the Japanese attack on the Hill resulted in the annihilation of four Japanese companies, General Sato soon countermanded his order to Miyazaki, instructing him to remain at Aradura with two battalions of 124 Regiment. I/138 was to cooperate with 58 Regiment under Fukunaga in Kohima proper.

General Mutaguchi was, of course, furious and indeed, if only one regiment had been employed against Kohima with the remainder directed against Imphal, Imphal might have been taken. But it was not, and 31 Division's declining state precluded any diversion, particularly as the whole Left Area unit was involved without hope of rations or ammunition.

The 15th Army Commander formally cancelled his order on 29 April, the date of the Emperor's birthday which the Army Commander had planned as the date for the capture of Imphal. General Slim's reaction to the captured Japanese order had been correct. He too, however, had problems, especially with 3.7 and 25 pounder ammunition and with smoke shells, which, according to rumour, were being diverted to the Congress Party for use against the Muslims in India. Whatever the reason, they were not getting through to the Burma front.

Notes

1. 33 Corps armour consisted originally of only five Lees of 150 Regiment, Royal Armoured Corps, commanded by Lieutenant R. H. K. Wait, manned by scratch crews including infantry and artillery troops: the regular crews were manning the Carabineers' reserve tanks at Imphal under the title of 'YL' Squadron. The situation improved on the arrival of 149 Regiment RAC, commanded by a Royal Tank Regiment officer, Lieutenant-Colonel F. W. B. Good, raised from the King's Own Yorkshire Light Infantry. 45 Cavalry Regiment was equipped with Stuarts, patrolling the Corps L of C in order to protect the road to Dimapur, carry supplies and cover the Zubza box. On 14 April, when the Japanese tried to break through with magnetic mines to Wait's harbour, they were twice driven off with severe losses. Later that day the original five tanks smashed in the Japanese bunker on Cameron Piquet, enabling the Camerons to storm it and open the way for the relief of Jotsoma.

   The Second Division Commander, Major-General Grover, sent his personal thanks to Wait as 'largely instrumental in getting 2 Div's troops through to Kohima in time'.

XXII

ADVANCE TO NAGA VILLAGE

VICTOR HAWKINS was a thoughtful soldier who, while warlike and professional, avoided 'unnecessary' casualties among the men he commanded, resembling Montgomery in that regard. He had fought in France with the BEF and was experienced in battle, but believed in the axiom that, although material could be rapidly manufactured, 'it took twenty years to build a good infantryman'. He was fit, tall, energetic, with a passion for physical exercise which his officers occasionally tried to evade.

On 21 April, when the Brigade began its advance towards Merema Ridge, its three Battalions were the Camerons, Worcesters and, on temporary secondment, the 1/8 Lancashire Fusiliers under Willie West presently relieving the Dorsets now on Garrison Hill with Shapland's 6 Brigade.

The Brigade's task was to cross the valley to Merema with little or no artillery support, and without engaging in a major confrontation. 'Infiltration' was to be the method, the objective to cut communications on the Bokajan route between Merema and Kohima, in order to prevent Japanese reinforcement on their right flank, while the rest of 2 Div attacked them from the left. In the event, the Brigade took thirteen hours in single file to traverse a valley not previously crossed by anyone except their guides, straight across the enemy's front, 'in defiance of Staff College doctrine' but actually unavoidable.

The first formations to leave Zubza were 'A' and 'B' Companies of the Camerons led by Major J. R. Somerville and Major W. D. Davidson under the overall command of Major A. J. J. Somerville-M'Alester, later Battalion Commander, who successfully occupied Japanese positions on the ridge from Merema village into the valley. It was then that Lieutenant Arthur Carbonell killed the Japanese bicycle despatch-rider and took the case containing Sato's orders. The Battalion Commander, Peter Saunders, followed with two more companies and on 22 April the Camerons were joined by two companies of Worcesters. The Brigade had been instructed to take a position 1½ miles from Kohima which was, in fact, the (pre-Siege) Army Reinforcement Camp, before moving to the road junction.

The rest of the columns, without the Camerons who had already left, marched off in cold, darkness and rain, taking eight hours to cover two miles, with one still to go. The 5th Field Ambulance was overloaded and the advance kept halting and bunching. At one point the Brigade was strung out in single file along a narrow track where they had to wait for five hours, 'straddling the trunks of trees', until the rain stopped and they could see where they were. It was not until 4 am, delayed by Colonel Bunting's Field Ambulance composed, extraordinarily, of fearless, unarmed conscientious objectors, that Hawkins could get going again with his Worcesters and Lancashire Fusiliers.

Even then, Hawkins' gunman, Private Hill, showed the Brigadier at dawn that there were at one point only ten men behind him, right in front of presumed Japanese trenches, daylight approaching. The Brigade, nevertheless, pressed on through thick jungle and across deep nullahs in the increasing belief that the guides had lost their way. The advance broke into two once more, but continued. A Worcester patrol bumped a Japanese platoon, apparently endangering surprise; but by daybreak on 25 April the Battalion was astride Japanese communications on Ms4 of the Kohima-Merema road, to be joined on 27 April by the Camerons. Peter Saunders, the Camerons' Colonel, had sent a message back that the terrain was too difficult for the purpose, but Hawkins had chosen to ignore it.

Because they would be cut off from Zubza's supplies, troops carried heavier loads than before: spare ammunition, rolls of barbed wire, larger water containers, ladders, ropes and food. In fact, they had eaten the rations before they reached the road. One Lancashire Fusilier, after drinking his first tot of rum, found it so devastatingly powerful that he feared he had been poisoned. It was not an easy journey. Corporal McCann of the Lancashire Fusiliers said, 'I looked back across the valley and saw, two miles away, the road we left nine hours ago, and we're not half way up the mountain yet.'

The first airdrop was comfortably achieved on 26 April, providing a degree of relative luxury. Two hundred and twenty Nagas, organized by Eric Lambert of the Indian Police, supplemented this channel, each with a 46 lb ration load on his back, two tins of 23 lbs, reaching Brigade HQ in two hours, not the four promised, with food, ammunition and medicine. But Captain Horton's mules with his Pathans had great difficulty on the slippery hillsides.

The contribution of the Nagas to victory has been recorded. It is worth adding that, as a tribute to their Intelligence activities and the three hundred men they offered as escorts, guides and sharp shooters, John Grover undertook to Lambert that their villages would not be bombarded unless occupied by the Japanese. Without Naga help in the evacuation of wounded British and Indian troops up and down the sodden hills, the death rate among Allied battalions would have been much higher. And thanks to the Nagas and their faith in the British, embodied in the great Charles Pawsey, the Japanese had to dilute their numbers further in foraging, thus weakening a strength already diminished in main battle as well as by Naga ambush.

On 25 April, Colonel Jack Stoker's second-in-command, Major Burrell of the Worcesters, who had led the guides to the rendezvous, was pleased to discover a Japanese officer paying out his men from a canvas chair at a table in the open. Burrell brought his patrol forward and eliminated the platoon and the paymaster with accurate Bren-gun fire, later removing documents, personal papers and cash. He also seized some mules to supplement the four hundred animals already under the Pathan muleteers of Captain Horton, the 'brisk individual with waxed moustaches'. Burrell was also able to secure the object of his patrol, a water point.

Enemy aircraft, for the first time in the Camerons' experience, flew over Zubza on 28 April. Hurribombers from Dimapur, on the other hand, continually attacked Japanese positions in Kohima with 500lb bombs, aided occasionally by Spitfires from Imphal and, later, by Vengeance dive-bombers.

The Lancashire Fusiliers, in defensive positions on arrival, encountered for the first time Japanese snipers tied into trees and suicide charges against wire by Japanese bearing explosives detonated to blow a gap. They met their first Banzai attacks, 'armed, screaming men, an officer in their midst brandishing a long curved sword in one hand and a Japanese flag in the other, concentrating their assault on a small portion of our position. The action was so frenetic that as the enemy's front men fell, others filled their place and continued the momentum until they were so close and intermingled with our men that weapon firing was almost impossible. The noise of guns was replaced by shouts of 'banzai', screams of pain and the moans of dying men.'

After this charge, the Fusiliers' 'A' Company had suffered twenty-four casualties, but had given no ground. There were many more such attacks in spite of the barbed wire, but, although the Japanese sometimes found a loophole and got inside the perimeter, the groups 'made good targets for our Brens, stens and rifles'. But the enemy's 75mm which when dismantled could be carried by mules, and an 'infantry gun' with a range of two miles and an 8-pdr shell caused trouble.

Until the main assault on Point 5120, the objective for Naga Village, patrol action was the principal activity. One Worcester patrol, led by a Lieutenant Phillips of Sherborne, with Sergeant J. J. White of Kidderminster and Corporals Webb and Gee of Bilston and Nuneaton, wiped out an entire Japanese platoon, who were then stripped of their papers and weapons, in a Bren, mortar, sten and rifle attack on enemy bunkers.

Corporal John McCann, a Section Leader, has said that, before reaching the crest of Charlie hill, the First Battalion of the 8th Lancashire Fusiliers deployed and rested while one company went forward to explore the higher ground. They listened for the sound of battle, but none came, so they advanced again, until the whole Battalion was on top of the hill. They did not like this because there was little cover from view, let alone cover from fire, and the sun was getting high. They felt naked, sure that they were being watched by thousands of eyes. It took an hour and a half for each Company to be allocated to the positions it should defend, but they dug in with a will, for they had been exposed too long.

The area allotted for 'C' Company was fully in the open. 'A' Company, who had originally taken up a 'reserve' position in the middle of the perimeter, came forward and started to dig in about twenty yards in front. 'C' Company had been chosen to attack the next hill at dawn on the morrow, and the enemy was known to be there. During the heat of the day they continued to dig, and when the time came for the sun to fade, the holes were deep enough to stand in.

No sooner had it become dark than the Japanese attacked 'A' Company. The latter knew better than to return the fire and thus expose their own positions. The Jap rifle and machine-gun fire was laced with tracer ammunition, and, when fired too high, resembled a good-looking fireworks display. After wasting his ammunition for half an hour, the enemy went away as silently as he had approached.

During the night a patrol led by Basher Bailey, a heavyweight boxer, lay quietly by the roadside at the foot of the hill. Sometime after midnight, Bailey heard the sound of footsteps along the road. The sergeant alerted his men. A marching column, three abreast, emerged from the darkness with one man leading them. For some reason which he could not explain, Basher thought they were British. He rose from his prone position, walked into the road, and peering into the officer's face, asked; 'Which mob are you, Sir?' The slanting eyes of the officer opened wide, but then he received a blow on the chin that lifted him from the ground and landed him in the roadside ditch. Before they could recover from their surprise, a few Bren-gun and sten-gun bursts had been sprayed among the Japs by Sergeant Bailey's men.

At dawn a great hullaballoo again broke out at 'A' Company's position just in front. Grenades exploded, rifles and machine guns cut loose and mortar bombs swished through the air, accompanied by high-pitched shrieking from the enemy. Cries of pain mingled with the other sounds, and, after half an hour, when the sun had begun to shed a little light, everything went quiet. The enemy had withdrawn leaving thirty-five dead bodies, unlike their usual practice. Normally, when an attack was unsuccessful, they would take away their dead in an effort to mislead. 'A' Company's losses were four dead, one missing and ten wounded. During the Jap bayonet charge, they had wounded Sergeant Ditchfield and dragged him down the hill. Thinking him dead, they went through his pockets for information: he flung them off, escaped and was rewounded by a grenade in the back of the leg, but not recaptured.

The next objective lay about a quarter of a mile to the south in the general direction of Kohima and was thickly covered with vegetation. The Battalion had to cross the road to get on to the lower slopes.

Thirteen Platoon, with Lieutenant John Fortune up front, led the way, Number One Section first, then Two, then Three Section. Getting to the foot of the hill, even crossing the road, was uneventful. The twenty men of Number One and Two Sections advanced, just ahead of the ten of Three Section and Company HQ, followed by Fourteen and Fifteen Platoons in fanned-out formation.

Half-way up the hill the men forward said, 'Bunker'. John Fortune told them to press on; 'You know what to do.' McCann took two men and approached the bunker at an angle from which he could see no firing slits. The entrance, a few yards away, was uncovered. This was a good sign, for, had the bunker been occupied, the hole would have been camouflaged. McCann dropped into the hole. It widened and bent like a tunnel. He had already taken the pin from the grenade and now released the spring. After counting three, he threw it round the bend and, in a further two seconds, the underground explosion echoed in the confined space, disturbing nothing but the earthworks. The leading sections approached the crest with extreme caution. When they reached it, it was not flat, but fell away steeply in all directions except the way up which the company had climbed. At an official briefing, they had been told that 30,000 Japs occupied and encircled Kohima, and when they found none holding the summit of this hill they were disconcerted.

John Fortune halted the two leading sections twenty yards beyond the summit, leaving a space between them for Three Section. In just a few seconds they were spaced satisfactorily in the undergrowth, the men about a yard from each other. Short sections of the road wound towards Kohima round the contours of the hill. The hill was itself covered with long grass, ferns, shrubs and a mixture of thin- and thick-trunked trees. From a standing position, one could see another standing figure at twenty yards; prone, visibility was down to nothing. John Fortune sent for Section Leaders and told them to make sure their men had a good field of fire. Everyone's position was adjusted slightly, so that one could see at least a few yards ahead when horizontal.

Then the pressure went off. Some unfastened equipment and took off steel helmets. They relaxed, knowing that in a few minutes they would be working hard with the picks and shovels from behind the hilltop where the remainder of the Battalion was deployed.

Shots rang out. They threw themselves down and peered into the bushes. There was nothing to be seen. A second salvo got one man in the shoulder and another in the wrist. Then a burst of machine-gun fire scattered leaves and twigs from a bush between Fortune and his men. That automatic continued to fire into the position, but the section held its fire. Two men on the left made a bet about which of them would get the first Jap. They spoke without looking at each other, for all eyes were to the front. Harry Judson, the second Bren-gunner, was hit by a rifle bullet that bounced off his wrist, leaving a nine-inch gash. He could not fire his gun and made room for Taffy Hughes, his Number Two on the Bren. Doctor Beckett did a good job on Harry Judson's arm, but Harry would not allow himself to be counted as a casualty and fought on, but was killed by a shell-burst ten days later. Meanwhile Taffy moved quickly behind the automatic, but before he could do more, his head and face became a mass of blood, the first of the Section to be killed.

With Taffy lying a few yards to his left, hatred welled up inside McCann, a feeling no amount of training could have instilled. It came like a big wave; he wasn't a boy any more; he wasn't a soldier in training; he wasn't even a soldier, or a man. He didn't know what he was, but those bastards had to be killed and he would kill as many as he could.

He threw a couple of grenades in the direction of the enemy machine gun. That was answered by a burst of fire that made more ribbons dangle from the little bush. There was a funny feeling at the back of his neck. He flung a hand round, expecting to find blood. It was only a leaf that had come to rest there. Since the first shot was fired no more than five minutes had elapsed, and, apart from a few rifle shots and a dozen grenades, they had held their fire. 'One bullet, one Jap' was the motto, but, as they couldn't see anything to fire at, they were frustrated.

Two men came over the crest of the hill behind him, asking about casualties. They were the stretcher-bearers, Bob Barwick and his mate, Frank Bamford. Instead of weapons, they carried a stretcher. When McCann pointed to where Taffy and Harry Judson lay, he heard them moving towards them. When they reached the spot, Barwick took a number of machine-gun bullets in his chest which finished him straight away, and Bamford fell with a rifle shot in his side.

Now McCann ordered his Section to blaze away into the bushes, and, under cover of this fire, Bill Whitehead, the Platoon Sergeant, miraculously got the dead and wounded back out of the line of enemy fire. Major Pearse, the Company Commander, crawled forward to lie by John Fortune. He carried his steel helmet in his hands. It was full to the brim with hand-grenades. John Fortune said, 'Can I take two men to wipe out this machine gun?' Pearse said a terse, 'No, you can't. You have to defend this line.' The Platoon Commander was clearly disappointed, but he spread the grenades among the men: 'Let 'em have these'. They threw them into the bushes where the enemy lay, and supplemented them with rifle and machine-gun fire.

John Fortune crawled back over the crest of the hill, returning in a few minutes with a bag full of machine-gun magazines and hand-grenades. When these had been distributed among the men, he gave the order to put all fire-power into the bushes for two minutes. They cut loose with all the resources of the Platoon. Thirteen Platoon threw hand-grenades and fired two-inch mortar bombs. The man with the discharger cap fired them from the end of his rifle and the riflemen fired their single shots with great rapidity. Those with automatics poured burst after burst into the bushes, and even the anti-tank gunman shot his large single bullets.

All was deathly quiet. A moment later a Japanese officer rose from the bushes no more than fifteen yards away. He wore a broad red sash across his chest and brandished a long curved sword above his head. He called his men, but before any appeared, he sank slowly from sight with much more red across his chest than his sash. 'That's for Taffy!' the Lancashires shouted.

The machine gun reopened fire, its bursts spraying around the Section, into the earth in front, below and beside. Splintered tree trunks and bushes brought down small branches and leaves that struck steel helmets.

Meanwhile Major Pearse ordered a section of Fifteen Platoon, commanded by Corporal Penkethman, to skirt from behind the crest of the hill and deal with the machine-gun crew and riflemen who were attacking. They were led by their Platoon Commander, Lieutenant Andrew Watson, who looked seventeen. Through gaps in the jungle, one or two heads were seen as they descended the hill. They were going too far down.

Eventually they turned inwards and, instead of surprising the Japanese Company that was lying slightly in front, they came upon the main body towards the foot of the hill. Penky took hold of his section's Bren-gun and knocked off six with his first burst, but was then fired on from a bunker. For the charge on the bunker, Andy Watson took the automatic and killed the occupants. Inside the bunker itself, he pushed the barrel through a firing slit. The small opening looked down on a crowd of Japs talking excitedly and running about with machine guns, rifles and swords.

Watson made the most of the opportunity by pouring bursts into them, at the same time shouting, 'Get a load of this, you bastards. Death from the Lancashire Fusiliers'. His fire was returned by the enemy in bushes near the bunker. He was hit in the left arm by two explosive bullets. He handed over the Bren gun to Penky but, still in charge, organized the move from the bunker, a dash of some ten yards into the nearby bushes. Seven men reached cover, but two were hit and lay in the open. A move to rescue them was aborted by enemy fire-power. Andy Watson, covered in blood with one arm hanging uselessly at an angle, sent a man to Company Headquarters to bring smoke grenades and seek reinforcements.

When the man returned with the grenades, he was accompanied by a party from Fourteen Platoon who had volunteered for the job, including Lieutenant Cameron, a Platoon Commander, and Bill Brazier, Platoon Sergeant. For two minutes all available fire-power was put on the Jap positions, ending with a smoke barrage in the space between them and the British wounded. Lieutenant Cameron and Sergeant Brazier dashed forward and took hold of a pair of arms. At the same moment, the enemy opened fire through the smoke-screen. Lieutenant Cameron got a burst in the backside and Sergeant Brazier was hit in the neck. He died immediately. The enemy fire had finished off the wounded as well. One of them was Tiny Henthorn from Royton.

Meanwhile Three Section's position had not changed. They were still under attack, and, between the bursts of machine-gun fire, heard orders in high-pitched voices and snatches of Jap conversation. Then came new sounds, plop, plop, plop, as discharger grenades flew from rifles, swishing in the air before landing. There was a clamour of voices in the bushes. Two hand-grenades landed, one on each side of McCann. He knocked the one on his right down the hill, where it exploded, but couldn't reach the other. He buried his head in his hands and hoped for the best. The grenade went off and sent up a great cloud of dust and smoke. He hadn't time to wonder whether or not he was wounded because, at that moment, the Jap let out his battle cry. A line rose from the bushes eight yards in front and started to rush forward. The bushes on both sides were alive with charging, shrieking Japs, with bayonets pointed at the Section, rifles firing. Their bullets thudded into the bank and whistled through the air, but the Section couldn't put their heads down.

Small holes began to appear in the Japanese faces. The tunics of the oncoming men ran with red blood. In ones, twos and threes, they crumpled before the Section, the nearest one three yards away. McCann was holding his sten-gun like a vice, but when he tried to relax his hold, his hands wouldn't let go. A thin column of smoke rose from the short barrel. He said some complimentary words to his personal weapon.

Looking along the line of his Section, he saw that Jennings, Gavin, Carter and Meachin were all right: they told him that Simmonds had survived too. The glances they exchanged spoke volumes. John Fortune, lying by his side in the middle of the line of men, was 'like a dog with two tails', but warned him to watch for the next wave.

About six months previously the sten-gun had replaced the Tommy-gun as the personal weapon of Section Commanders, and, on first sight of them, they had been amazed. The construction was in complete contrast to the workmanship and artistry of the Tommy-gun. Their rifles and brens, too, had quality and precision written all over them, but these sten-guns were like bits of old iron welded carelessly together. They needed to use them on the practice range often to gain confidence in them. Now McCann had confidence in his.

That 'bloody Jap machine gun' continued to fire into them. There seemed to be nothing they could do to stop it. John Fortune again asked Major Pearse if the Platoon could go down there, but, once more, was curtly refused. The Company Commander knew that John Fortune was fearless and would think nothing of his own safety. The order for him to stay where he was was very clear.

Although the machine gun was still in action, there seemed to be less rifle fire and there were fewer voices. The Section thought that there might not be another bayonet charge, but who could tell? Then there was shrieking as before from the scrub immediately in front, and they prepared themselves. Nothing happened, so they threw grenades, not to the full distance, but into the area from which the noise had come. There was moaning and movement of vegetation, but no other sign of the enemy.

Then complete silence. The silence continued. The enemy had gone. His last battle cry had been a ruse to take away as many of his dead as possible. Many were left. 'D' Company came over the crest of the hill to take over from 'C' Company, and after McCann had briefed their Corporal, Alf Priestly, they sat in a tight group, talked excitedly, smoked with relief, and gradually allowed the pressure to diminish.

He looked at his watch and found it was ten forty am. The battle had lasted three and a half hours. The remainder of the Battalion had been waiting for 'C' Company to do the job, and now the CO, Lieutenant-Colonel W. H. G. West, ordered the Companies to form a perimeter all round the summit of the hill. Part of the deployment was for 'C' Company to be reallocated the positions they knew so well. The hill became officially documented as 'Charlie Hill' in their honour.

Major Pearse had proved himself as Company Commander, active all the time, encouraging, bringing supplies of ammunition, guiding and instructing. John Fortune was one of the bravest, but would not put his men in jeopardy. He showed that the men of his Thirteen Platoon were very precious to him. Fifteen Platoon could fight, and Fourteen Platoon would come to the rescue when necessary. Thirteen Platoon was more closely knit than ever before, and the men in Number Three Section stood very high in their leader's estimation; no man had flinched.

The Section brewed up whilst the men of the Pioneer Platoon dug shallow graves. What value could one put on a mess-tin full of tea? When the digging of his Section's dug-outs was under way, McCann went over the hill to the line of his dead awaiting burial. Each body was covered by a blanket which he pulled back. Of course he had known them all, but, in particular, dwelt on Tiny Henthorn. He was six feet two inches, taller than the rest. McCann would never see him in Royton again, driving the Co-op butcher's van, or playing water-polo for the Royton team. He came to Taffy. Whatever else happened, he would always remember Taffy Hughes, the first of his men to be killed in action. They had marched hundreds of miles, sharing the load, had swum in rivers together, had sat over char and wads in canteens across Britain and India, laughing, arguing, falling out with each other sometimes. Taffy lived with his mother. His father was dead. He would sometimes read out bits from her letters. Not long ago she had written, 'When you come home, you must bring your pals from Number Three Section to visit us.'

He came to Bob Barwick. There was nothing spectacular about Bob, an ordinary lad, steady, compliant, reliable. He could never before recall seeing him without his glasses. Now they hung by the side of his head, held there by the strap of his steel helmet. Alf Harlow, Company Clerk, described how Bob Barwick died. As he had been lifted on to the stretcher, he tried to say something, but no sound came at first. Then with astonishing clarity, he got it out: 'Don't forget to pick up your empties, lads'. The expression had become a catchphrase, originating on the firing range, where troops had been exhorted to collect the brass cartridge cases at the end of firing. Alf said that Bob then smiled and closed his eyes for the last time.

He looked along the line of bodies. In about a fortnight their folk at home would know. He said a mixture of words, but he didn't know to whom he addressed them. They were blasphemous, obscene, angry, prayerful. Then Father Smyth arrived. He knew the right words. He went along the line, exposing the head and shoulders of each man, and prayed over him. At the end of the line he prayed in more general terms in the form of a little service.

The stretcher-bearers and pioneers could not do their work. Six inches of earth over each body was all that was needed. Later the War Graves people would come to make a proper cemetery. A small wooden cross with each man's particulars lay at the side ready to be placed at the head of each of these shallow graves.

Victor Hawkins commented, 'The Lancashire Fusiliers were not a very lucky Battalion,' and later events, alas, were to demonstrate the truth of this judgement. They were, however, an indomitable one.

XXIII

THE ASSAULT ON
NAGA VILLAGE

5 BRIGADE, consisting of 7 Worcestershire Regiment and 1/8 Lancashire Fusiliers, both TA units, and 1 Camerons, was advancing on
Kohima from the north, clearing the feature known as the Merema Ridge
on the way. There was sufficient armour, but tanks were confined to the
road. Artillery support was limited to the three Assault Field Regiments
RA, the 10th, 16th, and 99th, each comprising 2 × 25-pdr batteries, and
1 battery 3.7 in howitzer. The 3.7 howitzer was designed for mountain
warfare; it broke down into mule loads, but its range was limited and its
shell weighed only 10 lbs. At this stage there was no medium artillery,
apart from two 5.5 in guns which has been found in a railway siding at
Dimapur, with limited ammunition and manned by gunners from 2 Div
artillery. Gun ammunition was in short supply for both 25-pdrs and
3.7in howitzers, and neither was effective against bunker positions; at
one stage, the ammunition for the 3.7s ran out altogether.

The Japanese 31 Div was conducting an offensive defence of its
positions along the Kohima Ridge and, at this stage, had not committed
all its troops. Their artillery support was restricted to one mountain
regiment armed with 75mm guns deployed as single guns at very close
range, against carefully selected targets. Their effect was out of all
proportion to their numbers, since, at such short ranges, no ranging
procedure was required and every round caused casualties. Counter-
battery fire was ineffective, as the guns were dismantled and moved
before retaliatory fire could be brought to bear.

2 Div was therefore being asked to clear a well-entrenched and
stubborn enemy with minimal artillery or armoured support, and with
no preponderance in numbers. Indeed, it is probable that at this stage the
Japanese outnumbered the British in fighting troops in the Kohima area.
Of the Indian Army troops, 161 Brigade (Royal West Kents, 1/1 Punjabis
and 4/7 Rajputs) was in no state for offensive operations, and 33 Brigade
was still committed in the Dimapur area against any possible Japanese
attempt to disrupt the line of communication.

The Worcesters on 28 April mounted an unsuccessful action against
Firs Hill, a feature between 5 Brigade HQ and the main 5 Brigade
objectives of Church Knoll and Hunter's Hill at Point 5120. The road to

Kohima ran below both. Naga Village was built near Point 5120 in the vicinity of Kohima itself, separated therefrom by another valley, while Firs Hill covered the only route to 5120 (which, of course, denotes altitude), dominating Kohima.

The Lancashire Fusiliers then led the second attack against this feature, with increasing opposition from mortars and machine guns, 'B' and 'D' Companies in the lead with 'C' trying to outflank under very heavy fire. The Battalion withdrew temporarily to allow an artillery barrage from Lieutenant-Colonel Harry Grenfell's 10th Field Regiment. After that, however, snipers and mmgs screening the Japanese bunkers prevented the Fusiliers from advancing beyond twenty-five yards of the bunkers at the crest.

Before the advance, 'C' Company Lancashire Fusiliers, under Major Pearse, were still on Charlie Hill about 400 yards west of Firs Hill. When the company advanced at first light, it almost immediately became the target for the 75 mm on Merema. Severe casualties were caused, treated in Captain Mather's dressing station, attended by Father Smyth, 'the first clergyman I ever heard to use bad language, cursing the Jap in soldier-like manner'. Although a forward company eventually silenced them, Japanese machine guns firing on fixed lines at a bend in the road killed and wounded several men in 13 Platoon.

John McCann has written that the projected artillery bombardment of Firs Hill was largely ineffective due to a well-directed Japanese dive-bombing attack on 10 Field Regiment. The whole Battalion deployed in the thick scrub and 'brewed up', taking care that no smoke should escape. The noise of battle increased. 'C' Company was ordered up, first depositing haversacks at the foot of the hill, to find wounded and dead on the slope, particularly officers and NCOs from 'B' Company.

'B', 'C' and 'D' Companies advanced at noon, crashing through the scrub. The enemy opened up at the crest. Men began to stagger and fall. Major Pearse ordered, 'Take cover'. As they did so, 'a cloud of white smoke came towards them making human noises and as he came nearer, the smoke grenades in his pouch continued to ignite each other. As each one exploded, the density of the cloud increased and sparks of phosphorus flew from him . . . In the heart of the billowing smoke, a soldier was on fire. He had to wait until next day before dying.'

A section of 13 Platoon was ordered to take out snipers on the right edge of the hill. En route, they found a dead Fusilier officer with the back of his head shot away. They heard 'high-pitched voices speaking quickly and excitedly'. Japanese grenades rolled down the hill, but as the section could not have made it to the enemy up the steep banking, the platoon commander ordered a withdrawal.

10 Field Regiment artillery now began a high explosive barrage with

hundreds of shells that were eventually landing only about ten yards in front of the positions which the Battalion was methodically vacating. The explosions suddenly stopped, to be replaced by a smoke screen. Major Pearse called, 'Ten, nine, eight . . .' and at 'one' the Battalion charged, the sten-gunners firing in short bursts, the riflemen single shots. The men were still in line. They passed bodies of dead men in the Battalion, one glued together by congealed blood with a Japanese, another in the standing, firing position supported by branches with a jagged hole in his head.

Still they were not fired on, but, at the crest of the hill with the Fusiliers storming through the undergrowth, the Japanese opened up. Two Sergeants were the first to be hit, the first in the thigh, the second stunned by a grenade, then cut by shrapnel, pouring with blood but urging his men forward. After a few more strides, grenades and machine guns from the main enemy bunkers were fired from both flanks across the advance. All then went quiet except for the cries of the wounded and the noise of the retreat.

'C' Company, 'B' and 'D' no longer existed, not even coherent platoons, only a few officers and men escorting small groups or individuals down the hill, pursued by Japanese firing and throwing grenades. 'C' Company, almost dragging its wounded, ran through the Second Manchesters, through the Battle Platoon and the 3″ Mortar Platoon, who, with a well-positioned tank and a few individual Fusiliers, stood fast and gave cover to the fleeing men. The second-in-command by the side of the road produced order out of what had become a rout, directing the men back to the Battalion's position in groups of one officer or NCO and eight men.

Some got lost and finished up behind the lines. Officers and NCOs were disgraced, and Fusiliers suffered field punishment. This was the only battle lost by this gallant and over-tried Battalion in twelve months in the fighting zone.

Colonel West told the Brigadier that the Battalion had lost ten officers killed and wounded and many more other ranks. Although they *might* eventually be able to take Firs Hill, they could not do so that night. The foot of the hill, he said, was screened by Japanese machine gunners who warned their two hundred companions in the valley to the north of impending British activities. These would then move up to the summit where they were not only protected by bunkers, but by 150 yards of thick bamboo immediately covering the top of the hill. Although they had been stopped short only twenty-five yards from their target, the Fusiliers' withdrawal had left the Japanese position intact. On 29 April the Worcesters beat off a Japanese attack on the Brigade Box.

From their original rendezvous position among the bashas of the

Reinforcement Camp, under fire from both Firs Hill and a 75 mm at Merema, the Worcesters and Camerons continued active officer and other patrols to extract information about the Japanese Order of Battle in Kohima, including hours of activity, sleep and so forth. These patrols required courage, agility and clandestine skills. Another unsuccessful attempt was then made by these two Battalions to take Firs Hill. Hawkins could not yet solve the problem of occupying Church Knoll without first capturing the hill. The Cameron patrols under Lieutenant Angus McKay, Peter Cameron and Neil White were invaluable, providing details of tracks and paths which even the Nagas could not describe. At last, Angus McKay 'found a way round the Jap flank'.

On 28 April the 'little' monsoon had broken over Merema and its environs, rains hammering down in endless, unbroken sheets, the land turning to seas of chocolate mud. These conditions, with even heavier downpours, would continue throughout the battle, although back at Zubza 'the shadows come racing across the mountains in never-ending pageant of blues, mauves and deep purples', a rare day of sunshine and blue skies.

On 1 May General Grover instructed that Point 5120, including Church Knoll and Hunter's Hill, was the most important feature of the Japanese defence at Kohima. The Brigade was to try to get on to it and take Naga Village, built around these hills. Hawkins was to produce a plan which would be coordinated with the Divisional Commander's suggestions to be brought by a liaison officer (Major Robertson) on the following day.

The Brigadier, though expecting the order, was not sanguine. The Brigade would again have to pass across the Japanese front, this time right through their lines in the middle of the most important tactical feature of their position. An unpleasant time lay ahead. In considering whether to attempt yet another attack on Firs Hill, he consulted the commanders of 149 RAC and 45 Cavalry who had now reached his position from the Dorsets' area with Lees and other tanks. Their reply was that, without bulldozers, which the Brigade did not have, the armour could not get up the hill. The staff spent most of the day thinking about alternative methods.

When Major Robertson arrived, it was plain that Second Division's suggestions were based on incomplete information. Hawkins' 'bold plan' was therefore reluctantly accepted by 2 Div staff. It carried considerable risk, but Grover was under direct pressure from both Stopford and Slim to take Naga Village. He had faith in Hawkins, and the risks – of attack en route from Firs Hill and ambush on the track to the summit – were, after all, imponderable.

The assault on 5120 would take place on 4 May and would be led by the Camerons, Firs Hill by-passed, the lower slopes picketed by the Worcesters from the bashas to a point where the track to be taken by the Camerons crossed the road to ascend Point 5120. (This was the track discovered by Angus McKay.) As the Japanese tended to sleep between three and five am, and surprise was essential, the Camerons would wear gym shoes and carry nothing except ammunition and essential equipment. They would leave at two in order to cover the two miles to the target on time. Having taken the westernmost hill, they would move on to Church and Hunter's, the latter named *post facto* after Major Colin Hunter of the Camerons. If the Camerons were successful, the 1/8 Lancashire Fusiliers, the Field Ambulance and the small administrative tail would follow in support, the Worcesters behind them. PT shoes were issued, and boots and small packs were sent back to the Brigade base at Zubza where, needless to say, they were looted and everything of value or use abstracted. The Camerons were warned that there would be no artillery support whatsoever, as it was fully stretched in support of 4 and 6 Brigades on the other side of Zubza Nullah. This had dire consequences.

1 Camerons set off about 2359 hours on the night 3/4 May, delayed by a late start by 7 Worcesters. The moon was almost full. There was a thick mist, and dead silence, apart from an occasional burst of harassing fire from 3-in mortars away over on the Kohima Ridge. They were led by Neil White, a brave officer. A fighting patrol killed three Japs en route. By a miracle the enemy were not alerted. Movement was naturally slow, and the delayed start meant that it was getting light as they cleared the jungle and climbed the steep hill up to the Naga Village, slipping and slithering in their PT shoes, soldiers falling with a clatter every now and then, oaths and cries of 'Quiet!'. Eventually, in the grey light of a wet morning, they reached the top. The Naga Village had been bombed flat, and the ground was covered by sheets of corrugated iron from the house roofs. The Nagas' livestock, mainly pigs, lay dead all around. The stench was appalling, but, like Great War soldiers, the Jocks learned to live with it.

The Camerons' new Battalion Commander, 'the Rajah', Lieutenant-Colonel Peter Saunders, was forty-five and had commanded battalions in Syria and the Western Desert. His main interests now, apart from his wife and baby son in India, were sanitation and security, and bird-watching. In the first context, he took a particularly poor view of the use of air-letters from home as lavatory paper and, in the second, he would cry, 'Hark: a golden bulbul,' or whatever bird he identified during O groups and such. He later commanded 4 Brigade, for a week. But the latitude he gave to subordinate commanders was much appreciated by some of them, at least at Company level.

His orders on this occasion were imprecise, especially as he did not differentiate between large and small scale maps, companies thus finding themselves placed in the Bay of Bengal or China. The Battalion was to dig in literally along a contour line, 'D' Company (Colin Hunter) furthest east, 'A' Company to the north, 'B' to the south, 'C' closing up the rear, Battalion HQ rather distant and the HQ platoons acting as infantry. The mortar platoon, under Lieutenant (now Lieutenant-Colonel) David Murray of Lauder, had been on manpack since leaving Zubza: it was split, two sections forward, the remainder carrying the mortars and ammunition coming up with the Lancashire Fusiliers.

By five am the Camerons, in misty moonlight, had taken the western knoll without opposition and were moving on to the two others. By seven am the Fusiliers, covered by the Worcesters in the first stretch but later in full view of Japanese on Treasury Hill, had joined the Camerons without casualties. Up to this point the Battalion had achieved complete surprise, the Japanese asleep or, according to one report, some killed silently with the bayonet. The Lancashire Fusiliers held three sides of the perimeter, the fourth held by the Cameron Companies, 'D' on Hunter's, 'C' on the saddle, 'A' and 'B' in Naga Village up to Church Knoll.

The perimeter, however, was too large for one brigade to handle; at least Victor Hawkins said afterwards that if his formation had had another battalion it would not only have taken Point 5120, but held it. The jungle and the bashas also gave the Japanese exactly the kind of cover they enjoyed, while the saddle itself was open to enemy fire from North Spur and from Gun Spur to the south, including 75 mm.

As it got lighter, it became clear that the Battalion was in a commanding position, looking down along Treasury Ridge to the Kohima position. A few Japanese were moving about on Treasury. The Jocks took shots at them without orders, thus alerting them to the British presence. Thereafter the Japanese began to fight hard with infiltrated snipers and machine guns against the saddle linking Church and Hunter's, in particular against the Camerons' two forward companies. Both Allan Roy's 'C' Company and Colin Hunter's 'D' took severe losses from mortar and machine-gun fire. Hunter, clearing his spectacles of rain, was attacked with the bayonet by two Japanese infantrymen, just after enquiring, 'Are these ours, Sergeant-Major?'

It was also clear that the Battalion was out on a limb. No one was very worried. There was a general feeling that, if they had any sense, the Japs would withdraw. The Camerons still did not really realize what they were up against. As the morning wore on, it became clear that 'D' Company was not having it all its own way. The mortar position selected was on the Kohima side of the Naga Lookout, some hundred or so yards west of Point 5120, the highest point in the Naga Village, and past it came a steady trickle of wounded. The Japanese, from 124 Regiment, until then relatively uncommitted, but initially identified by the Camerons, were infiltrating with great skill up North and Gun Spurs. 'D' Company were having to contract the positions they held as casualties mounted. By midday all three platoon commanders had been killed or wounded, and Angus MacKay, second in command of 'D' Company, was commanding all three platoons as their strength steadily decreased.

About this time Dave Davidson (OC 'B' Company), and Jimmy Somerville (OC 'A' Company) attempted to persuade Battalion HQ to form a two-company position covering and including Point 5120 which was clearly the 'Vital Ground', but the proposal was not agreed. Brigadier Hawkins claimed that his first priority was to 'get the tail tucked in,' but did not use Colonel 'Bimbo' Howard, 2 i/c of the Brigade and a mountain gunner of impeccable manners, to that end, while himself continuing with a battle which was fast getting out of control.

Artillery support at this juncture, in conjunction with a sensible redeployment of 1 Camerons to hold Hunter's Hill and Church Knoll, with 1/8 Lancashire Fusiliers holding the Naga Village itself, would have totally altered the situation, but this was not provided. As Cavalié Mercer says of the Brunswickers at Waterloo, the command appeared to the Camerons to have taken 'spiritual leave'. The battle was left to the junior officers and soldiers.

It had rained intermittently all day, but, as evening came, the rain became a steady downpour. 'D' Company gradually withdrew until their forward positions ran along the crest of Point 5120. There seems to have been no attempt to relieve or reinforce them, although unescorted Dakotas of the Indian Air Force now appeared and carried out a supply drop at very low level. The Japanese opened fire with everything within range. With great gallantry the drop was completed, and the Dakotas flew off into the dusk. There was no possibility of collecting more than a proportion of the drop the Japanese got a lot – but those brave pilots had risked their lives to bring jerrycans of water and bales of warm shirts. What was needed was mortar ammunition and barbed wire.

In the later evening the lone 3-in mortar arrived with some 30 rounds of ammunition, and set about providing 'D' Company with *some* supporting fire. The Japanese artillery opened up at short range, but, by good luck, the mortar was well sheltered by the Naga Lookout, and was able to continue firing. Night then fell on a truly warlike scene, with Naga huts blazing, small-arms fire rippling from Point 5120, the crash and simultaneous whistle of the Jap 75mm, and the occasional cough of the forlorn 3-in mortar as 'D' Company called down fire in front of their position while the Japanese closed in. The mortar was firing at a suicidally short range, 100 yards plus, using only the detonating cartridge. The shells were hitting Japanese. 'D' Company could hear their screams. But ammunition was desperately short: 'Every round was one less.' No ammunition was sent from 1/8 Lancashire Fusiliers or 7 Worcester Regiment, nor, unfortunately did David Murray have the chance to request it. No fire came from the Assault Field Regiments.

At about two in the early morning of 5 May a tropical thunderstorm broke directly overhead. The thunder and lightning were incessant and the rain poured down like a burn in spate. Half an hour later there was a furious peal of thunder and a blinding flash of lightning, and, at almost the same moment, a scream like the fiends of hell let loose from the pit. The remnant of 'D' Company saw, by the glare of the lightning, two companies of Japanese rise from the ground and charge towards them, officers in front with swords drawn, the men with bayonets fixed, sliding, slithering, falling, but utterly determined to close and kill. This was the genuine 'Banzai' charge, the ultimate tactic of the Japanese infantry.

The Camerons of 'D' Company were at the very end of their tether, exhausted, famished and soaked to the skin. The Mortar Platoon nearest the enemy, and the flanks of 'A' and 'B' Companies, were in the air; they fixed bayonets and hoped for the dawn as the rain stopped and a heavy mist settled. Once it was light enough to shoot, they kept the forward slope of Point 5120 under rifle fire whenever a target appeared. At about 0700 a senior officer appeared, completely alone, assuring the men that the Japs they had been shooting were, in fact, the Worcesters. He ordered Murray to lead his platoon up to take over Point 5120 from them. Corporal Fergie of the Mortar Platoon then told the officer, 'If yon's a British officer, he's the first that's worn a sword since Waterloo!' and the men were spared.

The Battalion withdrew west of the Village, 'in close confused fighting among shouts, firing and the cries of the wounded' to the east face of West Knoll. The Japanese were in strength and no counter-attack was possible. A little later Hawkins ordered the Battalion to counter-attack Point 5120 by standing up and walking towards it in the Somme tradition, still without artillery support. A quick roll call then established that the rifle platoons, several commanded by corporals, now averaged twelve men, so Hawkins wisely let the matter drop.

The Worcesters, the Field Company Royal Engineers, the Field Ambulance and the Manchesters came forward and, by 5 May, the Brigade was reunited in its new position. Offensive operations against Point 5120 ceased. The main task became the evacuation of the wounded down the hill and across the valley, a six-hour journey at best. On occasion, because of the monsoon, the stretcher bearers could not get their charges down the slippery hillsides. The stretchers lay out all night in the driving rain. As the evacuation proceeded, Japanese bombardment became more persistent.

This was a period of waiting, either to join the Division or for the Division to rejoin the Brigade. Nevertheless, an Order of the Day on 5 May read: 'On no account will anyone retire from their position. If the area is overrun by Japanese or if they infiltrate through the position, they will be dealt with by bayonet at the first opportunity. This hill [the West Knoll] must be held at all costs.'

The attack on Naga Village had failed, bloodily repulsed, as did another attack by the Worcesters and Camerons on 18 May, and two assaults by 4/15 Punjabis some days after that with considerable artillery and Hurribomber support. Major-General John Grover took a more generous view: '5 Brigade's night march between located enemy positions was an epic performance. When the news reached me, I could hardly believe it.' 1 Camerons believe to this day, that Naga Village could have been taken, if 2 Dorsets had been back with the Brigade with artillery.

At least this Brigade had easier access than most to Zubza's canteen and its bath unit which included forty-gallon oil drums split in half and containing hot water. There was no water at all in the forward positions and frequently no lavatory paper, with obvious consequences for personal hygiene, including the spread of dysentery from flies. Everyone smelled and, although 'gradually one got used to one's own smell, except occasionally on bending down, the smell of other people was almost insufferable.'

But 5 Brigade's wounded still carried by Nagas across the Zubza valley had to undergo a terrible journey, borne under fire up and down the hills on unstable stretchers, then by spartan ambulance down the twists and turns of the road into the awful heat of Dimapur. 'I am,' said an officer, 'continually amazed at the patience of the troops: they lie still beneath the blankets, white with pain, but uncomplaining. It's a miracle that so many survive.' It was a particular miracle that they survived when the stretcher parties going down met a mule party coming up: then the Nagas would 'ease forward on the narrow track, gripping the cliff edges with their toes, and shuffle along . . . Then the next party came . . . and the next,' hoping that none of seventy mules would lash out with its back legs, kicking the wounded to death.

As for food, rations in the parachute bundles dropped at that time were K rations, mainly of American origin. Three small cartons, one for each meal, were contained in one larger cardboard box and comprised chocolate, chewing gum, four cigarettes, matches, a 4 oz tin of meat, sugar, coffee, salt, pepper, soup and four 'high protein' biscuits. The Chindits took soup as the first course, then the meat in a mess tin, turned into a sort of stew with water and broken-up biscuit. Pudding was biscuit mixed with chocolate powder, sugar and water.

'Compo Rations', in a four-gallon tin containing food for eight men per day, contained most of the above, plus luncheon meat (spam), bully beef or sausages, powdered milk, fruit, potatoes, vegetables and 'grain' for porridge. They arrived later in the battle and were more popular.

After these battles, extempore 'church' services were held, one a Communion in the trees behind the Battery for all those in a Royal Artillery Regiment who had been confirmed. All communicants carried arms, wore their tin hats and stood throughout the thirty-minute service.

'While we have time, let us do good to all men and specially unto them that are of the household of faith,' interrupted by the shouting of orders to the guns' crews through a megaphone.

'This day, the noise of battle . . .'

The clanging of four breeches slamming shut, the thunderous bang of four guns, the clatter of empty cartridge cases extracted from the breeches, again the shouting of orders and their acknowledgement, the usual pandemonium of an artillery troop engaged.

'Come near with faith and take this Holy Sacrament to your comfort . . .' The gunners prayed for the Second Division, especially the Infantry who faced the enemy eyeball to eyeball, the wounded, suffering, dying, and those who had lost their lives.

The firing ended.

'Greater love hath no man than this, that he lay down his life for his friends.'

XXIV

DEATH VALLEY

MAJOR-GENERAL John Grover's intention for 4 Brigade was that, through a left-handed sweep from Jotsoma via Khonoma to the south of Mount Pulebadze, it should come upon the Imphal road below Aradura Spur and cut it there. The terrain was very rough indeed – the Nagas said that, in the monsoon, even they might not be able to traverse it – dense jungle, steep sides to the high mountain (about 8,000 feet) and, in the rains, possibly impenetrable even by native bearers. For that reason, Second Division planned to supply by air-drop. Although the Spur as the crow flies was only seven miles distant, the march itself covered 15–18 miles.

The Brigade Commander, 'Willie' Goschen, was a Grenadier officer who had been ADC to the Viceroy. He was a grandson of the first Lord Goschen, Chancellor of the Exchequer, twice First Lord of the Admiralty, the model for 'the Ruler of the Queen's Navee' in HMS *Pinafore*, and Chancellor of Oxford University. The Brigadier's great uncle, the first Baronet, had served in the Diplomatic Service in Madrid, Buenos Aires, Paris, Constantinople, Lisbon and Washington; he had been Minister at Petrograd and Copenhagen and Ambassador at Vienna and Berlin. He became Gentleman Usher to the Sword of State and the family was presented with Schloss Tentschach in Carinthia by Austrian Goschens on the condition, never exerted, that they serve as officers in the Austrian Army. Uncle Willie was surely 'the only Grenadier officer within several thousand miles'. His efficiency, charm and old-world manners, unique in the jungly circumstances of North-East India, won him the respect and affection of 4 Brigade.

The Royal Scots, one battalion of his Brigade, which itself, however, lacked the 1/8 Lancashire Fusiliers temporarily with 5 Brigade, had been led during part of First Arakan by Lieutenant-Colonel A. G. Mackenzie-Kennedy. He was still with them. In that failure they had 'fought sturdily against vastly superior forces, inflicted heavy casualties, and withdrawn in good order'.

Thereafter they had undergone jungle training at Belgaum on lines laid down by Wingate and summarized by the slogan 'The Jungle is Your Best Friend'. Endurance, fitness, silence and trade craft were taught: no cigarette ends, no washing with soap 'downstream' in rivers, no talking or other sound, no footprints, no white clothing. They patrolled at night on exercises with natives in the jungle. They learned the use of kukris or of daos in clearing undergrowth, of compasses, of movement at night. They were taught about bamboo shoots, rice, the pulp, like melon, in banana stalks, the flesh of monkeys and mules. They knew about 'boxes', but learned more. They were educated in booby traps, in the bayonet, in Japanese habits and practices. Above all, they learned about action as individuals or in pairs.

Between 15–18 April the Battalion had moved from Bangalore to the Naga village of Khabvuma near Zubza, with the mountains around Kohima visible to the south-east. Here 'C' and 'D' Companies succeeded the Berkshires and here, in a couple of skirmishes without supporting fire, 'B' Company unsuccessfully attacked two knolls. Next day, after artillery and air attack, followed by mortar and machine-gun fire, a Royal Scots patrol determined that the Japanese had withdrawn, leaving many dead behind. In one grave, all the wounded had been decapitated to prevent them becoming British prisoners.

The Royal Norfolks, Goschen's other Battalion, had arrived at Priphema, 28 miles from Dimapur, on 13 April, less 'B' Company at Dimapur. An attack on 14 April by one hundred Japanese on 18 Platoon of 'D' Company, which was protecting a tank laager, was driven off by Sergeant Hazell's platoon, killing thirty Japanese with only three Norfolks wounded. Later that day 10 Platoon drove off a Japanese patrol without loss.

This Battalion was commanded by Lieutenant-Colonel Robert (Bob) Scott. Scott was a huge, noisy man, with large demands and appetites. He belonged, perhaps, in the Tudor or Elizabethan ages, his vast explosions of violence, rage and vituperation modified by a love of literature and music. He did not know the meaning of fear, danger his preferred circumstance. He carried the works of Shakespeare in his pocket.

On 17 April, 'B', 'C' and half the HQ Company under Scott moved to Jotsoma, leaving 'A' and the rest of the HQ Company at Priphema under Major Condor. On 25 April, the now reunited Battalion came under 4 Infantry Brigade and received its marching orders for Aradura via Khonoma and the Dzuna nullah, to seize and hold the Aradura ridge and thereby cut the Imphal road.

The country consisted of steep, rocky ridges covered by dense jungle, one steep khud after another. To quote Captain Horner of the Norfolks, now running his own Surveyors firm in Norwich, 'The physical hammering is hard to understand. The heat, the humidity, the altitude and the slope of almost every foot . . . You gasp for air, which doesn't appear to come, you drag your legs upwards till they seem reduced to the strength of matchsticks, you wipe the sweat out of your eyes . . . Your heart pounds, so that it must burst its cage; as loud as a drum . . . You reach the top of the hill, to find it is a false crest . . . All you can think of is the next halt.' The Nagas, however, could not understand why British troops were out of breath.

There were few known tracks. Most of the advance was made on game-tracks or paths hacked out by the marchers themselves in the jungle and in the 'putrescent' valleys. The Mortar Platoon, Manchesters and Signallers had to carry great weights, since there were no porters on the first leg. Steel helmets were worn despite Scott's preference for bush hats in jungle. Infantrymen had to carry a hundred rounds, two days' rations, a blanket, gas cape, rifle or automatic, two grenades *and* a pick and shovel over that ghastly terrain. The wet heat was intense in the valley; it was bitter cold on the ridges.

The Brigade was guided on its departure from Jotsoma on 26 April by 143 Special Service Company under a Royal Scots officer, Major A. K. MacGeorge, MC. This unit worked with Naga hillmen, short and strong, calf muscles so large they could not squat as do other natives. They wore ivory rings and necklaces, ivory rings also at the knee as garters. The headmen were draped in red blankets. They all smoked, Players, not Woodbine, for preference. The march was in single file and sometimes the men, not just the Nagas, had to pull themselves up the mountain by rope. The Nagas, although each carrying 80–100 lbs, complained about the British habit of halting for ten minutes on the hour or, eventually, even more frequently. They preferred to travel continuously for hours, then rest for hours, and in the end they were allowed to do so.

The Brigade bivouacked at night and marched by day. The nights, under only a blanket and a gas cape, were execrable. The Norfolks had no Tommy cookers, while fires, anyway, were not permitted. But a smokeless fire could be made by shaving bamboo, so breakfast could be done in mess-tins, of a crushed biscuit, porridge, salt and powdered milk. For tiffin, perhaps a bully-stew with leaves; a bit of cheese and biscuit for dinner.

After three days of endless rain, on slippery and dangerous tracks sometimes impassable to troops carrying such burdens, Goschen ordered a rest day in a dark valley known either, derisively, as Happy Valley or, more sombrely, as Death Valley. The ground was a quagmire, the men soaked to the skin, in dank, fungus-encrusted, stinking vegetation, some of which was 'luminous and glowed horribly at night. What a foul night,' wrote a Jock. 'The coldest, dampest, unhappiest night of all.' Here fires could not be lit, surrounded in the mist and rain by moss and rank shrubs with glaucous leaves. An icy stream poured down the steep sides of the sullen valley, a perpetual damp mist hung everywhere. Many of the troops fell ill, but could not go back to the aid posts.

The Norfolks left two days later for Pavilion Hill and Norfolk Ridge, eventually accompanied by the Royal Scots. Major Callender's 'B' Company with Brigade HQ and the Royal Scots Battalion HQ came between the Norfolks and the brilliant machine-gunners of the Second Manchesters. Major Menzies' 'C' Company later arrived. The road from Kohima to Imphal lay below them to the east.

The War Diary of the Norfolk Regiment asserts that, on 29 April, Operation 'Strident', the taking of Aradura, was cancelled because 6 Brigade had been unable to take Jail Hill, held in greater strength than had been thought. Whether this was the reason for cancellation, or whether the change was due to Imphal's need for all the air transport available, is not clear, but, on that day, Brigadier Goschen was ordered to go for Transport Ridge (GPT). Patrols went forward on 1 May to reconnoitre a route to 'Oaks Hill', the assembly point for the assault on GPT, but Goschen made plain to Division that he could not move, because the slopes were so steep, before 4 May. Actual steps had to be cut out of the ground on the precipitous hills, sometimes with hand-rails. This did not please General Grover, still less the Corps and Army Commanders, but on 2 May, the Norfolks, Royal Scots and 143 SS Company could cover no more than one mile on Pavilion Hill. At this point some Naga porters had been ambushed and, fleeing, had dropped their loads. The Jocks, in their turn, ambushed the Japanese who had come to collect the booty, killing several and acquiring a Japanese sword. Two platoons of a Royal Scots Company had been attacked by another Japanese Company, who, since they advanced up a hill in the open, were cut down by the Manchesters' machine-gunners. Surprise on Pulebadze was thus irretrievably lost.

Three more Japanese attacks developed in the next half-hour, the last of them overrunning a section in Major Menzies' Company with shouts of 'Banzai', grenades and machine-gun fire. The Japs were held by Lance-Corporal McKay, although wounded, and his Section, which drove them back. Before the night was out they were twice more repulsed by Lieutenant Colin Black's platoon. Black was awarded the MC and McKay the MM. The fighting was so close that two Company Commanders, Drew-Wilkinson and Menzies, could shout their messages to one another. Major Hayward, the Battalion second-in-command, was meanwhile priming grenades. Hugh Callender, commanding 'B', offered to do the same. When he said that he hadn't primed one since his course in 1939, Callender alleged that Hayward had made off at the double.

The Royal Scots held, losing only six men. The Japanese killed and wounded were in great numbers, either dead on the ledges or, having rolled down the hill, stopped by trees and bushes where they lay. The 4/1st Gurkhas of Loftus-Tottenham's 33 Brigade, previously before Zubza in order to deal with Colonel Torihai's 138 Regiment, had occupied Two Tree Hill to the west of Jail Hill, where they discovered after ambushing a Japanese line repair party (the Gurkhas themselves had cut the wire), the presence of Colonel Miyamoto's 124 Regiment. If, therefore, Grover had not changed 4 Brigade's plan from Aradura Spur, the Norfolks and Royal Scots would have been preempted by Miyamoto. Japanese forces in this area of the battle were stronger than 2 Div had expected.

The climb to Oaks Hill, the assembly point for GPT, was rigorous and steep, in thick jungle, the men overloaded with equipment. The reconnaissance party, at Scott's insistence, included eight representatives from the Norfolks. It moved off at 7 am on 3 May, escorted by 143 Special Service Company under Major MacGeorge, up the foothills of Aradura until Jail Hill could be seen, with a corrugated roof in front of it which was assumed to be on GPT Ridge. The party then went back, leaving the Commanding Officers of the Norfolks and of 99 Field Regiment (Lieutenant-Colonel James) to make a closer inspection.

Robert Scott flatly disobeyed Brigadier Goschen's order that fires were to be excluded. He insisted that the Norfolks should have tea before battle and had a deep pit dug, with a roof, which was filled with shavings. He had the fire lit at twilight, but, unfortunately, the Brigadier arrived, furiously demanding explanations. Colonel Scott said that the hot water was needed to treat scabies, septic prickly heat and other jungle infections. Fortunately, the Medical Officer was able to turn away Goschen's wrath by bringing forward a soldier who claimed to have been treated in that fashion. Scott's arrest, which had appeared imminent, although such seems unlikely on the eve of battle, was averted. Meanwhile, the only actual rations now remaining, which were issued to each man that day before the advance on 4 May, were jam, cheese, a little butter, bully-beef, biscuits, tea, milk and sugar.

Silence was stringently observed, orders for the following day being passed in whispers from company to platoon to section, a lengthy process. The attack began with a 45-minute shoot at GPT Ridge by two 5.5 inch guns with the 'cap on' so as to make large shell holes in which the Norfolks' advancing troops could later take cover. The Royal Scots took station to the north to block any Japanese infiltration before joining Scott.

When the Norfolks went forward from Oaks Hill at first light they were met by considerable rifle and machine-gun fire. 'D' Company (Major Hatch) outflanked one bunker; the next was taken by direct assault, with casualties. Japanese positions along the Spur enabled the enemy to cause severe casualties from above, many of the wounded falling in the undergrowth where the stretcher-bearers had trouble finding them. So many were there, and so fast the Battalion's speed of advance, that sometimes all the stretcher-bearers could do was dress their wounds and leave them for later recovery where they lay.

'The feeling of complete helplessness of a winding column in single file is not experienced in open warfare.' The targets were invisible, and so strict was British fire-discipline that little return fire took place until Robert Scott, vast and swearing horribly, initiated a rain of grenades against every possible source. These grenades, stens fired from the hip, and the course of the action itself reduced Japanese resistance and also brought the enemy into the open to be dealt with by automatic and rifle fire. 'A' Company, commanded by Major Swainson, with two platoons under Lieutenant R. Bothway, contained the enemy all day. Major Swainson was later awarded the Military Cross, but it is plain from the War Diary that the diarist, probably Colonel Scott himself, believed that many others, including Bothway, should also have been decorated. Advance was often by *crawling* through thick, drenched undergrowth in single file, fighting all the way.

The Battalion then drove on, almost at the double, with a reconnaissance party covered by the remaining platoon of 'A' Company and a platoon of 'B'. Despite minimal visibility in the jungle, but inspired by Scott with a bag of grenades and outlandish cries, the Norfolks overran Japanese positions, rushed a bunker, their impetus with the bayonet requiring no artillery support after the first superb barrage by 99 Field Regiment. The enemy was on the run. Personally led by their Commanding Officer, the Battalion took its objectives on GPT Ridge, although then coming under damaging sniper and machine-gun fire from bunkers on left and right.

A defensive box was formed. Every effort was made to bring back 'A' and 'B' Companies who had overrun the objective and were pinned down from a bunker ('Norfolk bunker') forty yards away. The stretcher-bearers and Dr Mather did magnificent work in recovering casualties under very heavy fire from these bunkers, housing them in slit trenches with little cover against the incessant rain.

Twenty-two officers and men had been killed and sixty wounded, including Scott himself. The Battalion had been in action for eight days, and under fire, in the most difficult terrain in Asia, for ten hours without a break. GPT had been won. When Scott called Division on the radio: 'I am on GPT, consolidating. My casualties are pretty heavy, but we've killed a hell of a lot of Japs,' Second Division replied that the Norfolks couldn't be on GPT, as they hadn't yet received the Fire Plan.

In the torrential rain, Brigadier Goschen that night made his Tac HQ with the Royal Scots 200 yards above the Royal Norfolks. Although the first remaining enemy bunker was eliminated, 4 Brigade had not yet understood that that was only part of a chain of inter-supporting Japanese bunkers stretching to the main road itself.

5 May, apart from Japanese snipers, was 'a quiet day', with only four killed and 36 wounded, including the second-in-command of the Norfolks, hit in arm and leg, who refused to be evacuated and sat in a slit trench all day reading, or pretending to read, Robert Scott's Shakespeare. He was eventually given a shot of morphia and sent back to the Aid Post. The serious problem facing the Battalion was that unless the main bunker, which a Norfolks' platoon had just failed to capture, was taken out, neither the supplies on the road nor Brigadier Warren's 161 Brigade on Congress Hill could get through. Until then the only access was through 4 Brigade's own assault route, dangerously exposed to Japanese attack.

The Divisional Commander's verdict was: '4th Brigade's march over the Naga Hills and through untracked dense jungle is an epic . . . Its attack was magnificent. Willie Goschen can't say enough for the Norfolks and for Robert Scott's personal leadership.'

XXV

THE RIDGE AGAIN

ON 30 APRIL, half the 1st Battalion of the Berkshires was still on Garrison Hill. The 2nd Dorsetshire Regiment had, as we have seen, recently arrived for the early attempts to send a tank up the Deputy Commissioner's drive. The first Royal Welch Fusiliers had just relieved the 2nd Durham Light Infantry after that battle which had so critically affected General Sato's plans.

In heavy rain the Sappers made the next attempt to haul a tank on to the tennis court. The cable broke. A light tank went up on 1 May and attacked the Japanese bunker on the court with its 37mm gun without substantive effect. Larger calibre was essential.

'B' and 'C' Companies of the Berkshires, who had stayed on Supply Hill (FSD) when the others left for rest on Piquet Hill, now also left after no less than twenty-four days in the lines. From Piquet, 'A' and 'B' were then able to see Colonel Cargill's 4/7 Rajputs repel a two-company enemy attack on Two Tree Hill, killing a third of the attackers for the loss of nine Rajput sepoys.

On 4 May the DLI returned from their short rest. The Royal Welch were ordered to take Kuki Piquet and Supply Hill with two companies under 6 Brigade, part of the Divisional operation to destroy the Japanese at Kohima. 4 Brigade was to assault Kohima from GPT Ridge and menace the Imphal road, while 5 Brigade was to press home its left hook against Naga Village, Perowne's 23 Brigade (Chindit) cutting the Jessami track. The DLI, less two companies, would attack and seize Jail Hill to link up with 4 Brigade on GPT and Congress Hill where they should have been in position.

At first light Hurribombers and Vengeances attacked Kuki, Supply and Detail, late because of bad weather and heavy mist, followed by 3.7 inch, 3″ mortars and anti-tank guns. Under the barrage, the Durhams were soon reported to have linked up with tanks on Detail. One company reached Supply where they were stopped by Japanese fire from Jail Hill. On the road, the other DLI companies debussed from the carriers, but came under such heavy LMG fire, with grenades also being rolled down on them, that Brigadier Shapland told Colonel Brown to withdraw through the Dorsets' position by the Deputy Commissioner's Bungalow since no further advance was possible on foot. A Company Commander and other officers were killed. Very accurate 37mm HE fire then killed the Battalion Commander, Lieutenant-Colonel John Brown, succeeded by Lieutenant-Colonel L. à B. Robinson of the Berkshires who at this stage was commanding a composite unit of the Berkshires and Durhams on FSD and Garrison, composite because both were so greatly reduced.

On the Ridge the tanks fired directly into the bunkers, destroying machine-gun posts in one bunker and in other positions. The Durhams and the Royal Welch had got up the hill across country. But one DLI Company trying to join the Royal Welch Fusiliers on Kuki Piquet found it still to be in Japanese hands, shooting into their and the Fusiliers' backs from concealed positions. Fire was poured on the British from the bunkers, terrible casualties inflicted from within the revetments. A company of the Royal Welch and the remnant of the Durhams dug in that night on Supply Hill under incessant attack. Many wounded could not be rescued, in the battered branchless wasteland. In one trench a soldier *stood* on a Japanese grenade which had landed between his feet sustaining only terrible bruising, although his comrades were badly wounded when it exploded.

The Royal Welch had already been caught on Kuki by sniping and machine-gun fire, the rear section of 12 Platoon being destroyed by machine-gunners. From the rest of the Platoon, only one Fusilier was ever seen again. 10, 11, 12 and 14 Platoons had been in the unsuccessful attack by 'B' and 'D' Companies on this hill, 13 and 15 engaged elsewhere. Five officers, including both company and three platoon commanders, and thirty-three other ranks were killed, twenty-two missing, one hundred and sixteen wounded. Only 30% of 'C' Company were unwounded. The two leading platoon commanders, Trigg and Smith, were found ten days later, dead on top of the Japanese position they had been told to capture. One MC, to Ogburne who had taken over the Company after Major Carrington's death, four MMs and a DCM, were awarded. A Durham company, of whom only fourteen men were left, found a gully containing hundreds of piled-up Japanese dead. What was left of the Durhams went to ground on Supply Hill with what remained of the Royal Welch, two platoons of one company. No supplies could reach them, and only a few wounded could be evacuated on tanks and stretchers. Next morning, 6 May, the DLI were relieved with the Welch Fusiliers by the Berkshires and 4/7 Rajputs. They joined the rest of their Battalion at Dimapur, not many left, just enough for three companies of two platoons each, although a draft of thirty joined them there.

The Japanese had again demonstrated, as they had before and would again many times elsewhere, that ill, hungry, short of ammunition, and with hardly any artillery or air support, these patriotic fanatics continued, from their deep inter-connected bunkers, to resist all the massive RAF, Royal and Indian Artillery and infantry assaults that the Allied forces brought to bear. It was becoming clear that, without consistent heavy and medium bombardment of the bunkers at point-blank range, the Japanese defences were going to remain impregnable. The first doubts about imminent victory were beginning to cross commanders' minds, but John Grover said only, '6 Brigade seems a bit under the weather; their plans for Kuki and FSD went badly wrong'.[1]

The same gloomy situation existed round the bungalow and tennis court, particularly the latter, where an attack on one bunker provoked return fire from supporting bunkers sunk so deep into the terrain that air-to-surface projectiles could not penetrate. Only tank fire from guns larger than 37mm would do.

The Dorsets' 'A' Company on the road junction by the DC's bungalow was being shelled by a 75mm gun at three hundred yards' range. DF was ineffective. Even their W/T had been out until a Corporal Mansfield (later Sergeant, awarded the MM), with two men, got through the Japanese lines to Colonel Jack McNaught with the old set and took back a new one. The outlook was unpleasant. Next morning, under smoke, Alan Watts' 'B' Company relieved John Bowles' 'A' Company which 'for five and a half days, had hung on by the skin of their teeth against almost overwhelming opposition in the most exposed position, killing a lot of Japanese'. 'A' Company climbed the hill to HQ, 'red-eyed, smoke-blackened,' twenty-eight survivors of one hundred men.

A successful patrol by Sergeant Seall of 'D' Company showed that the enemy were concentrating their defence of the spur, not by perimeter but on the tennis court through a sunken strong post under the Club, and by bunkers dominating the court. This confirmed the requirement for a medium tank (or man-handled gun) at close range against the bunkers, in conjunction with the infantry. On 3 May an RAC officer asked to try again to take a tank up the drive, guided by Captain Murrills who knew the hill very well.

Major Ezra Rhodes of the Royal Armoured Corps, after successive breathless attempts observed by the Dorsets from their trenches, reached the top of the drive and started to pump shells into the bunkers, inflicting heavy Japanese losses. The enemy, alas, soon came alive and the infantry (10 Platoon led by Dick Purser, killing five Japanese in the bungalow across deadly fire from the bunkers), had to retire, followed slowly by the awkward lumbering tank. The Dorsets had got closer than before to fulfilling their obsession. Next day they tried again, this time evading a newly dug but incomplete anti-tank ditch. The Lee tank could neither reach the terrace nor depress its gun enough to hit the machine gun holding up 'B' Company. 'B' had, nevertheless, already entered what used to be the bungalow and there killed ten Japanese. The tank and the Dorsets went in on 4, 5 and 6 May, but had to withdraw on each occasion. Meanwhile, 'B' Company still dominated the Japanese at the road junction until cut up as badly as 'A'. They were then relieved by 16 Platoon of 'D' Company under Lionel Halahan, an Anglo/Argentine.

General Grover now told Brigadier Wood, Chief of Staff of XXXIII Corps, that, because of his casualties, he needed reinforcements. He could not, in any case, mount further operations against Kuki Piquet, FSD or Jail Hill until 9 May, when he would have returned, at Stopford's suggestion, 1/8 Lancashire Fusiliers to 4 Brigade, and the Dorsetshires to 5 Brigade. Apart from the Corps Commander's wishes, the 4th and 5th Brigade Commanders wanted their own Battalions back; 4 Brigade now only had two Battalions.

Stopford would not wait until 9 May. He ordered forward Brigadier Loftus-Tottenham's 33rd Brigade comprising 1st Queen's Royal Regiment, 4/15 Punjabis, and 4/1 Gurkhas currently with Warren's 161 Brigade at Congress Hill. Grover, as indicated earlier, had been pleased by this move to a two-divisional Corps, eliminating the breath of Corps staff exclusively down *his* Division's neck.

But it was plain that relations between Stopford and Grover were deteriorating further. Stopford visited Second Division Headquarters on 6 May to give Grover his views in person, preceded by a rare and rather ineffective raid by a squadron of Japanese aircraft. Stopford urged the necessity of early and continual action against the enemy, from 33 Brigade against Treasury Hill and Jail Hill and from 4 Brigade down GPT Ridge to Congress Hill, these operations to begin on 7 May.

When he had left, Loftus-Tottenham arrived, 'a bulldog of a man, a noisy, beetle-browed giant, tenacious, stubborn, fine-looking, brave and dashing, a commander,' conditioned by his Great War experiences but also by the philosophy of Sir John Moore of conserving men's lives and wasting the enemy's. Warren of 161 Brigade also came up: he believed that as soon as 'Bunker Hill' (that Bunker Hill opposite the Norfolks) had been captured, Congress Hill could easily be taken. 33 Brigade could then move on Jail Hill. Although Loftus-Tottenham found the ordeal before his Brigade a daunting prospect, 'faced with clearing five or six strongly defended positions', after their experience in the major battle at Ngakyedauk Pass in the Arakan, he had no alternative but to send forward 4/1 Gurkhas and 1/1 Punjabis, still under Lieutenant-Colonel Grimshaw. The Punjabis would clear the bashas in front and then go on to contact McKenzie-Kennedy's Royal Scots, while the Gurkhas would clear GPT Ridge with the Royal Scots. The Punjabis would then take Congress Hill, while the Queens would occupy Pimple and Jail Hill.

The night of 6/7 May was dark, wet and cold. Next day, nothing fired by the Royal Scots and Gurkhas, whether spring mortars (PIAT), 2-inch smoke mortars, bazookas, grenades or machine gun, had any apparent effect on the Japanese bunkers at GPT Ridge. The first charge, by two officers, a havildar and eight sepoys, resulted only in the Commander's death and the wounding of four men. Since the Gurkhas had lost nearly all their British officers, the young Gurkha Battalion Commander, Colonel Hedderwick himself, in a bright green shirt, led a flanking movement. He drew sniper fire and was shot through the chest. Willie Goschen's orderly, a Grenadier guardsman, was killed trying to bring him in. Goschen himself was mortally wounded trying to drag the orderly back, and died in the arms of Colonel Scott of the Norfolks. 4 Brigade ordered the Gurkhas to retire, and Colonel Theobalds took over the Brigade.

Congress Hill had meanwhile been occupied. Loftus-Tottenham seems to have been unaware of the disaster on GPT, since he ordered a major Divisional artillery strike against Pimple and Jail. Nothing, it was again thought, would have survived the devastation, but when the Queens moved forward they came under Japanese machine-gun fire from bunkers on both flanks, on DIS and another spur south-east of GPT which defensive fire could not reach. Although the ranks of the Queens started to thin, they continued to advance with great courage, firing grenades directly into the bunkers' apertures and capturing two bunkers despite bad losses.

Sergeant Burt, bleeding and in great pain, shouted that he might be paralysed down one side, but he could 'still throw grenades: let me have some!' He attracted Japanese attention by hurling those grenades, while his platoon took the bunker in a flank attack.

The Queens took Pimple. There and on Jail Hill they came under 75mm fire over open sights, one officer and thirteen men killed, four officers and fifteen men wounded, only fourteen men in three under-strength platoons unwounded. On Loftus-Tottenham's orders, the Battalion withdrew. For their gallantry, Grover told Colonel Duncombe, their CO, to convey to them his congratulations and his thanks. But plainly Jail Hill could not be taken before GPT and DIS were clear of enemy.

Before 33 Brigade had set off, the Norfolks had attempted to take Bunker Hill with machine-gun cover on one flank in torrential rain and liquid mud. Here, too, the command had not understood the inter-locked nature of the extraordinary Japanese bunker system down the Kohima ridge. Thus the first bunker was quickly seized on the left, but the right-hand Norfolk platoon was stopped by fire from at least one other bunker. Captain Randle, the Company Commander, went with grenades and rifle, bayonet fixed, to the narrow aperture of the next one.

Hit repeatedly, he flung himself deliberately across the slit, preventing the enemy from firing out. He died there, permitting its destruction by a Norfolk platoon. Other bunkers off it, however, ran all the way down the spine. Three platoons were not enough to choke them off. As they covered Jail Hill itself, the Battalion was withdrawn until means could be devised to neutralize the enemy. Three officers were killed and wounded, twenty other ranks wounded and eight killed. Captain Randle was awarded a posthumous Victoria Cross.

Japanese bunkers and sniper posts had also been constructed along the supply route to 4 Brigade. The mules who provided the main method of supply could not get through. The Brigade was running out of water and food: the Norfolks had not had a hot meal for ten days. The Gurkhas as 'porters', escorted by the Punjabis, brought rations and a hundred gallons of water in tins, taking back casualties. The Indians, until they saw the number of Japanese corpses, initially resented this employment ('coolies for the British'), but their magnificent conduct in taking the wounded over country that none of our countrymen could so safely navigate earned the admiration of the Royal Scots and Royal Norfolks.

Grover now ordered the Sappers to build a new mule route as a permanent channel for supplies, including wire and flame-throwers for use against the bunkers.

Things, therefore, were very bad on the Ridge. Despite the efforts of Generals Giffard and Slim, the shells for the Artillery which alone could reduce the Japanese were not coming through from India. Without them, 2 and now 7 Division, in the shape of 33rd Brigade, were being reduced to half-strength battalions of as few as three hundred each. Not every battalion even had the right number of companies. Company and platoon commanders had been killed out of all proportion to their men. No way had yet been invented of breaking into the endless enemy bunkers without whose destruction victory was not imaginable. Stalemate and frustration seemed, indeed *were* for a little while, Second Division's daily bread.

As things stood, the half-moon formed in the 5,000-foot hills by the right and left flanks of 31 Division was intact. On the right, the steep jungle-covered slope of Aradura Spur sloped down via Transport Ridge and Pimple to the road. Beyond the road, and commanding it, was Jail Hill on the taking of which the Queens' plan had depended and that, in its turn, on the clearing of Issue, Supply and Point 5120. Three days of close and savage fighting had produced little but the knowledge that victory would not come until all the Japanese had been winkled out and exterminated to the last man in the honeycomb of bunkers and fox-holes: 'no quarter given, nor accepted'.

Conditions for the troops deteriorated as the monsoon wore on: cold food, drenched clothing, wet blankets, gas capes and groundsheets almost useless against the rains, the trenches water-logged. Life in an endless downpour on squelching mud became extremely depressing, approaching insupportable, but the soldiers kept on supporting it. Life in dug-outs, their roofs not more than thirty inches from the floor was slightly better, although no one left them except to squat over a hole. The British and Indians, however, resented 'roofs' as depriving them of full use of their personal weapons.

It should be recorded that 1st Assam Regiment, reformed at Piphema, now re-entered the battle. As they were still considerably under strength, the rifle companies were amalgamated on 7 May to form two strong companies at Ms 44 with Captain J. S. Taylor, Steyn, Khan and others under 33 Brigade. From Ms 44 they carried out a regular series of reconnaissances and ambush patrols.

In the thick, wet jungle with little visible except a curtain of green vegetation, they found an occupied oval bunker which had earlier caused trouble to 4/15 Punjabis from whom they had taken over. They dug in nearby, laid trip wire and had artillery defensive fire laid on round the bunker. At 10 pm the Japanese attacked and were driven off by 1st Assam supported by a 25 pounder. At dawn the Assamese captured the bunker with many Japanese casualties, one of whom had had his right hand cut off.

From the ring contour in steep, tangled jungle, Taylor sent out more patrols to protect the British right flank. Their morale was high and they killed Japanese, but the next bunker they were required to take, earlier occupied by the Royal Scots, was beyond their capacity. They found it abandoned, however, by the Japanese on 4 June. In these operations they were greatly helped by the Angami Nagas who provided tactical intelligence and made several kills, attested to by Japanese heads in sacks.

Major (later Lieutenant-Colonel) Gordon Graham, MC and Bar, was a Cameron, now a publisher living in Marlow, whose first wife died in childbirth in Bombay. As in *The Jewel in the Crown*, he returned to India to work as a journalist for ten years before residence in the United States and eventual return to the UK. He wrote a piece for the *Illustrated Weekly* of India on 10 December, 1944, which, although he was not in the action described above, showed the life of an infantryman in the Kohima campaign:

'Mopping-up operations continued in the Kohima area. Obviously nothing much doing there, concludes the reader. There is always something doing for the man on the spot, "at the front of the front" as Ian Hay calls it, with the Japs only a matter of yards away.

'He is wakened by a shake, while it is still dark. He is fully clothed, and probably has been for weeks. He does not sit up because the roof of the fox-hole is only two feet from the floor. Instead, he slides forward to his stand-to post, where the floor has been deepened. The other two or three occupants of the fox-hole are doing the same, pushing aside the slightly sodden blanket they have been sharing. One is already awake, as he was the last on "stag", or sentry. If possible, there should never be fewer than four in a fox-hole, or stag comes round too often. Even with four it will come round twice in a night, as it is forbidden to do more than one hour consecutively.

'Equipment on, rifle or automatic in the hand, grenades ready, all are now staring out into the blackness. It is the morning stand-to. In 15 minutes it will be first light, and in 15 minutes more it will be light enough to see and they will stand-down, that is unless the mist fails to clear. But all being well they can mount a single sentry at, say, a quarter past five, and the day has started.

'No one, however, gets out of his fox-hole, though it may be cramped and hurriedly dug. Fox-holes are all inter-supporting and integral parts of a defensive position, but in a way they are independent units. There should be no movement between them by night and as little as possible by day. One man may have crawled outside to perch over the hole dug to meet the needs of nature. Another will be preparing the morning "brew" with the aid of a Tommy-cooker, a tin with petrol or meths as fuel. It is the only method of cooking allowed when in contact with the enemy, as it is smokeless.

They are still eating yesterday's rations, – probably bully, biscuits, cheese and tea. These, along with a vitamin tablet, ten cigarettes and some sheets of toilet paper are issued in 24-hour packages.

Diet is not always so spartan. One may feed under primitive conditions and at long intervals, but when the situation permits, one eats well. Sometimes peaches and cream, or steak and kidney pudding are consumed within sight of the enemy. Food and sleep do not cease to be man's prime requirements, and an officer must see that his men get as much of both as possible.

'During an actual engagement, hunger is the last feeling that assails one, but after it is over everyone discovers a huge appetite.

'The arrival of the ration columns, whether by coolie, mule, motor transport or plane, is the main event of the day, not only because the actual rations are so important, but because along with them comes the mail, the rum issue and *SEAC*, the army newspaper. Mail is received like manna, for it is the only link with another world. *SEAC* is very popular and reaches troops engaged in actual fighting within a day or two of publication. So if one thought predominates in the mind of the man in the fox-hole, it is speculation as to the arrival of the ration column.

'Thoughts, generally, tend to be anything but profound, concerned either with one's part in the battle or with animal needs. At dawn the ration column will be leaving the admin area, but its arrival may be late in the day, depending upon the enemy, the weather and the distance to be covered.

'When the rations arrive, the quartermaster distributes them to companies, companies to platoons and platoons to sections. A fox-hole usually holds a half-section, with a corporal or lance-corporal in charge. They "muck in" on such cooking as there is to be done. Quite a reasonable porridge can be made by crumbling biscuits into hot water, and stirring in sugar and milk. With bully, one can do a variety of things. After the first two months, everyone has the same suggestion!

'But hot tea is the mainstay of any ration. It has an effect on morale quite out of proportion to its restorative or nutritive qualities. A wise officer knows this, and allows his men to "brew up" whenever possible. Plain food may become monotonous, but so does rich food, so it is better to keep to the plain rations in the end, and leave the palate unspoiled. The rum issue works out at a very small tot per man. A careful section commander will see that one member of his section always carries a water-bottle full of rum. A mouthful of this, taken unawares, will set you back more than you expect, for the rum is not the drawing-room variety!

'In the early morning, however, the arrival of the rations is in the vague future. The first business of the day is to get organized. Then, if there is nothing doing, rest. Always rest – at any moment it may cease to be possible. Organization may or may not include a cat's-lick wash. The water problem may be all too simple, but occasionally, for example when a defensive position is on top of a hill, it is difficult. Water then becomes part of the ration supply, and is used only for drinking. When necessary, quite astonishing refreshment can be obtained – a drink, clean teeth, a shave and a wash – all from a half mess-tin full of water.

'To shave or not to shave is debatable, for beards invite jungle sores and other discomforts. A careful soldier will wash his feet and change his socks whenever possible. It is pointless to wash the body when one has no clean clothes to put on.

'The task that is never missed is the cleaning and oiling of the rifle or whatever weapon a soldier carries. Oil and "four-by-two" (cleaning rag) are in daily supply; and in the monsoon particularly, when metal tarnishes within a few hours, a vital necessity. By, say, seven o'clock, tea and biscuit consumed, gun, ammunition and grenades clean, toilet, if any, complete, the soldier is ready for what the day may bring.

'It will probably bring a quick move. Junior officers and other ranks learn to keep an open mind about the development of the battle: even senior officers do not always know what is likely to happen. This does not mean that an intelligent soldier cannot form his own picture of the battle, but he must do so always with a reservation allowing for sudden, inexplicable changes.

'Disease is a deadly enemy in the field and the part played by the individual in combating it is as important a part of his training as any other. If everyone follows the basic rules of hygiene in the field, disease is minimized. In a jungle area, obedience to these rules is more important than anywhere else.

'Anti-malaria precautions are now almost instinctive, which means they will be carried out even under conditions of great discomfort. A good soldier is discriminating about what he eats and drinks, careful to bury all waste matter, human and other, and punctilious in rendering first-aid. The result of this, added to modern medical skill, is a decline in the incidence of disease.

'In the rest area the padre has an opportunity to hold church services. These are voluntarily attended even by the normally irreligious. Crowded church services are not generally a feature of army life. However great or absent a soldier's faith may be, nearness to danger makes him more consciously reliant on God. When in a few days the unit goes "up" again, he knows from past experience that he will need something more than human resource to protect him from harm.

'Successful soldiering is largely a matter of adjustment. Everyone has his own way of adjusting himself, but the man who cannot adjust himself does not last. If a new perspective is gained, events which would otherwise be soul-shaking find their correct relation, and life is curiously normal. Selfish cowardice does not win battles nor is sustained heroism expected. It is the average man doing ordinary things well who achieves victory.'

Notes

1. By dusk on 4 May the 2nd Durham Light Infantry and the 1st Royal Welch Fusiliers less the remnants of two companies on Supply Hill, were on Garrison Hill. 60 ORs of the RWF and five officers had been killed and wounded, 30 ORs

and four officers of the DLI were dead. Two Grants in 149 RAC had been knocked out by mines, 1 Stuart in 45 Cavalry and 3 armoured cars in 11 Cavalry knocked out. The Japanese strength had been badly under-estimated. This bloody operation had the code-word 'Key'.

XXVI

LIEUTENANT-GENERAL SATO VERSUS GENERAL MUTAGUCHI

IN THE initial stages of the Imphal campaign there is no doubt that every Japanese Division made strong advances. 31 Division entered Kohima on 6 April and the advance forces of 33 Division reached areas looking down on the plain of Imphal by the beginning of April. Although in the third week of the month 15 Division had stopped attacking north of Kohima and was seeking reinforcement from Sato, it was at least firmly dug-in.

But Sato knew that Mutaguchi had missed his target of 29 April for taking Imphal. He knew that the British south of Imphal on the Shenam Saddle and to the west of Bishenpur were offering stubborn resistance to Yanagida's 33 Division. He knew that Yamauchi and 15 Div had been defeated at Nungshigum. He knew that Yanagida had been dismissed by GOC 15th Army and, if the latter's increasingly paranoiac orders meant anything, that Yamauchi (15 Div) soon would be. He knew that the Chindits had inflicted 12,000 casualties on the Japanese divisions, and that they and the Americans were moving on Myitkyina.

He knew, above all, that his own Division, which had started off with over thirteen thousand men, had now been substantially reduced. There are no reliable figures for the date in May which this narrative has attained but, by June 22, the losses suffered had brought the Divisional strength to 6,500. 15 Division at the same time was down to 7,500 from 15,000; the numbers in the Yamamoto detachment of 33 Division had also been halved. He had consequently disobeyed the GOC's order to send the Miyazaki detachment to the aid of 15 Division, while the two battalions of that detachment would fail in a final effort against British armour to cut the Imphal–Kohima road.

When Sato heard of the dismissals of the commanders of 15 and 33 Divisions, he said openly, 'This is shameful. If Mutaguchi considers himself a knight, he should apologize for his own failure to the dead soldiers and to the Japanese people. He should not try and put the blame on his subordinates.'

For Sato, Mutaguchi's 'failure' was his total neglect of the supply factor. Lieutenant-General Kunomara, Chief of Staff of 15th Army, had promised that 31 Division would receive ten tons of supplies a day after they had arrived at Kohima and a total of 250 tons up to 25 March. Nothing arrived except 500 rounds of mountain-gun ammunition, some sake and cigarettes which were brought up in seventeen jeeps by Lieutenant-Colonel Hattori at the end of April, five of them to Tactical HQ at Chakabama and twelve to Tohema. Three more jeeps with 'camp comforts' arrived on 24 May.

These contributions did not significantly affect the artillery's performance and did nothing for the rations. The food brought with them by the Division in their epic march from the Chindwin was long since exhausted and neither foraging nor captured British stores had been able to fill the gap, at least for 124 Regiment, the main body. On 25 May, only two weeks after the point now reached in this story, Sato signalled XV Army:

'My Division's rations are now exhausted. We have completely used up ammunition for mountain artillery and heavy infantry weapons. The Division will therefore withdraw from Kohima by June 1st at the latest and move to a point where it can receive supplies.' Mutaguchi's reply was judged by Sato to be both discourteous and threatening. It seemed to him, furthermore, that 'Army cannot grasp the real situation: no supplies, and men wounded and sick'. In fact, despite Kunomura's later assurances on a visit to 31 Division in early June, there were little or no supplies at Sangshak or Humine even when the division got there. Sato told Mutaguchi that he would certainly not disobey orders, but 'first we have to eat. Carrying out Army orders comes after that'.

On 4 May Sato protested to General Kawabe, Burma Area Army, that 'XV Army had failed in its responsibilities towards his Division and that no supplies had arrived', complaints that he subsequently repeated to Count Terauchi, Commander-in-Chief South-East Asia and to the Imperial General Staff itself in Tokyo.

The Japanese had lost thousands of men and were losing more by the day; they were ill, weak, under-nourished, if not yet all starving. Some could hardly stand up in their bunkers. Before the next Allied attacks began on the three sectors – the Ridge, Naga Village, and Aradura Spur – Sato had issued an emergency Order of the Day:

'The enemy are superior in weapons and fire-power. Each and every man must look after his rifle as a mother her child. An uncared-for arm is a criminal offence, and anyone found with an unserviceable rifle, or no rifle at all, will at once be shot by his officer. You will fight to the death. When you are killed you will fight on *with your spirit*.' On 13 May, after the central section of Kohima, less the tennis court, had fallen, he told Mutaguchi that because of 'heavy rain and starvation . . . this Division, accompanying its sick and wounded, should move to a point where it could receive supplies.' Mutaguchi refused, citing prospects for 33

Division under General Tanaka, its new commander, more imaginative than actual, which Sato indeed discounted as fantasy.

Nevertheless, as a senior Japanese officer he was not yet ready totally to flout his Commander-in-Chief. In any case, despite his losses and his defeat all along the ridge, he still held the 'half-moon' anchored so far at Aradura Spur and at Point 5120 by Naga Village. On 14 May, however, he was to lose even the tennis court, and the core of Kohima had at last been consumed. The Japanese, so long as they remained in their bunkers, and their illness often gave them no choice but to remain, could hold on, even against bombardment of up to four thousand shells a day, as long as they could pull a trigger. An officer of 58 Regiment said:

'Even the invalids and the wounded were driven to the front to help supply manpower. Even those with broken legs in splints were herded into battle, the malaria cases too. I have seen these go forward with yellow faces, the fever still in their bodies. I saw one man whose shoulder had been fractured stagger forward to the front.' It was widely believed among the rank and file that they would soon be relieved by another division. But these men were neither supermen nor automatons, only human beings devoted to a creed which, however misguided, produced courage and tenacity across a wider spectrum than in most other races.

Field-Marshal Slim stressed the 'theatricality' of the Japanese; public execution, bayoneting and the officers' habit of striking their men in punishment. He emphasized their patriotism also, its spirited base persisting even when the individual was alone. ('In this situation, we remembered our duties to our ancestors.') Courage was individual, not group. They would fight on alone rather than surrender. Their resistance and endurance were often incredible.

They had no fear of death. Here the Field-Marshal would cite the 'human anti-tank mines', the detachment of fifteen Japanese marching into the Irrawaddy in full kit and drowning there, 'soldier-ants', the disciplined acceptance of any order, the belief that although 'the Division might be annihilated, Japan would win' ultimately, should Japan be invaded, from dug-outs and caves in the homelands. Their chief professional fault was over-confidence, glitteringly exemplified by General Mutaguchi and his complete failure to provision his men.

Slim, although stressing the individual basis of Japanese courage and tenacity, recognized that Japan was a group society. Officers and men tended to come from the same regions, to share everything, to consolidate these 'unit' qualities in formal meetings in the evenings. One result was that, though 150,000 Japanese were killed, only 1,700 prisoners were captured, of whom only 400 were not very ill or wounded. No one above the rank of Major was taken prisoner, and no regular officers at all. When addressing the Japanese Staff college, Slim said, 'Well, of one thing I am certain. Next time I would want you on my side. It was a tough business. Let's keep together now.'

So it is easy to see that 2nd and 7th Divisions still had a hard fight ahead of them at Kohima.

XXVII

THE JAPANESE HOLD THE BUNKERS, BUT THE TENNIS COURT FALLS

BY 10 MAY, after the vicious, unsuccessful actions on GPT, Jail, Detail and Supply, those close, often hand-to-hand battles preceded by everything that the guns, mortars and, now, flame-throwers could do, the Japanese held their bunkers. Every time the British and Indian infantrymen – through the mist and rain, bent khaki and green figures with fixed bayonets – scurried up to the defences, remorseless fire was unleashed from ahead and from the flanks. There was neither respite nor apparent hope now of breaking through.

In these gigantic hills, men began to doubt even the possibility of victory. Too many officers and men were dying, battalions halved, some more than halved.

Colonel Scott had said that the bunkers on the vital GPT and Detail Ridges could not be taken 'by mere assault'. Grover told Stopford, to the latter's chagrin, that nothing could be done against Jail Hill until GPT had been neutralized. 11 May was the earliest date for the next stage which would then also include operations against Jail, Detail, Supply and Pimple Hills. Stopford was, of course, under renewed pressure from the Army Commander, concerned to reopen the Imphal road before the borrowed aircraft had to be returned to the Middle East, and before IV Corps' reserves at Imphal were exhausted.

The Corps Commander now brought Major-General Messervy's 7th Indian Division into the battle with its 33 and 161 Brigades. The sweep projected was to be from Naga Village on the left to Mao Song Sang, south of Kohima. But this sweep could not even be contemplated until the Ridge, Naga Village/Point 5120 and the Aradura Spur had been conquered.

A six-pounder gun was brought up against the bunkers on GPT Spur. It was ready on 9 May in a pit dug by the Sappers, to be manned by Gordon Highlanders of 100 Anti-Tank Regiment. Two attacks by 'C' Company of the Royal Norfolks to exploit this shelling were unsuccessful, the first being driven back by a heavy counter-attack mounted by fifty howling Japanese armed with grenades. The next morning a grenade severely wounded Brigadier Theobalds, now commanding 4 Brigade.

Robert Scott took over again, insisting that tanks were essential if bunkers were to be blown in and the battle won.

The Royal Scots on Pavilion Hill, whose kit had all been destroyed in Death Valley by damp and insects, had occupied the past days successfully hunting snipers in perpetual rain and cold. They only had half a blanket each which were usually passed on to the wounded. Fortunately the QM found new clothing for them in Dimapur.

Major Menzies, then commanding 'C' Company of the Royal Scots, was the next to attack the bunkers, 'a rabbit warren with passages that linked bunkers and concealed weapon replacements, highly elaborate, burrowed out of the steep hillsides and reinforced within'. Nothing was visible on the outside except for camouflaged loopholes for those rifles and machine guns which had themselves almost destroyed the Norfolk Company.

The damage inflicted on Menzies' Company was grave, twenty-five casualties including ten dead, from the bunker in front and from cross-fire, machine guns and artillery. Colonel Scott withdrew them a few yards. 'We were still so close to the Japs,' Menzies said, 'that we tried to burn them out with petrol tins which we set alight with Verey flares. The trenches began to fill with water. Soon we were standing on dead bodies to get a foothold. Nobody could sleep or even rest.' Lance-Corporal Canham climbed up to a loophole and forced his Bren through it, firing twenty rounds before being killed.

'D' Company under Major Russell then succeeded Menzies. Grant tanks got to within thirty yards of the bunkers and blasted them. The First of Foot went forward with fixed bayonets, then digging in to prepare for the forthcoming attack on Aradura Spur. The 'Norfolk' bunker and GPT were in British hands by 14 May after 25-pounders had destroyed a Japanese 75mm which had been brought up on an elephant under a shell-proof cover.

On 10 May Grover said, 'It must be exceptional for a Divisional Commander to be able to coordinate a Divisional battle personally, with all Brigade commanders, the CRA, tank commanders, machine-gun battalion commanders, from a perfect viewpoint from which we could look down with impunity into the whole battlefield set out in panorama, and to be able to look into the backs of the enemy positions.'

Jail Hill was to be attacked on 11 May by the Queen's Royal Regiment on the right, and the Punjabis on the left. Because enemy patrolling had robbed them of sleep, and because the rains had again begun beating on the sodden earth,they were exhausted before they started up the steep hillside. The Punjabis' Adjutant, Major R. A. J. Fowler, had translated into Urdu, a practice of his, 'Come the three corners of the world in arms, and we shall shock them. Nought shall make us rue,' which greatly affected the jawans. The Berkshires and 4/15 Punjabis were to go for FSD and DIS, 1/1 Punjabis for the Pimple, the Royal Welch Fusiliers for Kuki Piquet.

The Queens moved up on the difficult, undefined track to Jail Hill through thick undergrowth until they reached their forming-up point. The barrage broke the quiet darkness with a tremendous crash, lighting up with 'one red glow' the whole of Jail and DIS Hills. The Battalion stormed the first bunkers, firing from the hip, but, as usual, Japanese fire came down from the crest. Next morning the bunkers on DIS and GPT were still manned. The Japanese and British lines were close, and the grenade battle which followed was described from Battalion Head-quarters as 'if a snow fight were in progress with grenades instead of snowballs'.

Jail Hill was a very dangerous place. The Norfolks and Royal Scots had not yet eliminated the bunkers on Transport Ridge. Jail was unlikely to fall until these had been taken. The Berkshires had taken some bunkers, but not those on the reverse slopes of Supply Hill. On Detail, the original 4/15 Punjabi charge under Colonel Conroy with drums and pipes playing 'The Wounded Heart', led by Jats and Sikhs 'carrying their religious books' and shouting war cries, had been followed by the Mussulmen, enfiladed from FSD and Jail, suffering 130 killed and wounded. They and a company of 4/1 Gurkhas started to dig, using anything they could lay their hands on to get below ground level.

The Punjabis, the old '28', were a very grand Regiment. 'Even the junior NCOs had seven or eight years' service and the VCOs and havildars a good deal more.' They had no blankets at all, only gas-capes. When all the Platoon Commanders had been killed or wounded, Major Johnson rallied the Battalion from the position near the bunkers on the reverse slopes where they and the Queens were pinned down by grenades and machine-gun fire from the flanks.

About twelve Japanese were shot running away on the left when Major Lowry's Queens' Company reached the crest after dawn. Ahead were three bunkers blocking the advance and others further up. Using grenades, Lowry took a party forward to within ten yards of the nearest bunkers, engaging them for nearly six hours, actually going into one before mortars and flank machine-gun fire caught them. Mist came down at about 10 am, enabling the men to dig in and to get the stretcher-bearers away with the wounded. When Major Johnson extricated his battered Punjabis, the north-west part of the hill was in the hands of the Queens and 4/1 Gurkhas. The Queens had lost Captain J. H. A. Scott, Lieutenant Ingham and, later, Major M. L. Mansell.

Lowry needed to get at the bunkers on the reverse slopes. He called for smoke. The terrain was very difficult, 'horizontal tree trunks and the odd trench,' and the men were caught again in cross-fire, followed by a sniping duel and continued grenade exchanges lasting a considerable time. As the party was down to six or seven, the assault was halted and the Queens dug in, having joined up with 4/1 Gurkhas. They were observed by the Gurkhas to have indeed taken 'one third of the south-west part of the hill,' but strongly enfiladed and with no cover whatsoever. Any movement was met by a hail of bullets from the Japanese bunkers.

A Queens' officer who wished to give an order to a Gurkha Subedar, but could not make himself understood, had to do so through a field telephone to Major Thompson at Battalion HQ, Two Tree Hill, who passed on the order in Gurkhali to the Subedar waiting at the Queens' position. But digging-in under this hail of machine-gun bullets was not easy for either unit. A 3-inch mortar screen was laid and some slight gains made in thick mist and heavy rain. Food, ammunition and rum were brought forward for the Gurkhas, but the Queens, often only fifteen yards from the Japanese, got little rest that night. They had lost seventy men.

On 11 May Major T. S. May's Gurkha Company took a bunker on the forward slope after two attacks against grenade and machine-gun fire from in front and on the flank.

Next day, the Grant tanks came up.[1] They and the Artillery shelled Japanese bunkers on the reverse slopes only 15 yards from the forward units of the Queens, who had to lie under the barrage to avoid the debris and the shells. Two bunkers were abandoned by the enemy, caught by the Manchesters as they fled. Fifteen minutes later, 4/1 Gurkhas went in against heavy opposition and with great courage captured two more bunkers, closely investing the third on the forward slope. Twenty Japanese were seen running down the far side of the hills, a newish phenomenon. 'A bunker by the road was shot to bits and the corpses were seen to be blown clean up in the air.' Major Fowler, the translator of Shakespeare to the Punjabis, remained in a tank throughout the action, pointing out the bunkers to the guns' crews. Many Japanese were found dead in their positions, shot or burned alive. But DIS, FSD and Jail were still in enemy hands, and still they fought.

The Berkshires had started against their FSD objectives after an artillery and mortar concentration before coming up against a bunker. The Company Commander put his hand through a firing slit, grabbing a Japanese officer's arm, but a pole charge was required. Next day the Battalion, with two tanks, went forward to capture the rest of Supply Hill. Sergeant Garrett, pushing forward after a reconnaissance, directed the tanks on to the bunkers, followed by a company attack by Major Walem. Although the tanks were firing point-blank, the Japanese still resisted, shooting out the periscopes of one Grant. The tendency to jam of the British 75mm guns was infuriating.

The Berkshires had lost two officers and fifty-six men killed, fifteen officers and 239 men wounded, and sixty sick in five weeks' fighting.

On 13 May Sergeant Garrett went forward without orders, reporting that the enemy had vacated their positions. The Berkshires went after them until they were instructed not to continue the pursuit uncontrolled. Forty Japanese, not including those entombed in their bunkers, were buried. The Battalion captured one 75mm gun, two regimental guns, six heavy and twelve light machine guns, plus papers from a Battalion Headquarters 'as big as a cathedral and full of galleries'.

The 1/1 Punjabis had captured Pimple Hill on the evening of 11 May and on 12 May the Royal Welch Fusiliers took Kuki Piquet, preceded by pole charges and tank fire. Here they found the skeleton of a Royal West Kent private. He was tied to a tree and had been used for target practice by 58 Regiment.

At dawn on the same day patrols from the Queens and the Gurkhas found that all the twenty bunkers on Jail Hill were similarly deserted. For his part in this action Private Easton of the Queens, for six hours under continuous mortar and machine-gun fire, received the MM. The 4/15 Punjabis reported that the enemy bunkers on DIS were empty, although, like Supply Hill, full of documents and equipment. The Queens and the Gurkhas said that ten of the unoccupied positions on Jail Hill had been booby-trapped; they were, however, able to do a great deal of damage to fifty Japanese running from Treasury Hill. They themselves were still under sniper fire from GPT Ridge until a 4 Brigade tank shot up a bunker on the south side of that feature. Jail Hill was a loathsome place, battered, barren, scattered with debris and thick with flies.

The main bunker on Jail was deep into the hill and fortified with steel shutters, removed from Assam Barracks on Treasury, which could be closed, against grenades. It was, like many of these Japanese redoubts, of great complexity. On 14 May 1/1 Punjab and a company of 4/1 Gurkhas took over Jail Hill from the Queens. The latter had lost four officers and 57 ORs killed, six officers and 106 men wounded. A warning order that Treasury was the next target was received. Two Companies of 1/1 Punjab relieved 4/15 Punjab on DIS.

13 May, unlike the terrible 13 April on Garrison Hill, was a good day for the British, embellished by the Dorsets' eventual victory at the tennis court. There Indian troops of the 4/7 Rajputs had recently cut down some trees in order to build dug-outs. As a result, the then second-in-command of the Dorsets, Geoffrey White, later Battalion Commander, noticed that the DC's bungalow and compound were now visible through the thinned forest.[2] Three-quarters of the tennis court, the lower terrace,

the bungalow and drive could all be seen. For the first time the Dorsets really knew where they were. A secondary significant advantage of this discovery was the opportunity for return sniping at the Japanese in the 'early morning, the time that the Nips chose to move around and behave as human beings instead of the sub-human hole-dwellers which made them such first-class soldiers in defence'. The Intelligence Officer, Norman Havers, believes he killed seven of the enemy with a captured Bren.

Passwords, incidentally, in Kohima liberally employed the letter 'L', a Japanese shibboleth: Lilliput, Lollipop, Lullaby, Lahore, Calcutta, Absolutely, and so forth.

The Battalion objective was the tennis court, the point of attack against the bungalow terrace, linked with 'D' Company on the spur. Above the road one section would launch a left hook from the Club square to take the bunker at the north-east end of the court while others would drop from the Club square on to the court eliminating the Japanese by the water tank and below the Club. Another platoon would get round the Pimple and attack from the south.

Surprise, unfortunately, was lost and the 11 May attack was repulsed by fire from near the water tank and from 'a very suspicious clump of bamboo' in the DC's once ornamental gardens.

On 12 May the Sappers had succeeded brilliantly in building a track up Hospital Hill Spur along which a Lee/Grant medium tank was brought, to repose that night outside the Dorsets' HQ cookhouse. The plan of attack remained the same. The infantry, with supporting fire from the Lee, would take the bunker, another platoon seizing the water tank and the shed on the southern end of the tennis court. A third platoon would pass across the court to the bungalow terrace joining 'D' Company on the spur. A 3.7 inch gun was dragged by Major Law (10 Field Regiment) up to the Pimple with two hundred yards between it and the installation on the tennis court, the Lee to fire from the opposite direction and at the suspect bamboos. The 3.7 is the gun in the famous Cuneo oil paintings.

Next day Sergeant Waterhouse of 149 Royal Tank Regiment 'waddled his Grant over the edge of the bank and slid down on to the tennis court'. There is no evidence that this AFV inadvertently *fell* on to the court, as some accounts have suggested. Waterhouse slowly trained his turret and opened fire with his 75mm directly into the bunkers at no more than twenty yards range, the 3.7 inch firing fifty rounds simultaneously from the other quadrant. Platoons of the Dorsets, led by Sergeants Given and Cook, then exploited the complete surprise that the armour and artillery had achieved, while the great, lumbering tank, its turret turning from target to helpless target, loomed over the triumphant riflemen. 'Figures moved with an unexpected lack of haste . . . the enemy had been overwhelmed.'

Small arms fire from the Dorset platoons harried the fifty-odd Japanese abandoning their bunkers at the double for the temporary safety of Treasury Hill. Those of them who remained received pole charges of ten pounds of ammunition through the loop-holes, initially with twenty-second fuses which the enemy tore off. These were then replaced by four-second fuses which the Japanese could not remove in safety. The officer in charge of mopping-up, Major Chettle, from a manorial village of that name near Blandford Forum, crammed ammo down any likely Japanese fox-hole. Sixty Japanese dead were counted, apart from those buried in their bunkers. Only one Dorset was killed and four wounded but, over the whole three-week battle, they had lost seventy-five men in their dogged and imaginative struggle.

Only a chimney stack remained of the DC's bungalow. The earth was broken by shell holes, trees were no more than broken stumps, bodies and smashed equipment littered the garden. Debris and filth were everywhere. Flies and rats infested the grotesque landscape.

Now, for the first time since 5 April, there was no fighting on Kohima Ridge. General Stopford said, 'It was exactly like the Somme in 1916. One could tell how desperate the fighting had been . . . Our operations have been the biggest offensive show that the Japanese have yet had to face . . . I feel very exhilarated by the magnificent show which all battalions have put up.'

He added, 'There will be much hard fighting ahead,' a comment echoing General Slim's 'The capacity of the ordinary Japanese soldier to take punishment and his fanatical will to resist were unimpaired. I know of no Army that could have equalled them.' He and Stopford might also have emphasized the British shortage of artillery ammunition and its effect on the ability to take the bunkers, Second Division's permanent responsibility for keeping open the road to Dimapur as well as fighting the war and the shortage, in comparison with the European theatre, of men and material. Generals, as well as tailors, have to cut their coats according to their cloth, and Grover's, although he was dismissed after victory by Stopford on 4 July, was good cloth. One sour joke was no longer made: 'Knock, knock, who's there?', 'Two Div', 'Two Div what?', 'Too difficult – send for 5th or 7th', according to taste, 'Indian Division'.

Notes

1. Three tanks of 'A' troop, 149 Regiment RAC were knocked out. 'B' troop followed a converted minesweeper into enemy lines until the sweeper was blown up: the

leading Grant tank of the troop then had its right track blown off, slewing into the mountainside, so that neither the 35mm or 75mm could be used. Two other tanks were similarly damaged and blocked the road. When the crew of the lead tank, which was driven by J. H. Adderley, a militant member of the British Communist Party, bailed out, through the door, not the turret where the Japanese expected them, the door swung wide open under its own weight, exposing the crew to the concentrated fire of the two trenches of Japanese. Adderley held them off with a Thompson sub-machine-gun, which he had found behind the driver's seat and which he had had no idea how to use, until they could run for shelter behind the tank. The tank commander had fainted. Adderley smugly quoted Gorki to himself: 'Man's greatest possession is life and it is only given him once,' before pulling him clear.

2. Geoffrey White, among other distinctions, was an Olympic hurdler, while Nishida to whom reference has been made at Sangshak and who will be noted at Gun Spur, pole-vaulted for Japan in the 1936 Olympics. Nishida was hit by seven bullets at Sangshak; when asked by a British officer after the war whether he had been sent to the rear as a result, he replied that there were no medical facilities to which Japanese wounded *could* be sent.

XXVIII

DEREK HORSFORD TAKES POINT 5120

BRIGADIER VICTOR Hawkins, commanding 5th Brigade, was badly wounded on 12 May, just as 33 Brigade was making decisive progress elsewhere against Detail, Supply, GPT and Jail. He was the third Brigadier of his Division to become a casualty, Goschen having been killed on GPT the week before, and Theobalds wounded the same day as himself. Two Battalion commanders, Hedderwick of 4/1 Gurkhas and Brown of the Durham Light Infantry, had been killed, and the explosive Scott of the Royal Norfolks wounded. When Grover saw Scott's bloody bandage, he remarked, 'Perhaps you'll now apologize for your truculence when I asked you to take steel helmets on Pulebadze.'

Hawkins was succeeded in Naga Village by Mike West, later to hold such distinguished appointments as GOC Austria, Commander Commonwealth troops Korea, Commander 1st British Corps BAOR, GOC Northern Command, Commandant, School of Infantry. He married Christine Oppenheim and became rather a glamorous figure, a 'political' soldier who enjoyed relatively High Society or at least sensibly enjoyed social life amongst the Austrian *Erstegesellschaft* and their English and European connections. He was also, however, a professional soldier. There is no objection to the military expanding their horizons or, for that matter, to diplomats learning something about the military.

His objective was the capture of Church Knoll and Hunter's Hill, against which the Worcesters, Camerons and Lancashire Fusiliers had come a cropper on 4 May after the earlier set-back on Firs Hill. The Camerons had since 4 May sustained 105 casualties, including 35 killed and ten missing, with more on 7 May from the shelling of Battalion Headquarters and from a Japanese machine-gun attack on a patrol. Lieutenant J. A. C. Carbonell, who killed the despatch-rider carrying General Mutaguchi's crucial order to General Sato, himself died during this period, after being severely wounded and developing gas gangrene while his stretcher lay in the rain.

Hawkins, before he was wounded, sent out regular officer and other patrols to these two hills in order to monitor Japanese bunker and dug-out construction. He concluded that a full-scale attack with up to two battalions, plus tanks and artillery, would be required to take the position. As this strength could not currently be provided, he decided that a night infiltration should be attempted by the Camerons, against the time when the whole Brigade could attack from the north and formations of 2 and 7 Divisions from the south.

On 15 May two Camerons platoons got on to Church Knoll, but lost surprise. Although they killed five of the enemy, their fire activated a major Japanese response with grenades and machine guns which, *inter alia*, set fire to a basha containing petrol. The lurid glare added to the tracer in a grotesquely illuminated blaze. Captains Neil White and Peter Cameron withdrew their units.

After a conference between John Grover and Mike West, two tanks were brought up to 5 Brigade in order to move up a track built by the Sappers. The entire Brigade now formed a perimeter round Naga Village, while Church Knoll, on which the Japanese had a firm base, was only two hundred yards away. Both sides occupied bunkers, 'like rabbits', as the Worcesters' Regimental History fastidiously remarks. The British were supplied by air, the drops sometimes, and sometimes not, falling within the perimeter. If they fell outside, collection awaited mist or darkness; occasionally the bundles were unreachable and had to be destroyed by rifle or other fire.

On 18 May a concentrated Hurribomber air strike thoroughly frightened the Worcesters, who feared that bombs were bound to fall short against targets only two hundred yards away. They fortunately did not and, on 19 May, preceded by an artillery barrage, two companies of Worcesters went forward. Once again withering fire from mutually supporting Japanese bunkers, from the terraces above as each lower terrace was scaled, and from the bunkers on the reverse slope which DF could not reach, ended another failed asssault. The 6-pdr anti-tank guns with HE or AP shells were found to be the most damaging weapons against the bunkers. Flame-throwers into the loop-holes were effective, but only at point-blank range where they cleared at least one bunker. Pole charges were used, tank and anti-tank fire was laid down on call, but there were no less than five connected bunkers on the reverse slope as well. The Japanese were 'nipping out of bunkers, hurling grenades and then disappearing into fresh holes'. As it seemed unlikely that the Worcesters could hold even the forward slope that night, they withdrew under artillery covering fire, forty lives lost.

On 20 May West had to tell Grover that there was no chance of building a track for tanks round to the reverse slope of Church Knoll. As there was also no possibility of acquiring the Medium Artillery which *could* deal with the bunkers, Grover only ordered 'patrolling and offensive action against any accessible bunkers'. The Camerons, now under Lieutenant-Colonel Somerville-M'Alester, known to officers and men alike as 'Sporran Jock', moved to Jotsoma after a few days' patrolling on relief by the 4/15 Punjabis. The Worcesters moved back three miles for a short rest, relieved by the 1st Queens Royal Regiment.

A Japanese prisoner from 58 Regiment at this time said that he had surrendered because his company no longer had any officers, was commanded by a sergeant and reduced to forty men. It had been demoralized by air and artillery bombardment and only had salt and rice to eat. This was encouraging news, but the behaviour of the enemy within their bunkers was a more accurate indicator of morale and determination.

Commander XXXIII Corps now instructed that Major-General Messervy's 7 Division, including 33 Brigade, should go for the Naga Village and Point 5120, while 2nd Division should attack Aradura Spur, employing 4 and 6 Brigades.

At dawn on 23 May, a Punjabi patrol sighted twenty-five Japanese in a cookhouse, drinking tea. A bombardment by the 5.5 inch guns of 5/22 Medium Battery then caused what appeared to be the total disintegration of the bunkers on Church Knoll, Hunter's Hill and North Spur. Earth and beams flew in all directions. Again it seemed to observers that no one could have survived under the ruins. Another barrage, followed by Hurribomber strafing on 24 and 25 May preceded the assault on Church Knoll by 'B' under Marment and 'D' under Fowler of the 4/15 Punjabis with an accompanying 25-pounder barrage, plus tanks. The shells, with one exception which wounded several of the most forward Punjabis, fell just ahead of the advance. The troops then came under machine-gun fire from a flank, but it was not until they reached the crest that the enemy once more beat off this allied assault with rapid, well-directed and unexpected counter-fire from hidden bunkers. Even with the 5.5s, the Medium Artillery requested by Grover, the famous 4/15 Punjabis had failed, just as the Camerons and Worcesters had also failed. The casualties when they withdrew at dusk were eight killed and 58 wounded.

After this set-back, on 28 and 29 May General Messervy called up the tanks, Hurribombers and artillery for yet another strike on Church Knoll and Hunter's Hill. The 4/15 Punjabis went up the hill. 'Every face showed that he was sure of his part.' Men were seen falling, but none ran back under the rain of Japanese mortars and grenades. The Sikhs, hand-in-hand, went for Church Knoll and those not hit were seen on top of the objective, the Punjabi Mussulmen making for Hunter's Hill. Major Thomas took the Jats of 'C' Company to reinforce 'A' and 'B', but, although reaching the crest, they could not dig in on the rocky earth. Colonel Conroy, who had been wounded, arrived, and Major Marment then brought up 'B' Company before 33 Brigade ordered a general withdrawal. Brigadier Loftus-Tottenham was somewhat surprised when a 4/15 Punjabi orderly, 'hopping in and out of the shell holes', brought to the command post sandwiches with the crusts cut off on a china plate bearing the regimental arms. Twelve were killed, 83 wounded and one Sikh Company had only eighteen men left. The Battalion had shot its bolt.

Some of the reasons for this depressing, even desperate, situation have been suggested in the earlier chapter on contemporary Japanese morale and practice. They included the 'security' felt by the enemy within, but not without, their bunkers, their positive inability, due to disease and starvation, to *leave* their bunkers, their belief in imminent relief, iron discipline and devotion to the Emperor.

Whatever the explanation, Second and Seventh Divisions were halted where they stood in front of unassailable Japanese positions. No gains had been made, no defences taken. Despite their desperate physical conditions, the enemy could still hold off the exhausted and reduced battalions of the Second, and now the Seventh Divisions, all of them engaged in fierce close-contact battles for five long weeks, and some since August, 1943. The Japanese lines, if not solid, still held. The commanders wondered for how much longer these British and Indian regiments could be asked, in the appalling conditions of the Burmese monsoon, to live, fight, sleep and die against an implacable and apparently invincible enemy.

Stopford, Grover and Messervy had a conference after this latest battle, not a hopeful nor a constructive one. The Americans had agreed to let SACSEA keep the eighty air transports for another two weeks, but if the Kohima–Imphal road could not be opened by 15 June, supplies, including rations for IV Corps at Imphal, would be very tight indeed. 33, now under Tanaka, and 15 Divisions were pressing on the defences; 17, 20 and 23 Indian Divisions could not hold for ever without supplies of ammunition and food. One observer has said that the Generals, in discussing all the prospects, feared that even if XXXIII Corps were to break through at Kohima, 'the enemy had a series of magnificent defensive positions running almost back to Imphal: Viswema, Kigwema, the great height of Mao Song Sang, and the Ridge at Maram.' Time was running out for Slim's splendid, battered XIV Army, plagued by inadequate armour, not enough men, fragile communications and shortages of ammunition, food and water. The battle of attrition against these stubborn Japanese might take too long to save Imphal and, hence, communications with China, even India itself. A pulverizing victory was essential to win the campaign. None was visible.

At this depressing moment, almost of despair, hope was born. Without the brilliant tactical success now described, it is far from certain that the victory of Kohima could have been achieved in time also to secure victory at Imphal.

Major Derek Horsford, second-in-command of the 8th Gurkhas, was brought out of the Arakan to command the Fourth Battalion of the First Gurkhas in 33 Brigade after Hedderwick's death from the sniper on GPT Ridge. From 12 April, when he took over, 'Lieutenant-Colonel Horsford created a magnificent fighting unit, leading the Battalion from strength to strength' and, in the process, winning two DSOs. The Battalion had been classified as 'suffering from malnutrition as a result of the Arakan privations', and was not supposed to go into action until September! Slim refused him an initial DSO on the grounds that 'for so young an officer' (he was only 27) 'to command a Gurkha battalion was sufficient reward'. Horsford lives today near Shaftesbury, a former Colonel of the King's Regiment and the Gurkha Transport Regiment; he is a Major-General now who, like others, was deprived only of the luck and opportunity to reach the very pinnacle of his profession, a summit that he deserved more than most.

The enemy was concentrated on Church Knoll and Hunter's Hill to the north-east of Treasury Hill. Horsford had noticed that, although all previous patrols from the 5 and 33 Brigade box had said that Treasury was held in strength, no patrol had actually reached the position, nor could anyone remember actual firing from the hill. One of his Gurkha patrols reported that there were Japanese there; two said that there were none.

Acting on his own judgement, Horsford then moved the entire Battalion to Treasury, finding it empty. There they remained for thirteen days, raided every night, shelled and mortared every day. The Gurkhas behaved impeccably. 'They were first-class. As soon as the shelling stopped, they got straight out of their semi-dug trenches and continued to work on the defences.' Six Gurkhas were killed and nineteen wounded during this stage.

So many frontal attacks had been made on the Japanese bunkers and other features at Church Knoll and Hunter's that when Brigadier Loftus-Tottenham ordered another, this time by the 4/1 Gurkhas, Horsford demurred. The Brigadier had originally not wished to use the Battalion here, after its ordeal in the Arakan and after the devastating losses suffered by his other two Battalions, Queens and Punjabis. Horsford believed in 'getting round behind the Japanese' as the training manuals instructed. His plan was to infiltrate the high and forested Gun Spur by night so that, once in position, his Gurkha riflemen with artillery support could dominate the reverse slopes of the target. The features on the Spur, which lay to the south-east of the objectives, were running south from Hunter's Hill – Basha, Nose, and False Crest, all easily observed from

Treasury Hill. On that hill Derek Horsford had had just enough time to think about his operation, and plan for it with unhurried subtlety. It was vital to discover the Japanese strongpoints, if any, so that they could be by-passed as the Battalion advanced. Surprise was essential.

It is difficult to say why no one other than Horsford could reach a decision so vital but at the same time so 'conventional' and in accordance with doctrine.

Patrolling took place day and night, ambushes at night. Four Japanese prisoners were captured on Treasury. Three days and nights were given the Battalion to find a weak point in the defences through which a force could be put strong enough to hold until the entire Battalion advanced. Two-man patrols of one NCO and one rifleman went out every night with the specific task of discovering which of the three features were occupied by the Japanese, in what strength and condition. The patrols left Treasury immediately darkness fell. They were then required to quit their objectives before the enemy could see them at first light next morning.

False Crest and Nose were clear of Japanese on that first night, and on the second. Basha was defended strongly by bunkers, probably inter-connected, containing about thirty Japanese, a 'garrison' which had increased to forty the next night, with a similar force on Ring off the Spur to the south. Road blocks and bunkers were found in the darkness nearer Kohima to the west and a hundred yards east of False Crest. Patrols monitored the defences again on the third and last night.

On 25 May at 7.45 pm, Major Sir C. J. Nixon occupied the empty False Crest. Captain R. S. R. Carr's company, starting at 10 pm, had taken Nose by 4 am on 26 May. The companies had had to advance down a very steep slope with a dry nullah at the bottom and then up another hill, both units having Carrier, Pioneer and Escort platoons. Behind Carr, Major M. J. T. McCann's 'B' Company formed up on Nose in preparation for the assault on Basha which still held its forty Japanese in their bunkers. Communications were provided by Gurkha signallers reeling out cable as they went, connected to one terminal of a field telephone. An earth wire was connected via the other terminal to a spike on the signaller's boot. When the spike was driven into the ground, the circuit was complete and Company Commanders could talk to their Commander.

At first light McCann passed through Nose and attacked the main Japanese position after a twenty-minute concentration from medium artillery, 25-pounders, 3.7 howitzers and tanks. The Company advanced to within fifty yards behind the barrage, and tanks firing high explosive 'to clear the jungle', and armour-piercing to destroy the bunkers, changing to Browning machine guns over the Gurkhas' heads to prevent the enemy from moving out in counter-attack. But as the Battalion went in, the tanks fired armour-piercing shells only ten yards ahead of the Gurkhas.

The leading files were wearing white towels on their backs so that they could be seen by the tank commanders. There occurred a sudden cloud-burst during which the Commanding Officer lost sight of the white towels, assumed 'B' Company was late and so continued with the barrage for another five minutes. The Company was not late, however, and the Japanese were still cowering, in no state to resist when the attack came in. Twenty of them were killed by bayonet or grenade while huddling in their trenches. Twenty more were killed later; twenty escaped. Six mutually-supporting bunkers were sighted on the top of Basha, and the company dug in. Only six Gurkhas were wounded, none killed.

'A' and 'C' Companies, after their silent night infiltrations by sections, platoons and, finally, the whole Company, to Nose and False Crest, had formed defensive positions with all-round defence. Now they made their way up Gun Spur, consolidating under accurate, harassing Japanese mortar and grenade dischargers, driving off three Japanese counter-attacks. This process continued for three days.

Between 29 and 31 May the Battalion destroyed sixteen bunkers with pole charges, flame-throwers and tanks. The flame-throwers were unreliable, and were indirectly responsible for the wounding of Captain Green. As he knelt under a hail of bullets to apply his weapon to a loophole, he and his No. 2 were hit by machine-gun fire from the flank, the No. 2 riddled by bullets. Subedar Narang Ghal raced to Green, bound his wounded leg and carried him for one hundred yards in full view of the Japanese before rolling with him into a bomb crater under showers of dirt and tree splinters. Narang received the Military Cross.[1]

Digging and wiring, since the Basha was overlooked, took place at night only. The Japanese were certainly diminishing in number, but patrols from 'D' Company discovered that they were still in strong possession of Hunter's Hill, the Battalion's objective.

Derek Horsford described 1 June as 'the highlight of the whole operation'. Jemadar Patirquam Gurung with a platoon of 'C' Company raided Ring, a small forested hill, the position of which has been already described, occupied by thirty Japanese. He was ordered to kill as many as he could, but not to try to capture the position.

Preceded by a tank firing HE, the Jemadar led his men up the hill, tossing grenades into a machine-gun post and killing four Japanese within. His 'A' Section then rushed a 75mm gun and killed with their kukris a further four enemy gunners, also stuffing five grenades down the barrel of the gun. The platoon then withdrew to the Battalion, having killed twelve Japanese without loss. Patiram received a Military Cross. All the other platoons begged to be allowed to do a raid like it.

On the same day three Sherman tanks came up along the Jessami track to join the Gurkhas. The cross-fire between the Battalion which had now been joined by the CO's Headquarters and the Japanese on Hunter's Hill, was fierce. It was only after another Hurribomber attack, followed by more artillery and tank fire, that Hunter's Hill could be taken. The victor was Captain W. G. Hughes with his 'D' Company of 4/1 Gurkhas.

Meanwhile on 30 May 'B' Company of the Queens had met 4/1 Gurkhas on the Jessami track, and had pointed out targets for the tanks. Two platoons of the Queens then attempted to infiltrate a bunker on Church Knoll from which they were driven off twice by Japanese artillery and mortar fire. At 1030 next day, under mist and heavy rain, they took the Knoll without opposition, finding the main position empty at last; the 4/1 Gurkhas destroyed guns and mortar positions there in a night action.

The Japanese had evacuated Naga Village. Gurkha casualties had been five killed and thirty-five wounded, including one British officer. The 4/1 Gurkhas were relieved on 2 June by 4/5 Gurkhas, the Queens by 2nd South Lancashire Regiment. The Royal West Kents, back in the line, occupied Firs Hill, while Warren's 161 Brigade took three tactically important features on the left flank. 33 Brigade had won the battle: 7th Division could start the left hook southwards ordered by Montagu Stopford. There was now a chance, which could not come soon enough, of reopening the road.

At the height of the siege of Imphal the RAF had been asked to feed 155,000 men, of whom 30,000 were British, and 11,000 mules and horses. Food and supplies, including oil, petrol, ammunition, clothing, weapons, reinforcements, field guns, AFVs and jeeps amounted to 750 tons a day or 157 daily transport aircraft flights. Some squadrons were flying three, four, even five sorties each day, supplies in, wounded and sick out, against continual pressure from the Chiefs of Staff to return the borrowed aircraft.

The RAF 221 Group's performance was magnificent, both in supply dropping and hostile action, 2,200 sorties against 31 Division in April and 400 tons of bombs in support of Kohima. Aircrew losses there and on the Tamu–Palel road were considerable. They had delivered by the end of the battle for Imphal 14,000,000 pounds of rations, nearly one million gallons of petrol, 1,200 bags of mail, forty-three million cigarettes, twelve thousand reinforcements. They had evacuated thirteen thousand casualties and forty-three thousand non-combatants.

Notes

1. Green subsequently changed his name to Rodney Needham. He became Professor of Oriental Social Anthropology at All Souls. There he was visited by a Captain Susuma Nishida of 58 Regiment who commanded the unit which wounded him, the same Nishida who had led the monumental reconnaissance of the Somra and Naga Hills before the battle, in which 2 Company of III Battalion of 58 Regiment had destroyed V Force HQ, disabled all V Forces' communications and thus blinded IV Corps on its north-eastern front. Nishida was also present, with Shosaku Kameyama, at the Battle of Sangshak.

XXIX

THE JAPANESE LEAVE
ARADURA SPUR

THE SECOND curve of the Japanese half-moon, that based on Aradura Spur, had now to be eliminated if 4 Brigade (Royal Norfolks and Royal Scots) were to mount a frontal attack through to the Imphal Road. 6th Brigade – Durham Light Infantry, Royal Welch Fusiliers and Royal Berkshires – were allocated to this task under their Gunner Commander, a nice man with two daughters, Brigadier J. D. Shapland. (Shapland had been CRA of 2 Div; he was sound, not dashing, later becoming Major-General (Admin.) Rhine Army.) What followed was one of the most disastrous episodes in the Kohima campaign, rigidity personified.

These three Battalions, accompanied by the 1st Burma Regiment, were assembled on GPT Ridge. The DLI consisted of only two companies and an HQ Company, the Battalion already having lost 175 men and eleven out of fifteen officers. Although it was gravely below strength, it gave the lead to the Berkshires and the Royal Welch, participating fully in the ghastly march, even taking over at one point from the Burma Regiment.

For the Durhams, 'The Spur was covered with thick jungle . . . A party under Jack Burman found Japs cooking a meal and attacked them with grenades, putting an end to their destructiveness, with only one man wounded . . . The advance was by leapfrogs, with a steady drain of casualties from snipers. It rained almost continuously and the jungle tracks consisted of mud and water . . . Wherever we went the Jap was always up hill, a beastly situation. All supplies were carried by mule or the gallant Nagas, two steps up and sliding back one . . . a number of mules fell over the side, one carrying the telephone exchange.'

Brigadier Shapland's plan was to attack Aradura where the road passed round its northern end to the eastern side of the mountains. 6 Brigade would attack the village and crest from the west, 4 Brigade assaulting the lower slopes. The Berkshires would take the crest, the RWF dealing with positions named after three apostles, 'Matthew, Mark and Luke', before both Battalions occupied 'John'. Unfortunately Shapland intended to proceed by an artillery tactic called 'stepping-up', which meant that Companies were not 'firm' at the point of change. He also proposed to advance in single file. Colonels Bickford and Garnett Braithwaite took extreme exception to these proposals, not quite to the point of disobedience or of reference to Grover. (It is hard, in fact, to see how they could have advanced on those tracks other than in single file.) There were other doctrinal points to which the infantrymen objected, nor did they approve of senselessly taking points high in the jungle from which the road was invisible. (The maps, and the aerial reconnaissance conducted by David Wilson, the Brigade Major, could not help greatly, although Naga interpretation shed some light on things.) But Shapland's orders stood.

The Berkshires started up the hill in a tropical downpour, carrying mortars, ammunition and machine guns and guided by Major Mac-George's Special Service Company in vulnerable single file. Progress was slow through the dripping mass of vegetation, thorns and creepers. The ground was slippery mud and men could not keep their footing, sliding back on those behind. Their loads often forced them to climb by rope. Visibility was down to twenty yards. Leeches penetrated unsecured clothing, to be removed only by lighted cigarette ends with, at best, discomfort and inconvenience, the whole business miserable. 'It could take four hours to move one man and his mortar a quarter of a mile, with or without the aid of a mule.'

The track rose and fell continually, dipping and sometimes climbing almost vertically, so that the men had to be hauled up as if mountaineering. MacGeorge told Bickford that he could not find the way to the crest, nor did he even know his and the Berkshires' present position. Bickford then asked the guns to put fire down on their objective. He hoped to find his location by judging the direction of the sound. 143 Special Services and the Berkshires then formed a box from which they patrolled unsuccessfully to find a track. Nothing was seen of the HE and smoke then fired, but, from their sound, the crest was a long way away. The W/T set had got wet and was not working but a signal line had been paid out behind the Battalion, so that it was possible to communicate with Brigade. The troops dug in, wet, tired, braced against trees so as not to slip down the hill. Some dozed but no one slept and, next morning, there was heavy sniping against the climbers.

The Royal Welch Fusiliers, already having suffered severe casualties and under great strain, took over from the Berkshires, believing that they were six hundred yards from the crest. A company of the Worcesters relieved the DLI perimeter defence while the Durhams moved forward and took over from 1st Burma. The Berkshires – and the Royal Welch Fusiliers, reduced to three Companies of *thirty* men each and a Company HQ – also advanced, but then dug in. The Royal Welch Box came under very heavy cross-fire, sniping, machine gun, grenades and mortars: 'The Japanese occupied the whole jungle in an arc facing this Battalion.' 'A' and 'B' Companies were overrun, with 90% casualties.

The RWF, in slit trenches vacated by the Berkshires, had used all their ammunition. Colonel Garnett Braithwaite ordered them back. Shapland, severely wounded in the neck, said that they 'gave'.[1] Although they, and the 2nd Manchester machine gunners, *were* shaken and in disorder, their Commander said that most of them were wounded and therefore seeking cover. He had withdrawn to avoid 'obliteration and the continued and unnecessary slaughter of these wonderful men who had always fought so bravely. They had been led into a trap.' Whether they had been caught in a prepared counter-attack or a local tactical success, the Aradura operation was ruined. Michael Demetriadi, the Intelligence Officer, carried Shapland to the rear. (Demetriadi and David Wilson used to play the penny whistle and the bagpipes respectively to one another on the field telephone.) Braithwaite was succeeded in the field by Jack Stocker of the Worcesters. The Royal Welch at Kohima, and after, were the bravest of the brave, but right now they had had too much.

Wilbur Bickford and the Berkshires were further up the mountain in thick jungle where they too had dug in. MacGeorge said that his Company had, indeed, found Japanese along the crest, but that troops with such loads as 6 Brigade's could not get at them through the mud and undergrowth. The Battalion, in thunderous rain, heard increasingly heavy firing behind them. Next day they were ordered to withdraw. In the meanwhile, 1 Burma Regiment retook the area previously held by the Royal Welch Fusiliers. They were attacked in greatly superior numbers and forced to withdraw on 2 June, but then continued to patrol, trying to reach the crest. The Royal Welch, after the most exiguous of 'rests', took over on the same day from the Worcesters who had moved into 6 Brigade area on 28 May.

The Berkshires had suffered terribly, losing 28 killed, 87 wounded and no less than 92 sick from scrub typhus, dysentery and malaria.

4th Brigade, with the Royal Scots under MacKenzie-Kennedy and Royal Norfolks under Robert Scott, were no more successful. It will be recalled that this Brigade was to conduct frontal attacks on the Spur, 6th Brigade covering their right flank. Charles Hill, Bare Hill and Basha Spur were attacked with artillery support at 7.30 am on 28 May while 6 Brigade were fighting their doomed right hook through the jungle to link up with 4 Brigade. The attack was, of course, a repeat of 4 Brigade's tumultuous earlier action on Transport Ridge, but the Japanese were ready for them this time. No companies of the Norfolks had more than two platoons: their total strength was no more than 380 men. Although many of these, because of filthy conditions in the positions on GPT occupied by the Japanese, had dysentery, a high proportion refused to go back to the Regimental Aid Posts.

The Norfolks made some gains, but from below the ridge they could not even see the enemy. Movement became impossible. The Royal Scots quickly occupied Basha, but a 75mm on Big Tree Hill caused casualties. Advance on the remaining features was strongly opposed sixty yards from the crest itself by a defiladed Japanese machine-gun position on Charles, and from weapons on the reverse slope of Bare Hill. The Royal Scots and Norfolks reformed one hundred and fifty yards from the crest. Very accurate machine-gun and artillery fire was directed at the bunkers, but both Battalions were still held up, 'spreadeagled on the slippery slope . . . against swarms of Japanese in thick jungle on higher ground'.

Colonel Peter Saunders, temporarily commanding 4th Brigade before succession by Theobalds, recognized that had the companies led by Majors Greene and Murray-Brown of the Norfolks and Menzies and Russell in the First of Foot remained under Japanese fire from above they would have been wiped out. 'Reluctantly, quietly and in good order, they withdrew to GPT.' Padré Crichton Roberts, after burying the dead, called the place 'the Hill of Death'. The Royal Norfolks' casualties in the whole Kohima battle were seven officers and 79 other ranks killed, and thirteen officers and over 150 other ranks wounded: the Royal Scots had 17 killed and 54 wounded. The 1/8 Lancashire Fusiliers took over.

The lessons of these failures were learned and applied later during the Emergency in Malaya. They included the need for closer co-ordination and understanding between higher and lower formations; the right of subordinate commanders to carry out their orders in their own way and time; the vital necessity for reasonable intelligence before action; practice in infiltration; time to be allowed for consolidation; comprehension that armour cannot go or climb *everywhere*.

It was, incidentally, in this battle that the extraordinary Robert Scott, cursing on his weak, exhausted and depleted companies below the crest of Charles Hill, pulling out grenades and hurling them over the ridge to the reverse slope, was hit and fell back severely wounded down the hill. There is no further reference to him in Swinson or in the Norfolks' War Diary. The Royal Scots Regimental History has it that he commanded 4 Brigade in the chase after 5 Brigade down the main road to Imphal. This is not confirmed by Louis Allen, who lists McNaught (Dorsets) as taking over the Brigade from Theobalds.

Now, 33 Brigade having taken Church Knoll and Hunter's Hill and brought about the retreat of the Japanese from the vital point of Naga Village, General Stopford decided to go for the 'present centre of the Japanese line', taken to be three features on a ridge south of Kohima, Dyer Hill, Pimple and Big Tree Hills which had held the 75mm firing on the Royal Scots. If they could be taken, the road would be open to Pfuchama at 5,000 feet and to Phesema on the Imphal Road. The Japanese on Aradura would have been cut off, further direct assault on that murderous spur thus rendered unnecessary. General Grover gave the task to Brigadier Mike West and 5th Brigade, the Dorsets, Worcesters and Camerons, who knew one another and fought well together, three formidable British Regiments, now better accustomed to their circumstances.

Patrols from the 268 Brigade, Bombay Grenadiers, chiefly used to provide reliefs for battalions in 2 Division, and from 114 Brigade, claimed that Dyer Hill and Big Tree Hill were free of Japanese. On arrival there on 3 June, an officer of the Dorsets, 'Snagger' Highett, reported that he had, however, been shot up from both Big Tree and the Pimple. 'False-reporting' in these conditions of rain, mud and vertical movement was endemic and caused pain, even if sometimes the cause was Japanese 'deception'. The Dorsets under McNaught set up a perimeter including the Camerons, in slit trenches filled with water, and with no food. Next day at first light, 'cold, soaked through, stiff and breakfastless,' the Dorsets occupied Dyer Hill, the Japanese having evacuated the position during the night, leaving a strong bunker on the reverse slope. A barrage was laid down on Pimple but, after initial success, the enemy, as was so frequently their custom, 'came alive' at the crest and forced the Dorsets off. Captains Michael Morice and David Purser were killed in these actions. On 4 June the Camerons took Pimple and, after an artillery and 3″ mortar concentration, their 'C' Company, supported by Sherman tanks, attacked Big Tree Hill. The conditions were foul and the steep slopes shiny with mud. The enemy, who had killed the Cameron Highlander's second-in-command Angus Douglas, were in some strength. The main assault was deferred until the next day.

On 3 June Lieutenant-Colonel Bradford's 2nd Reconnaisance left the heights (approx 7,500 feet) of Mount Pulebadze after more than ten days and another nine on Aradura Spur. They had been in frequent action, killing a number of Japanese on the way up and down, Sergeant-Major 'Posh' Price particularly distinguishing himself. Major Ken Hook, the second-in-command, won an MC; he said the views from the top, even through cloud, were spectacular.

On 5 June, after extensive artillery, mortar and machine-gun preparation, the Camerons took Big Tree Hill without difficulty. Their casualties, since leaving the start-line this time, had been three killed and seven wounded. The Battalion was then relieved by the Bombay Grenadiers, moving on to Garage Spur which the Punjabis had already found clear of Japanese. No movement could be seen on the Kohima–Imphal road.

On 30 May, when organizing the withdrawal of 31 Division, Lieutenant-General Sato Kotuku arranged to leave behind rear parties, including a rearguard on Aradura Spur of about 600 men, (1 company 58, 1 battalion, 124 Regiments, and the 31 Engineers Regiment) under the excellent Major-General Miyazaki. At some time after midnight on 5/6 June a patrol of 1/8 Lancashire Fusiliers found that, because of 5 Brigade's successes on 31 Division's last line, this detachment had silently pulled off the Spur. The Fusiliers' patrol found a dead Royal Norfolk whose boots and socks had been stolen by the Japanese. The Japanese fought, however, at Viswema and Mao, before being finally broken up at Maram on 20 June by the Worcesters.

Men had been fighting on these hills and ridges for sixty-four days in conditions of mud, rain, fire and blood as bad as the Somme and Passchendaele. But now the Battle of Kohima had been won.

Notes

1. Shapland was succeeded by a brilliant Australian officer of the Indian Army (1 Punjabi and Tochi Scouts), Bill (W. G.) Smith DSO, whose only weakness was a dread of his own Generals. He was never to be found by his Brigade Major (David Wilson, formerly 8th Argylls) when the Generals came to call, drawing on Wilson, now retired at Lamberhurst, Grover's lofty disapproval.

XXX

GENERAL SATO
GOES HOME

ON 25 MAY Lieutenant-General Sato learned from 5th Air Force Division, possibly because of requirements against the Chindits, that no supply aircraft could be expected for 31 Division. He therefore sent the signal to XV Army already quoted but deserving repetition:

'My Division's rations are now exhausted. We have completely used up ammunition for mountain artillery and heavy infantry weapons. The Division will therefore withdraw from Kohima by 1st June at the latest and move to a point where it can receive supplies.' A XV Army staff officer had anticipated this, advising his superiors that the division should be sent to Ukhrul, to shorten the supply routes. Mutaguchi, as will be recalled, disregarded the question of supply and told Sato to hang on for a further ten days. Sato regarded this as discourteous, informing XV Army that he would act on his own initiative, an unheard-of proposal in the Japanese Army.

It has been said that Mutaguchi threatened him with a court-martial, to which Sato responded that he would 'bring Mutaguchi down with him'. After his order for withdrawal, it is alleged also that he signalled: 'The tactical ability of the XV Army staff is below that of cadets'.

On 31 May he *did* act on his own initiative, ordering the division to move to Chedema. 'Shedding bitter tears, I now leave Kohima. The very thought is enough to break a General's heart.' He then sent a battalion from Miyazaki's command to protect 31 Division's withdrawal on the right flank, leaving to Miyazaki the rearguard detachment already described.

On 9 June Mutaguchi ordered him to proceed to Ukhrul and, 'after receiving supplies', to join 15th Division and attack Imphal. Four Infantry Battalions and one Mountain Artillery Battalion from Miyazaki's column should come directly under XV Army and, at Aradura Spur, halt the British advance to Imphal, orders impossible to execute by the date given, 10 June. Sato recognized them as designed to deprive him of independent authority.

The monsoon had made the Humine–Ukhrul road impassable for lorries so that, on arrival near Ukhrul, 31 Division found that the small quantity of rations which had been portered there had, anyway, been removed by 15th Division. When Sato reached Humine there was only enough rice for two days, and 'between Humine and Tamu there were absolutely no stocks of rations at all'. When urged by Mutaguchi's Chief-of-Staff, the wretched Kunomara, to obey orders, i.e. attack Imphal, it will be remembered that Sato replied, 'We will go where there is something to eat. I have not said I will not carry out Army orders, but first we must eat. Carrying out Army orders comes after that.'

Thereafter, although he sent two battalions to Major-General Yamamoto's Force in 33 Division, Sato ordered the main body of his Division into the hills to gather unhulled rice, and the rest to the Chindwin. He was dismissed from command on 7 July and denied the court-martial he so keenly sought.

'It is clear,' he said in a farewell speech to his staff, 'that this operation was the foolish desire of one man, Lieutenant-General Mutaguchi. I do not intend to be censured by anybody. Our 31st Division has done its duty. For two months we have defended our positions. None of their men (the British) passed down the Imphal road.

'Before God, I am not ashamed.

'Now I must say goodbye to you. I remember the hard time we had at Kohima. I thank you sincerely.

'I ask the forgiveness of those who lie dead at Kohima because of my poor talent . . . Nothing can separate those of us who were tried in the fire at Kohima . . . I cease to be your commander, but I hope we shall meet again at the Yasakuni Shrine. Goodbye.' Sato then left for the Chindwin, accompanied by his batman.

On 4 June Mutaguchi had issued a Special Order of the Day, in which he 'withdrew his troops from Kohima with one great push to capture Imphal. If a decisive victory is not obtained, we shall not be able to strike back again. On this one battle rests the fate of the Empire.'

It was not, however, until 8 July that he withdrew his troops east of the Chindwin in what a Japanese writer has called 'the worst military defeat yet chronicled in the annals of war'. An overstatement, but Sato said that he had realized in May that there was no possibility of success. The Army was acting for 'face', heading inexorably for massacre. He had to stop the crazy Imphal tragedy. Sato therefore moved his Division to the rear, deliberately to collapse the front and save his Division from annihilation and XV Army from associated destruction.

In the end, they were no longer soldiers but 'a herd of exhausted men waiting to be taken across the Chindwin. British planes swooped down on them. The river banks were heaped with corpses. It was impossible to tell whether the piles of mud and blood, eaten up by maggots, were the corpses of human beings, or heaps of earth . . . As the British planes left, their place was taken by flocks of vultures. We had no ammunition, no clothes, no food, no guns . . . all we had was grass and water. And there were jungles, great mountains and flooded rivers barring our way . . . malaria drove men mad; dysentery, men going forty or fifty times a day, most of them with blood.'

Even before the next phase began, of extermination, the Japanese had lost 30,000 dead and 23,000 seriously wounded out of 84,000. Still today there are letters, even articles in the Tokyo press about Kohima, but Japanese do not talk willingly of 'that great bitter battle'.

Some strategists blame Sato for his failure immediately to exploit 31 Division's early arrival at Kohima, when the British had nothing. Others, like Mutaguchi, blame Sato for his later refusal to commit troops to Imphal. Others attack Miyazaki and other officers who allowed themselves to be 'diverted' at Sangshak, at Jessami, Kharasom and Phek. Some accuse General Kawabe, GOC Burma Area Army, who would not allow Sato to seize the railhead at Dimapur and block the routes to both India and Ledo. Others point to the original plan which presupposed that, after Kohima was taken, Imphal, not Dimapur, would be the destination for 31 Division's disposable strength. Harry Seaman thinks that Sato quite simply 'funked' the move on Dimapur, fearing that a trap would be sprung on him from behind if he advanced.

Mutaguchi himself never had any doubts. 'Why should you stay at Kohima? The enemy will be running away to Dimapur. Your job is to get after them.'

But the Indian and British soldiers did not run back to Dimapur, and Kohima never was taken. For the rest, let us not blame the Japanese for everything. Let us remember that, for reasons which time may not have yet ratified – weakness is no reason for lack of valour – our interests may not have been served in the 1920s and 1930s by actions seen as an unprincipled abandonment of friends. Such betrayal, normal since 1945, was then sufficient cause for a *renversement des alliànces*, or, at least, fierce self-reliance.

On 14 April, 1991, at the dedication of the new Roman Catholic Cathedral of Kohima attended by 15 veterans from 31 Division and 17 from 2nd Division, one of the British delegation walked over in front of the whole congregation and held out his hand to the leading Japanese delegate. Then both groups moved together to shake hands.

But no one attended from the Fourth Battalion of the Queen's Own Royal West Kent Regiment.

XXXI

IV AND XXXIII CORPS MEET

MEANWHILE, SOUTH of Imphal, Mutaguchi had ordered 33 Division to 'sweep aside the paltry opposition we encounter and add lustre to army traditions by achieving a victory of annihilation'. The Division moved on 7 March, Yamamoto's combined column advancing against Douglas Gracey's 20 Division, other units cutting the road from Tiddim to Imphal at several places.

17 Division's move back to the plain was somewhat later than expected, and fierce fighting, aided by two Brigades of Ouvry Roberts' reserve 23 Division, was required before Cowan could cross the Manipur bridge on 17 March and begin the breakthrough. On the night before, V Force and the 9/12 Frontier rifles had spotted 15 and 31 Divisions crossing the Chindwin on their floating boat bridges for the march to Kohima and the Imphal road.

By 29 March Gracey was firmly established on the Shenam Saddle and by 4 April, when Lieutenant Smith was taking his carrier up to Kohima, General Cowan had brought 17 Division into the plain, to be temporarily relieved by 23 Division. 15 Japanese Division was between Litan and Kanglatongbi, and 33 Division, although hammered on the Tiddim road, was far from out of action. A serious threat at Nungshigum to the whole IV Corps' position was removed on 6 April when the 1/17 Dogras defeated the Japanese there.

The front was a horseshoe from Kanglatongbi through Nungshigum and the Shenam Saddle to Torbung. 20 Division at Shenam covered Tamu and the eastern approach. 23 Division was holding 33 Division, while 17 Division rested and 5 Division under General Briggs dealt with 15 Division in the north. When 17 Division, refreshed, came back into the line, Cowan and Gracey 'held the ring' from Shenam to the Tiddim road, while Briggs' and Roberts' Divisions (5 and 23) began to destroy 15 Division on the Mapao Ridge and on the road to Ukhrul.

The fighting between 20 Division (and, later, 23 Division) and Yamamoto's column at Shenam (Nippon Hill, Scraggy, Gibraltar etc), and between 33 Division and Cowan and Gracey's formations in the Tiddim road and the Silchar track was ferocious and incessant. Four Victoria Crosses were won.

Scoones brought the entire 5 Division onto the Kohima road to break the Japanese block at Kanglatongbi, while 20 Division left Shenam for Ukhrul. No progress was made by Yamamoto at Shenam or by Tanaka (33 Division) at Bishenpur. By 3 June the Battle of Kohima was over. The Allied advance to the Chindwin and the rout of 15th Army began, at the end 53,000 dead or missing Japanese out of 85,000, nearly all the rest wounded or starving. British casualties had been 17,000, most of whom recovered, thanks to greatly superior medical care.

As the battle at Imphal turned increasingly against the Japanese, 5 Division had moved north to clear the Manipur road, while 7 Division moved south-east and south from Kohima astride the Jessami track, cutting the Japanese off from the Chindwin as they retreated east through the jungle. 2nd Division thrust straight down to Imphal to re-establish the road and make contact with IV Corps, led by an armoured column, small by the standards of the Central European plain, but with tanks, armoured cars, carriers under a screen of guns, mortars, dive-bombers and fighters.

23 Brigade of Chindits (Border, Duke of Wellington and Essex columns) had operated ambushes in the Somra Hills including Jessami, Phek and Kharasom since 26 April. They continued to do so until July, aided by Nagas and supplied by the RAF. The Brigade claimed 1,000 Japanese killed to eighty killed and wounded of their own. The Japanese denigrated these claims, alleging successful 'Beau Geste' responses with dummy men.

The road to Imphal was cut out of the cliff. Movement off the cliff was therefore vertical, up and down. The mountains were immense. Locating the enemy was like finding a needle in a haystack: battalions could be swallowed up on any one of them. Adding to the difficulties were such incidents as, at Khuzana, a Japanese with a magnetic mine round his waist who leapt onto a tank, blowing it and him up together, while his colleagues ambushed the leading Durham Light Infantry.

On 7 June, a Camerons patrol pushed through to Pfuchama where the village itself was clear. The crest was not clear. It contained light machine guns covering the withdrawal of the main Japanese body eastwards. These caught the Dorsets in the flank after their stiff climb up Warno nullah. (Since leaving Kohima, this Battalion had suffered two more killed and twenty wounded: evacuation and treatment were still at an early stage, and the journey back could be agonizing for patients). The Worcesters moved to Pheswema.

On 8 June the Dorsets met some opposition at Kigwema as well as the familiar spectacle of Japanese officers blowing themselves up with their own hand grenades. The Worcesters joined them there, having laid a road block south of Phesama. The Camerons occupied Pfuchama, now completely cleared, and moved on to Phesama with Mike West's Brigade Headquarters. 4 Brigade passed through the Dorsets and Worcesters: on 6 June the men heard with delight the news of Operation Overlord, the Allied landings in Normandy.

'C' Company of the Lancashire Fusiliers under Captain Sam Caloe at one point led 2 Div's breakout, 13, 14 and 15 Platoons and their sections in single file on either side of the road, some of the sections with as few as four men. When the Battalion left England in 1942, their strength, including a reserve company, had been 999. Now they were between 130 and 150 strong. Behind 'C' came 'A' and 'D' Companies, similarly strung out on either side of the road, with 'B' Company riding on tanks.

After some distance, they were approached by a large van with a crew of women from the Women's Auxiliary Services who unloaded food for them. They were now within a mile of Viswema, the road following the hills, and the land dropping sharply into a deep and narrow valley, with the mountains rising starkly opposite. It was here that the two Scouts in 14 Platoon, Fusiliers Wardle and Knight, were picked off, and the Battalion ambushed with many killed and wounded in that action and in the subsequent attacks against the Japanese bunkers. An enemy 75mm gun killed Colonel Willie West, the Fusiliers' Commanding Officer, before the Battalion settled into a defensive position three hundred yards from the ambush area.

On four out of the five days of the Viswema battle the rain poured down continuously. The mud was ankle deep. When the men were dug in, the water came up to their knees. Shelling was continual, 'the screaming missiles tearing through the air . . . loud thuds as the shells exploded around us . . . the earth vibrated and shuddered as the bursting shells ploughed into the ground . . . We could hear whizzing pieces of murderous shrapnel flying through the air above our heads and wondered if this was the end'. All the Bren-gunners in 'D' Company were blown to bits by cannon.

Viswema was strongly defended and the Dorsets had to climb, 'hanging on to one another's water bottles', to Shaving Brush Spur in order to reinforce the 2nd Norfolks. The march was in pouring rain, through jungle and slippery, scarcely visible tracks, the troops heavily laden: 'the most unpleasant, dense jungle' that Captain Joe Chamberlain had ever seen.

Here, in a space two hundred yards wide, two hundred deep and within one thousand yards of the Japanese, were packed in artillery, including 3.7 inch howitzers of 16 and 99 Field Regiments, fifty 3 inch mortars and a squadron of Lee tanks. They were visited on Shaving Brush by Generals Grover, Stopford and Slim, the Army Commander himself.[1] The Camerons, who had lost four killed and seventeen wounded, nevertheless got above the Norfolks and Dorsets on 13 June with their three companies, now of only seventy men each. The Dorsets themselves, Geoffrey White commanding vice McNaught now in charge of 4 Brigade, were reduced to six weak platoons, 92 killed, three dead of disease and 235 wounded, two men in five killed or wounded since their arrival at Kohima.

The main and successful attack on Viswema village was made by the Worcesters, Camerons and Royal Scots with artillery, tank, machine-gun and mortar support. After a night at Tuphema, severely bitten by fleas in Naga huts, the Camerons moved to Maram via Khuzama and Mao Song Sang, supporting the Worcesters in glorious mountain country.

On the way south from Viswema, a young British officer of Prince Albert Victor's Own, an Indian Regiment, was observed sitting in a stationary armoured car. An Indian civilian wearing a pugri, plainly his body-servant, set up a small table, laid a white cloth with good china and silver, placed a book-rack on the table with a book and book marker, put out a glass of orange juice, and subsequently toast, butter, marmalade, bacon and eggs. The officer descended from his turret, sat down and consumed a leisurely breakfast. The watching Jocks were speechless.

Miyazaki's tactics were excellent, blowing up bridges and so forth on a very twisting road which contained a great many of those artefacts. Although 2 Division developed effective sapper and infantry flanking counter-measures, progress was initially very slow. It was not much helped by the insistent pressure from the Staff to open the road before the borrowed aircraft had to be returned. These SACSEA proposals, often hysterical, included the mass slaughter of cattle (in a poor Hindu country) to eke out the rations at Imphal which were, indeed, running low; opening the Bishenpur track, whose suspension bridge had been blown up and was still not repaired; 'forcing a convoy through to Imphal as convoys were forced through to Malta'. Neither did the Chiefs of Staff understand why 'fighting was characterized by company and platoon action'. Giffard had again to explain that *each* Japanese had to be killed, if necessary in his fox-hole. Slim also intervened.

Mao fell on 18 June, but after the battle on 19 June at the ridge of Maram, a great feat of arms by the Worcesters under Mike West's direction, one officer of the Durham Light Infantry described the advance as 'like walking-up partridges'. Casualties in this Battalion had nevertheless again been heavy, one company reduced to forty-seven men. As the Durhams moved on, they were opposed only by emaciated walking wounded from a Japanese hospital, determined to fight until they were killed and, indeed, all of them were. Naked corpses, discarded arms and ammunition lay along the tracks – no more than 'quagmires in the valleys and mud-slides on the slopes' – off the Manipur road. All were beaten, starved, half-dead with fatigue. Miyazaki's forces too had faded away at last.

On 22 June the DLI, preceded by armour of 149 Regiment, Royal Armoured Corps, met tanks of the 3rd Carabineers at Ms 109 on the Kohima–Imphal road where elephant grass gave way to trees: XXXIII Corps had met the advance elements of IV Corps. Imphal had been relieved. 'We sat alone in the sunshine and smoked and ate. Soon the staff cars came purring both ways. The road was open. It was a lovely day.' Imphal had ceased to be a fortress under siege and was to become the main base for the total destruction of the Japanese Burma Army.

Kohima had locked and unlocked the door, both at the right time. In 1951 a contributor to *Dekho*, the Burma Star magazine, wrote, 'In those days our Commander said: "You may not think much of yourself as you walk down Chowringhee in your battered bush hat and jungle battle-dress, enjoying a delicious "V" cigarette. There may be smarter gents in town who'll have annexed the available girls but one day, soldier, back in Blighty, someone will say to you, "If you were in the XIV Army, you must have been a pretty good chap: have a drink on me".'

Notes

1. At this point Slim personally suggested the use of 105mm guns mounted on tank chassis and of 37mm guns over open sights. The CRA, unaware of the instigator, arrived during the subsequent bombardment. 'What fucking fool ordered this?', roared 'Hair-trigger' Stevens. 'I am afraid I did, Brigadier,' said the Army Commander. It was also at this moment that, questioning the rush for Imphal, David Wilson was told by General Slim, 'Young officers shouldn't argue with Generals.'

ENVOI

THESE WORDS are carved on the Memorial at Kohima to the Second British Division:

> When you go home
> Tell them of us and say
> For your tomorrow
> We gave our today.

The men of that time looked different, as if they were enjoying themselves. Confidence was part of it, acceptance – not dependence, not even reliance – of things like God and the King before those concepts were polluted by *bien-pensants*. Dependence on administrative arrangements like the Welfare State was not yet possible. Nor was Empire one of the 'things': most of them knew that that was doomed and, anyway, if Burma was the Empire, they could do without it. They were neither bosses nor serfs. There was trust and equality between them . . . certainly dependence in *that* regard. Through their officers, the men had a 'vote'. The accountability to them of their superiors may have been silent but it was there, the opposite of Democratic Centralism.

Look at their faces. They may not *always* have been happy. That would be a bit much in the Hukawng valley or even a mess-deck in Trincomalee. They complained all right, they complained the whole bloody time, but they complained about incidentals, as a matter of routine, corrigible or not. They knew that what must be endured was a good deal better than what would be imposed on them by others not their own. They laughed a lot and told jokes because they were in their skins and jokes both passed time and lifted the spirits. They were tough, and simple, recognizing pretence and ignoring it.

They were very decent. The jokes they told really were not about dishonourable things. They were not, perhaps because the causes against which they fought were so dreadful, at all cynical. I do not mean that they endlessly praised God or abused Fascism, only that they were sure of who they were, of the officers who led them and of the country to which they belonged. They loved their country and returned to it with such joy. I did not know one of them who did not.

As to the Indian Army, John Masters said, 'Past the ruins of the Empire the Japanese had tried to build there, it took possession of the Empire *we* had built, in its towering, rising dust clouds India traced the shape of her own future. Twenty races, a dozen religions, a score of languages passed in these trucks and tanks. . . . The dust thickened under the trees lining the road until the column was motoring into a thunderous yellow funnel, first the tanks, infantry all over them, then trucks filled with men, then more tanks, going fast, nose to tail, guns, more trucks, more guns. . . . This was the old Indian Army going down to the attack, for the last time in history, exactly two hundred and fifty years after the Honourable East India Company had enlisted its first ten sepoys on the Coromandel Coast.'

APPENDIX 'A'

GARRISON COMMANDER'S CONCLUSIONS

SOME OF the lessons drawn by Colonel Richards from the Siege and its preceding engagements were:

'Untrained' troops cannot withstand a full-scale Japanese attack. To be able to 'handle a rifle' is not a sufficient condition to qualify as a trained infantryman. And even fully trained infantrymen cannot give their best in composite or hastily assembled units, short on NCOs and with officers unknown to the troops.

Shell and mortar casualties were very heavy because bunkers were inadequately roofed. A hollowed-out communication trench is not a bunker. The latter must be an independent unit with immediate access to the trenches. A bomb in a communication trench could kill all the occupants: a bunker must be deep and contain a bursting course of logs, impossible to construct in Kohima before the Siege because of the fluctuating Garrison and inability to identify likely sites until the last moment.

It is essential to provide water storage and supply, and enough covered bunkers for the wounded and for ammunition/POL in *all* Boxes.

On Japanese tactics, Major Calistan said that:

Before any heavy attack, they would attempt to identify enemy positions, drawing fire by the use of automatic weapons including blanks, and by putting forward very small and light parties to spy out the land. After a preliminary reconnaissance, the Japanese would employ mortars, grenade dischargers, 75 mm and very large numbers of grenades during the attack itself. (The shouting and yelling had little effect.) They were very adept at spotting and destroying mortars in open pits: the latter were suicidal and should be avoided at all costs in future.

In their use of MMG, the Japanese used belt after belt without any attempt at camouflage or disguise.

When they found a weak link, they hammered it. Even when driven out with casualties, they would counter-attack using cover and dead ground, right up to the Assam positions before bombing.

The Japanese had bullets which exploded on impact, causing awful wounds.

Wire was essential in defensive positions. Had there been enough at Jessami – only 30 bundles – the enemy might never have broken through, nor in many positions at Kohima.

Japanese booby traps were D.I.Y., grenades in milk tins hidden in trees with string or wire from the grenade to another tree, quite effective. They used our grenades, from V Force or Treasury dumps: on the first night, they threw them with the pins in, while others had 'string' round the grenade securing lever.

They wore captured British uniforms on occasion. Their own was a dark-green or khaki battledress, not unlike the British. They wore soft, felt peaked caps, high crowned pith helmets or well-camouflaged steel helmets, resembling our own, studded boots, high US-type puttees/gaiters, leather belts and two inferior quality leather pouches. They carried haversacks. Their weapons were well made, but other manufactured goods were not good.

Japanese ambushes were well organized, but their fire tended to be wild.

The defence must observe wire obstacles day and night. There must be no uncovered dead ground within the bombing range of any foxhole: when sighting, the eye must be at ground level. Fire from foxholes must be possible in all directions, especially on the uphill side of bunkers. Calistan advocated single-man foxholes with roofs proof against 3-inch mortar, as opposed to many-men trenches.

Fire discipline was vital. There should be no wild firing, into the air or wherever. Fire only when the enemy was in view. The first Punjabi losses at the tennis court were caused by the platoon opening up with all its machine guns, giving away its position. The Japanese then threw gelignite bombs into the trenches with horribly effective results.

W/T sets (No. 48 sets were no use, inaudible over a quarter of a mile) must have their own generators, batteries and chargers. There must be designated call signs for both air and ground communication. There was no functioning W/T at Kharasom, and lack of the equipment and call signs referred to above caused confusion at Jessami.

APPENDIX B

A PRIVATE of the Royal West Kents wrote:

'Colonel Laverty said that our task was to guard the Imphal–Dimapur road at Kohima. That was our objective and that was where the Royal West Kents would stay.

'The Japanese came at us on the Ridge in hundreds. Sheer manpower pushed us back from one trench to another ten feet behind: we were overrun by manpower, gradually into one small perimeter less than ½ mile square. In that perimeter, we stopped the Japanese Army. We were told that the Second British Division was on the way to save us and on the fifteenth day it did save us. Meanwhile, Laverty said: "If you let go, India will fall".

'Imagine fifteen days without hardly any water, no lavatories, dead Japanese in front, our own dead and wounded all around us. We were frightened but, if we were to surrender, we would be tortured, tied up with wire, shot. We stayed in our fox-holes and prayed to God for 2nd Division to come and get us and, thank God, they came.

'Padré Randolph and Colonel Laverty saved India, the Padré through prayer for the strength for us all to hold on.'

APPENDIX C

INITIAL ATTACK ON THE DC'S BUNGALOW, NIGHT 26/27 APRIL, 1944

April 26: 'A' and 'C' Companies of the Dorsets received orders to proceed to Garrison Hill. At 1300 hours orders were given by the CO for an attack on the DC Bungalow.

1st Task: 'A' Company to capture and hold east end of Garrison Hill Spur, to cover the road junction so that AFVs could reach 5th Infantry Brigade.

2nd Task: 'C' Company to strike from north edge of Spur towards Tin Hut area and Long Tin Hut area. Little was known of enemy positions and ground so the plan had to be somewhat vague. However, with the help of a plan provided, Platoon objectives were allotted.

Phase 2: Royal Berkshire Regiment were to attack from the Pimple towards the Tennis Court area. One Platoon of 'A' Company, providing initial success was achieved, would strike the DC's Bungalow.

THE ATTACK

Phase 1 ('A' and 'C') 'A' Company moved off at 0245 hours. The advance progressed very slowly over difficult terrain and, after fifty yards, an LMG opened fire from top of bank causing a further delay. An attempt was made by Corporal Hill and two men to silence the weapon. The attempt was abortive owing to presence of LMG 15 yards away to a flank. The Company crossed the lane of fire in short rushes. Two further lanes of fire were encountered, crossed by the use of folds in ground.

'A' and 'C' Company Commanders liaised at this stage and 'C' Company planned their attack and struck south.

The Company moving in rear of 'A' had the Company Commander and two Platoon Commanders with their runners leading. It soon became obvious that 'A' Company were under fire from a bunker position in 13 Platoon area. This they silenced but were unable to occupy.

Phase 2 ('C'): 'C' Company having reached the top of the high bank came under LMG fire from three or four different directions.

The bunker on south end of the Tennis Court was silenced by 13 Platoon. During this stage, the Platoon Commander and Platoon

Sergeant of 13 Platoon were killed. The Platoon Commander of 14 Platoon was wounded and also the Company Commander. CSM Keagan took over the Company and made a further attempt.

Phase 2 ('A'): 7 Platoon pushed on round the edge of the Spur to contact the road junction. 8 Platoon moved out to the right and made for the same point. 9 Platoon followed by Company HQ moved forward behind 7 Platoon.

Company HQ stopped by a large tree as decided in the original orders.

7 Platoon reached the road junction and dug in without opposition apart from sniping coming from the DC Bungalow area.

8 Platoon under Lieutenant Murrills formed up in the area above the crossroads and moved forward two sections and Platoon HQ up towards the DC Bungalow, leaving one section on the right to cover them in. At the same time, Sergeant Varley was trying to recce a route for AFVs which were to come up at first light. Two leading sections crawled within 15 yards of DC Bungalow and halted whilst two Pole charge men moved forward and exploded their charges in the Bungalow. On the charges exploding, the two sections assaulted the Bungalow, meeting no opposition, and reformed west of the Bungalow.

It was fast becoming daylight and extremely heavy fire was opened from the Tin Hut area pinning the two leading sections and the third section which had moved forward to the ground. The Platoon Commander signalled the rear section back over the crest and he himself crawled out, there being no hope of recovering the leading sections. Meanwhile, 9 Platoon moved round above the road until they contacted 7 Platoon and commenced digging in. Company HQ dug in above the road due north of the DC Bungalow as previously arranged, dawn breaking as this operation started. As the light strengthened, the Company Commander realized that the post which he, wireless operator, and his batman were occupying were completely commanded by the Bunker on the north edge of the Tennis Court. At approx. 0530 hours, OC 8 Platoon asked for a section to move round the south edge of the Spur with a view to silencing the opposition he had met from the Tin Hut area. He proceeded along the north road towards the crossroads and came under LMG fire from a bunker on the tip of the Spur. Lieutenant Murrills and Corporal Softley rushed and liquidated the position killing seven Japs and capturing a British bren gun also discovering that a two man post of 7 Platoon was digging down directly into the bunker itself. At the same time, a party of about five Japs ran from the south side of the Spur across the road and into a bunker opposite the one being attacked. They did not in any way interfere with our operations. The section then moved round to the first ramp as shown on the plan. Corporal Softley was killed trying to locate the guns on the top. The

233

section then came under heavy fire and withdrew, linking up with 7 Platoon. At approx. 0900 hours, the Company Commander decided that he commanded the crossroads and said AFVs could proceed. At shortly after 1000 hours a message was thrown to him in an empty cartridge case stating that 8 Platoon were now dug up. The message was passed immediately to Battalion HQ.

32 British and 32 Japanese had been killed, 41 British and an unknown number of Japanese wounded: the figures do not include Japanese heard screaming in three bunkers which had been blown up.

Lessons

1. The attack launched with little information as regards enemy opposition and ground.
2. The attack should have been closer to the Artillery barrage, especially with the difficult terrain over which we had to move.
3. The time allotted between Z hour and dawn was insufficient.
4. The failure of a Honey Tank Commander to realize that the drive leading to the DC Bungalow was not only wide enough to take his tank, but would take a Grant tank as was proved a week later.
5. LMG fire does not stop an advance but time must be allowed to pass through the belts of fire.
6. It is fatal to select a prominent object for Company HQ.
7. Even though sniped, a Platoon or Company occupying a position must search the immediate area.

Captain R. D. Castle
Captain Jock Murrills

APPENDIX D

WHAT FOLLOWS, the work of Major Gordon Graham, MC and bar, once a company commander of the Cameron Highlanders at Kohima, later a journalist in India, ultimately becoming Chairman of Butterworths, was published in *The Times* of 18 August, 1954 after he had revisited the site of the battle.

'The trees are all young on Garrison Hill, and in Naga Village children are playing. The wet earth and the sprouting shrubs have the same spring-fresh smell. And there is no stench. Grass-filled foxholes still pose forgotten firelanes, and some rusty ration tins and leather straps have escaped, as too worthless to pick up, a decade of scavengers.

Beneath the Hill lie the graves. One thousand, three hundred and eighty seven of them, in orderly, impersonal, endless rows. In this geometrical panorama there is no heartbreak, no rebuke, no regret. It is a design of peace, the pious peace that follows war, the revulsive peace of "Never Again". It is the mute attempt to express the inexpressible by those who, helpless, are left behind. It has the same conscious inadequacy as the "Remarks" column in the Visitors' Book, where a sudden embarrassment catches the pen which has written smoothly the name and address and then stumbles to an anticlimactic "Very impressive", or, "A fitting resting-place for heroes". But one ex-soldier had written in a flash of perceptiveness, "I wish my name were here."

On bronze plates row by row are inscribed the parting messages of those who loved. Some are inspired; some are simple and heartfelt; some are superstitious; some are blank, like the blank spaces in the Visitors' Book, stifled to silence by the despair of incomprehension. Mute or vocal, all concern those who stay behind, and we are left wondering what may be the response of those who are gone before. Do they know too much to keep their treasures in the crumbling storehouses of memory? Or do they go on unforgetful, yet untrammelled, by past happiness? Killed in Action. April 18 1944. Aged 27. "Good Night, Daddy". Killed in Action. April 21

1944. Aged 29. "A very parfit gentil knight". Killed in Action. May 5 1944. Aged 35. "Beatae memorias; quis nos separabit?". Killed in Action. May 6 1944. Aged 23. "Our only beloved son, who died that freedom might live". As one steps haltingly from stone to stone, tears defy detached appraisal. One walks quite quickly, so that numbers may smother the sense of individual tragedy. It is a relief to meet the Anglo-Indian Clerk of Works and the beaming Sikh contractor, who apologize for the unfinished state of the construction. "Only another 50,000 rupees, then it's done".

Statistics can be comforting. Fifty thousand rupees; 200 saplings; 36 tons of cement; 1,387 graves; and ten years. Like the poignant milestones, past which the country bus had driven in as many minutes as the advancing troops had moved in days, these figures measure the thinker, not the thought. To the visitors of today they are mere computation; to those who were there, they are the sight, smell and touch of a forgotten battlefield. Just as, at the summit crossroads where the bus groans to a standstill, the level space above is to some that which was once a tennis court and is now a war cemetery; to others it was a point of dominating destiny. Behind lies the tortuous mounting road. Before lie the jumbled blue forests and hills of Burma. Above the crossroads is the memorial, its message unread by those who pass by, but commanding and holding the gaze of those who pause:

"When you go home
Tell them of us and say,
For your tomorrow
We gave our today."

Round the memorial are written the names. Brigadiers, privates, tank drivers, stretcher-bearers, signalmen, riflemen, captains, corporals, names from every corner of England, Scotland and Wales. For our tomorrow, they gave their today. Do we handle our heritage with reverence due? A heritage given from the stark values of the battlefield can rust unheeded in the lumber room of peaceful living.

One of tomorrow's children guided me to the memorial on the Naga Village height. "5120" we called it. With proud knowledge he explained the bullet-riddled sheets of corrugated iron. The track which the bulldozers drove up the mountainside is now a leafy lane. Houses identical with those which the battle obliterated have hidden the pattern of war till it can no more be traced. Red-blanketed Nagas, cheerful rebels now as then, stared in unbelief as I panted upward behind the nimble barefoot urchin to the place which I should have known better than he and which I knew before he was born. The Highlanders' memorial is in a houseyard, a confusion of fencing, pigs and hens. McCassey, Mackay, Mackinnon, Macmillan, MacNaught, in bronze alphabetical permanence. Here eighty three were killed and eight were missing. Beneath the names is the title of the Cameron lament, "Lochaber No More".

The wail of the bagpipes from the Assam Rifles' barracks on the ridge below was almost too timely a background to reverie. So, too, was the bugle sounding reveille when, stumbling through the thickets in the mist of a rainy dawn, I looked for ghosts and found none. We are the ghosts, called forth by our own memories, investing each impersonal inch of soil with our own personal meanings; these meanings our self-conjured mists in which, wraith-like, we startle only ourselves.

But as the mists are swept clear of the heights above by the rushing winds of an oncoming monsoon, there, where we stare uncomprehendingly at the sudden call for vision – still too sudden, too fleeting, but unutterably certain – is the great meaning we seek. For the trees are all young on Garrison Hill, and in Naga Village children are playing.'

A service of Remembrance was held at Kohima on November 9th 1969 to commemorate the 25th Anniversary of the Battle and the opening of the road to Imphal. (Strict security was observed because of Naga dissidence against the (Indian) Nagaland and Central Governments). The Cemetery maintained by the Commonwealth War Graves Commission, covers the DC's Bungalow Spur; the Cross of Sacrifice on the crest of the spur, beside the tennis court. The Stone of Remembrance (Second Division) is a little to the south and the Second Division Memorial is at the foot of the spur overlooking the road junction to Naga Village. Wreaths were laid there by the commander of the Indian 8th Mountain Division (Major General Makshi), by the GOC Nagaland, by former members of 2 Div and by the Chief Minister of Nagaland.

There are other memorials, Assam Regiment, Assam Rifles, Royal Welch Fusiliers, Durham Light Infantry, the Dorsets, Berkshires, Queens, the Gurkha Regiments, finally the Royal West Kents and 161 Brigade, including 1/1 Punjabis and 4/7 Rajputs.

161 Brigade's stone was a commemoration by John Wright, a hero of the Siege, of Naga 'virility'. It reads:

At KOHIMA in April 1944 the Japanese invasion of India was halted.

APPENDIX E

CAPTAIN JOHN LAWRENCE SMYTH, 1st Battalion Queen's Royal Regiment, son of Major General Sir John Smyth VC MP was killed on May 7 rallying his company with a hunting horn.

His brother, Robin, once Foreign Correspondent in Paris of the *Observer*, remembering their days together in the Hebrides, wrote:

> 'What if the sun should rise above those eyes
> And be no longer seen. If rain at night
> Comes silently to where his body lies,
> Unmindful of the passing of the light.
> If he should never hear the winds rejoice
> On the grey crowned moors at break of day,
> Should listen to his hounds' unhurried voice.
> Yet he had cheated death in his own way.
> For surely these strange rocks will not forget
> The one who loved them, and who cast his net
> Between the Isles, among the magic seas?
> For I remember how in summers past
> His horn awoke the sullen Hebrides.'

BIBLIOGRAPHY

Allen, Louis, *Burma, The Longest War*

Barker, A.J., *The March on Delhi*, Faber

Bell, *History of Manchester Regiment 1922–50*, J. Sherratt

Bellers, *History of 1 KGV Gurkhas Vol II*, Gale and Polden

Birdwood, Lord, *History of Worcestershire Regiment, 1922–1950*, Gale and Polden

Blackwood, William, *Historical Records of the Queen's Own Cameron Highlanders*

Blight, *The Royal Berkshire Regiment*, Staples

Campbell, Arthur, *The Siege*

Evans and Brett-James, *Imphal*, Macmillan

Foster, *History of the Queen's Royal Regiment Regiment of Engineers (Volume 8)*, Gale and Polden

Graham Bower, Ursula, *Naga Path*, John Murray

Havers, Norman, *March On*

Hutton, J.H., *Angami Nagas*, Macmillan

Kemp and Graves, *Red Dragon (Royal Welch Fusiliers)*, Gale and Polden

Kemp, P.K., *The Royal Norfolk Regiment*, Royal Norfolk Regiment

Lewin, Ronald, *Slim*, Leo Cooper

Lucas Philips, C.E., *Springboard to Victory*, Heinemann

Lunt, James, *Hell of a Licking*, Collins

McCann, John, *Echoes of Kohima*, John McCann

McCann, John, *Kohima*, John McCann

McCann, John, *Return to Kohima*, John McCann

Muir, Augustus, *First of Foot (Royal Scots)*, Royal Scots History Committee

Pakenham-Walsh, *History of Royal Engineers*

Rissick, D., *The DLI at War*, DLI

Roberts, M.R., *Golden Arrow*, Gale and Polden

Rooney, D., *Burma Victory*

Seaman, Harry, *The Battle for Sangshak*, Leo Cooper

Shakespear, *History of Assam Rifles*, Macmillan

Slim, *Defeat Into Victory*, Cassell

Steyn, *History of Assam Regiment*, Orient Longmans

Swinson, Arthur, *Kohima*, Cassell
White, *Straight on for Tokyo (2nd Dorsetshire Regiment)*, Gale and
  Polden

Despatches
of General Sir George Giffard (11th Army Group) and Admiral Lord
Louis Mountbatten (Supreme Allied Commander).

Combined Historical Section, India and Pakistan, *Reconquest of Burma
  (Volume I)*
'GWR' in *Dekho, The Gunners in the War with Japan, Part II*
Hingston, Lt Col W.G., 1st Punjab Regiment, *Kanglatongbi*
Houston, Major R.B., late 10th Gurkha Rifles, *Imphal Campaign*
Indian Army Review, October, November 1946, *The Story of 'V' Force*
Kirby, Woodburn, *The War Against Japan, Volumes I, II and III*,
  HMSO
Mackenzie, Compton, *All Over the Place*

War Diaries
1st Assam Regiment, Burma Rifles, Carabineers, 1st Royal Berkshire,
2nd Royal Tanks, V Force, Worcesters, 3/1 Gurkha, 1st Devonshire, 2nd
Dorset, 2nd DLI, 4th Royal West Kent, 6th Field Ambulance, 75th
Indian Field Ambulance, 49 and 53 Indian General Hospitals, 2, 11 and
12, and 20 Indian Mountain Batteries, 24th Mountain Regiment Indian
Army, 1/1 Punjab, 4/7 Rajput and 4/15 Punjab, 149 Royal Armoured
Corps, 2nd West Yorkshire, Lancashire Fusiliers, 4/15 Gurkha, Queen's
Own Regiment, 1st KGV Bengal Sappers and Miners (2nd) Field
Company Indian Engineers.

Imperial War Museum
All material below can be obtained from the Imperial War Museum using
the reference numbers given.

516. 81	E7315 Siege Of Kohima, QO Gazette
516. 158	59082 Four Samurau
516.322 'Dirty Half Hundred' Queen's Own Gazette	
	Vol LXXII No 1 1956
116. 322 4 Battalion QO Queen's Own Gazette	
	Vol LXXV No 2 1969
516.322 Great Men	516.81 Queen's Own Gazette
	Vol LXIX No 5 1952
516.322 Epic of Kohima Queen's Own Gazette	
	Vol XLVIII No 4 1951

516.322 Kohima Queen's Own Gazette
　　　　　　　　　　　　Vol LXIII No 4
516.322 Kohima Army Quarterly
　　　　　　　　　　　　Vol LIV(3) 1945
O1/5(591)52.2 Kohima, How I Got There,
　　　　　　　　　　　　Richards, Brig HU,
　　　　　　　　　　　　Vol 8 Ap 85, Issue
　　　　　　　　　　　　3, 204–07

Individual written and oral records
Boshell, Col Francis (Royal Berkshires)
Charles, S.T., OBE (Chairman, British Campaign Fellowship Group)
Clinch, Sgt (HQ Company, 4th Royal West Kents at Kohima)
Cropper, Lt Col, Randle, (Notes on Japanese Prisoners)
Cropper, Lt Col and Good, Col H.W.W. (Notes on Health, Hygiene, etc. in Burma)
Easton, Col D., MC (Company Commander, 4th Royal West Kents at Kohima)
Fletcher, J.S. (Life in Kachin Country, 88/19/1)
Franklin, Lt Col P.H.A.L., DL, (2nd i/c, 4th Royal West Kents at Kohima)
Hirakubo, Masao (Secretary of British Campaign Fellowship Group and Supply Officer, 58 Regiment)
Hogg, Capt T. (4th Royal West Kents at Kohima)
Horsford, Maj Gen D., CB, DSO
Laing, Dr S.R.C., MA, MB, MRCS
Mountstephen, Capt P.K. (Intelligence Officer, Kohima Garrison)
Murray, Lt Col D.
Norman, Cpl H.F. (4th Royal West Kents at Kohima)
Patrick, Capt J. (1/7 Gurkha)
Rome, Major P. (Durham Light Infantry)
Seaman, H., (author of *Battle for Sangshak*)
Slim, the Viscount (Chairman, Burma Star Association)
Slim, Field Marshal (Letters to Colonel Gibb, 6/Gurkhas, and to Lord Birdwood)
Smith, Maj H.C. (HQ Company Commander)
Steyn, Maj P., MC (Assam Regiment)
Wilson, Brig A.D.R.G., CBE (Cameron Highlanders)
Wilson, C.O.J.R. (V Force, 88/19/1)
Winstanley, Maj J., MC, TD, MB, FRCS (Company Commander, 4th Royal West Kents at Kohima)
Wright, Capt J. (1st KGV Bengal Sappers and Miners, (2nd Field Company, Indian Engineers))

Taped Narratives
2827   Collins, Gunner
11516/4/3–4   Hirakubo, Masao
2847   Honda, Maj
2561   McNaught, Col, DSO
2562/FA   McNaught, Col, DSO
2562/B   McNaught, Col, DSO
2562F/D   McNaught, Col, DSO
2562E/E   McNaught, Col, DSO
2866   Okada, Teryo

AL 2549 General Aung San and Burma Independence Army
AL 5248 15 Army Order of Battle
AL 5296 33 Division
AL 5217 55 Division
Lieutenant-General Mutaguchi's report on Operations in North Burma in Spring 1943
Japanese Opinion on: Allied Qualities
Japanese Account of Battle of Sangshak
Japanese Account of Imphal Operation 2/51 Infantry Regiment, 61 Infantry Regiment
OB of 15, 31, 33 Divisions on 22 June plus Miyazawi and Yamamoto Dets
A1 5214 Wingate and 5 (Jap) Air Division
AL 5030 Comments on Chindits by 15 Army
AL 5244 Japanese Air Strength diverted by Chindits
AL 5011 Imperial GHQ Army Directive 1776 of 7. 1. 44 on Imphal
Williams, Maj JHF (23 Brigade Chindits, events in the Naga Hills)
The Papers of Sir Charles Pawsey

Bibliography of Japanese Books
58th Infantry Regiment and Masao Hirakubo, *Burma Front*, Tokyo
Imai, Yukihoko, *To and From Kohima*, Tokyo
Kase, Toshikasu, *Eclipse of the Rising Sun*, Cape
Tagaki, Toshiro, *Imphal*, Tokyo

Japanese Accounts in Imperial War Museum and Elsewhere
AL 5245 31 and 15 Japanese Divisions
SEATIC 27 X 45 (827/11) History of Japanese 15th Air from March 1944
(827/2) History of Japanese 15 Army (report by HQ18 Area to HWALFSE)

Field Marshal Terauchi's report on Japanese Operations in Burma (20 10 45) to Saigon Central Command

827/20 Japanese account of Burma Operations (Dec 41–Aug 45) to HQ 12 Army Japanese Studies in WW2 No 89 Part II – Operations

5009/7 Interrogation of Lt Gen Sato Kotoku

5009/1 Interrogation of Gen Kimura Hyetaro

5016 Japanese Monograph 146, Political Strategy before outbreak of WWII, Part II, 1940

5049 Japanese Monograph 144 Political and Military Strategy 1931–39

5074 Japanese Monograph 133 Burma Operational Records

5239 Japanese Planning in Burma for 1944

5241 Battle of Kohima and Japanese 31 Division, Japanese Research Division

5245 Order of Battle and Progress of Operations 15 Div. Advance to Kohima, March–May 1944, Japanese Research Division. Japanese Monograph 134, Burma Ops record, 15 Army Ops in Imphal Area and withdrawal to Northern Burma. Jap Bulletin 240 Item 2208 Relations between 15 Army Cdr and 15, 31 and 33 Div Commanders. The Retreat.

AL 5009/7 General Sato Kotoko

AL 5002 Comments of Jap Higher Command on Indian National Army; Wingate; Strategy for defeat of British/Indian Forces.

Maps of 31 Div area of Battle

Japanese Generals on Kohima (Bulletin 247, pps 19, 20, 24, 27)

Account of 33 Div's actions with 15 Div under 15 Army during Imphal ops.

App 2 of JM Research Study (Decision at a Conference between Imperial GHQ and Government on 27 July 1940) for future Japanese military and political Strategy

INDEX

245